THE CAMBRIDGE
CLASSICAL LIT

General Editors
P. E. EASTERLING
Professor of Greek, University College London
E. J. KENNEY
Fellow of Peterhouse, Cambridge

Advisory Editors
B. M. W. KNOX
formerly Director of the Center for Hellenic Studies, Washington
W. V. CLAUSEN
Pope Professor of the Latin Language and Literature, Harvard University

VOLUME I   PART 2
Greek Drama

THE CAMBRIDGE HISTORY OF
CLASSICAL LITERATURE

VOLUME I: GREEK LITERATURE

THE
CAMBRIDGE HISTORY
OF
CLASSICAL LITERATURE

VOLUME I   PART 2
Greek Drama

Edited by
P. E. EASTERLING
Professor of Greek, University College London

and

B. M. W. KNOX
formerly Director of the Center for Hellenic Studies, Washington

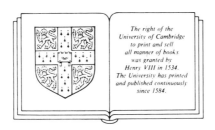

The right of the
University of Cambridge
to print and sell
all manner of books
was granted by
Henry VIII in 1534.
The University has printed
and published continuously
since 1584.

CAMBRIDGE UNIVERSITY PRESS
CAMBRIDGE
NEW YORK   NEW ROCHELLE   MELBOURNE   SYDNEY

Published by the Press Syndicate of the University of Cambridge
The Pitt Building, Trumpington Street, Cambridge CB2 1RP
32 East 57th Street, New York, NY 10022, USA
10 Stamford Road, Oakleigh, Melbourne 3166, Australia

First published 1985 and reprinted 1986, 1987, 1988 as chapters 10, 11, 12 of
The Cambridge History of Classical Literature, Volume I
First paperback edition 1989

Printed in Great Britain by
Redwood Burn Limited, Trowbridge, Wiltshire

Library of Congress catalogue card number: 88–6123

British Library cataloguing in publication data

The Cambridge history of classical literature.
Vol. 1 [Greek literature], Pt 2, Greek
drama.
1. Classical literatures, to *c.* 500 –
Critical studies
I. Easterling, P. E.   II. Knox, Bernard M. W.
(Bernard MacGregor Walker)
880'.09

ISBN 0 521 35982 1

CONTENTS

CONTENTS

PLATES

ABBREVIATIONS

BT	Bibliotheca Scriptorum Graecorum et Romanorum Teubneriana (Leipzig & Stuttgart)
Budé	Collection des Universités de France, publiée sous le patronage de l'Association Guillaume Budé (Paris)
Bursian	Bursian's *Jahresbericht über die Fortschritte der klassischen Altertumswissenschaft* (Berlin, 1873–1945)
CAF	T. Kock, *Comicorum Atticorum Fragmenta* (Leipzig, 1880–8)
CAH	*The Cambridge Ancient History* (Cambridge, 1923–39)
*CAH*²	2nd ed. (Cambridge, 1961–)
CHCL	*Cambridge History of Classical Literature* (Cambridge, 1982–5)
CGF	G. Kaibel, *Comicorum Graecorum Fragmenta* (Berlin, 1899)
CGFP	C. F. L. Austin, *Comicorum Graecorum Fragmenta in papyris reperta* (Berlin, 1973)
CIL	*Corpus Inscriptionum Latinarum* (Berlin, 1863–)
CVA	*Corpus Vasorum Antiquorum* (Paris & elsewhere, 1925–)
Christ–Schmid–Stählin	W. von Christ, *Geschichte der griechischen Literatur*, rev. W. Schmid and O. Stählin (Munich, 1920–24) 6th ed. (Cf. Schmid–Stählin)
Diehl	E. Diehl, *Anthologia Lyrica Graeca* I (2nd ed. 1936); II (3rd ed. 1949–52)
DTC	A. W. Pickard-Cambridge, *Dithyramb, tragedy and comedy*. 2nd ed., rev. T. B. L. Webster (Oxford, 1962)
DFA	A. W. Pickard-Cambridge, *The dramatic festivals of Athens*. 2nd ed., rev. J. Gould–D. M. Lewis (Oxford, 1968)
DK	H. Diels–W. Kranz, *Die Fragmente der Vorsokratiker*. 6th ed. (Berlin, 1951–2)
EGF	G. Kinkel, *Epicorum Graecorum Fragmenta* (Leipzig, 1877)
FGrH	F. Jacoby, *Fragmente der griechischen Historiker* (Berlin, 1923–)

ABBREVIATIONS

FHG	C. Müller, *Fragmenta Historicorum Graecorum* (Berlin, 1841–70)
FYAT	(ed.) M. Platnauer, *Fifty years (and twelve) of classical scholarship* (Oxford, 1968)
GLK	H. Keil, *Grammatici Latini* (Leipzig, 1855–1923)
GLP	C. M. Bowra, *Greek lyric poetry*, 2nd ed. (Oxford, 1961)
Gow–Page, *Hell. Ep.*	A. S. F. Gow–D. L. Page, *The Greek Anthology: Hellenistic Epigrams* (Cambridge, 1965)
Gow–Page, *Garland*	A. S. F. Gow–D. L. Page, *The Greek Anthology: The Garland of Philip* (Cambridge, 1968)
Guthrie	W. K. C. Guthrie, *A history of Greek philosophy* (Cambridge, 1965–81)
IEG	M. L. West, *Iambi et Elegi Graeci* (Oxford, 1971–2)
IG	*Inscriptiones Graecae* (Berlin, 1873–)
Kai	G. Kaibel, *Comicorum graecorum fragmenta*, 1 fasc. 1 *Doriensium comoedia mimi phylaces* (Berlin, 1899)
KG	R. Kühner–B. Gerth, *Ausführliche Grammatik der griechischen Sprache: Satzlehre.* 4th ed. (Hannover, 1955)
Lesky	A. Lesky, *A history of Greek literature*, tr. J. Willis–C. de Heer (London, 1966)
Lesky, *TDH*	A. Lesky, *Die tragische Dichtung der Hellenen*, 3rd ed. (Göttingen, 1972)
LSJ	Liddell–Scott–Jones, *Greek–English Lexicon*, 9th ed. (Oxford, 1925–40)
Loeb	Loeb Classical Library (Cambridge, Mass. & London)
OCD²	*Oxford Classical Dictionary*, 2nd ed. (Oxford, 1970)
OCT	Scriptorum Classicorum Bibliotheca Oxoniensis (Oxford)
Ol	A. Olivieri, *Frammenti della commedia greca e del mimo nella Sicilia e nella Magna Grecia* (Naples, 1930)
Paravia	Corpus Scriptorum Latinorum Paravianum (Turin)
PLF	E. Lobel–D. Page, *Poetarum Lesbiorum Fragmenta* (Oxford, 1963)
PMG	D. L. Page, *Poetae Melici Graeci* (Oxford, 1962)
PPF	H. Diels, *Poetarum Philosophorum Graecorum Fragmenta* (Berlin, 1901)
Pfeiffer	R. Pfeiffer, *A history of classical scholarship* (Oxford, 1968)
Powell	J. U. Powell, *Collectanea Alexandrina* (Oxford, 1925)
Powell–Barber	J. U. Powell–E. A. Barber, *New chapters in the history of Greek Literature* (Oxford, 1921), 2nd ser. (1929), 3rd ser. (Powell alone) (1933)
Preller–Robert	L. Preller, *Griechische Mythologie*, 4th ed., rev. C. Robert (Berlin, 1894)

ABBREVIATIONS

RAC	*Reallexikon für Antike und Christentum* (Stuttgart, 1941–)
RE	A. Pauly–G. Wissowa–W. Kroll, *Real-Encyclopädie der klassischen Altertumswissenschaft* (Stuttgart, 1893–)
Roscher	W. H. Roscher, *Ausführliches Lexikon der griechischen und römischen Mythologie* (Leipzig, 1884–)
SEG	*Supplementum Epigraphicum Graecum* (Leyden, 1923–71; Alphen aan den Rijn, 1979–)
SH	P. J. Parsons and H. Lloyd-Jones, *Supplementum Hellenisticum* (Berlin & New York, 1983)
SLG	D. L. Page, *Supplementum Lyricis Graecis* (Oxford, 1974)
SVF	H. von Arnim, *Stoicorum Veterum Fragmenta* (Leipzig, 1903–)
Snell	B. Snell, *Tragicorum Graecorum Fragmenta* (Göttingen, 1971–)
Schmid–Stählin	W. Schmid–O. Stählin, *Geschichte der griechischen Literatur* (Munich, 1929–48)
Spengel	L. Spengel, *Rhetores Graeci* (1853–6); I ii rev. C. Hammer (Leipzig, 1894)
TGF	A. Nauck, *Tragicorum Graecorum Fragmenta*, 2nd ed. (Leipzig, 1889)
Walz	C. Walz, *Rhetores Graeci* (Stuttgart, 1832–6)

EDITORIAL NOTE

Updating of bibliographical material in the paperback edition has been undertaken where possible in references to recently published texts and commentaries. This edition also incorporates corrections received by the editors after the 1986 reprinting of the one-volume hardcover edition.

1

TRAGEDY

I. THE ORIGINS OF TRAGEDY

The documented history of Greek tragedy begins in 472 B.C. with Aeschylus' *Persae*. Of his earlier career we know little; we know something but not much about one or two of his contemporaries; we have a date (536/533) for the institution of a competition in tragedy at the Great Dionysia. The origins of tragedy lie in the sixth century. So complex, however, and so obscure is the evidence, so various are the theories advanced, that the hardened scholar approaches this subject with dismay.[1]

The surviving plays of Aeschylus tell us what needs to be explained. There is a chorus, dramatized as the play demands. Their songs are elaborate and bulk large and, in pre-Aeschylean tragedy, may have bulked larger, since Aristotle informs us that Aeschylus reduced the choral element and 'gave the leading role to the spoken word'.[2] For the earlier plays two actors are required (either of whom could, with a change of mask and costume, take more than one part). Aeschylus is said himself to have added the second actor and either he or Sophocles the third, and Aeschylus uses three in his later plays.[3] The actors deliver speeches, often of considerable length and formality, but also enter into dialogue with the coryphaeus (chorus-leader) or with the other actor. Particularly characteristic are passages of line-by-line interchange (stichomythia) which, like the narrative speech, remains a formal convention of tragedy as long as we know it and may well go back to its earliest beginnings. The plays (except *Agamemnon*) are of moderate length, rather over 1,000 lines. In what kind of performances did plays like these originate?

It is easy to list contributory influences. (i) Tragedy took its stories, with few exceptions, from mythology. These stories had been treated by the epic poets, Homer and the Cycle and other epics now lost; and Aristotle, with a sure instinct, regarded the Homeric handling of myth as a prototype of tragedy.[4] But myth

---

[1] For bibliography see Appendix.   [2] *Poetics* 1449a17f.
[3] *Poetics* 1449a18 (with note in D. W. Lucas's edition).
[4] *Poetics passim*. A famous Aeschylean trilogy now lost clearly followed the plot of the *Iliad* very closely.

had also been treated by lyric poets. It seems that, from an early stage, it had been characteristic of hymns and other types of choral lyric poetry to contain a narrative; and Stesichorus had developed lyric narrative on a big scale. One could say that the stories came to the tragedians rough-shaped for drama by epic and lyric poets. (ii) The choral songs of tragedy, metrically complex and linguistically rich, written in a literary dialect which is not pure Attic (using, for instance, the α of the lyric *koine* for Ionic-Attic η),[1] are clearly indebted to the choral lyric tradition of the Peloponnesian and western Greeks: Attica had no great tradition of the kind. (iii) For a noble rhetoric in spoken iambic trimeters we must look elsewhere. Aristotle thought – it may or may not have been a guess – that the original dialogue metre of tragedy was the trochaic tetrameter.[2] Both the tetrameter and the trimeter had developed in Ionia, at the hands of Archilochus and his successors, but tragic trimeters may have owed most to Solon who, at the turn of the seventh and sixth centuries, had elevated the metre to be a medium of political exhortation.

It is easy to list these influences: but on what were they brought to bear? Few today would agree with Murray in deriving tragedy from a ritual passion play.[3] Aristotle, on what evidence we do not know, believed that it originated by extemporization on the part of 'those who led the dithyramb'; and the dithyramb was a choral hymn to Dionysus, which is likely to have included a narrative. Ignorant as we are about early dithyramb, it seems likely that the burden was carried by the leader and the main function of the chorus was to utter conventional refrains. But how does a choral performance, even with mimetic dancing (the extent of which we cannot judge), become a drama? There was a tradition, known apparently to Aristotle (though not mentioned in his extant works), current in the Hellenistic period and adopted by Horace in his *Ars poetica* (275–7), which ascribed this development to a certain Thespis from the country-deme of Icaria in Attica. There are many obscurities in the various accounts, but we must suppose that he separated himself from the chorus which he led (what kind of chorus we are not told), assumed a dramatic role and addressed speeches to the chorus: in other words, he stopped singing a story and began to act it. He brought his new invention to Athens, in mid-sixth century or later, where he acted before and after the institution of competitions.

The role of the actor was at first strictly relative to the chorus. The word for actor is *hypokrites*, the sense of which is debated. Some scholars think that it means 'interpreter': the actor elucidated the complexities of the mythical story, partly perhaps through a spoken prologue. (Whether early tragedy had a prologue is itself debated, since two of the surviving plays of Aeschylus, including the earliest, open with the entry of the chorus.) There is still, how-

---

[1] Cf. Björck (1950).   [2] *Poetics* 1449a21.
[3] For criticism of this and other theories see *DTC* 174ff.

ever, much to be said for the view that *hypokrites* means 'answerer'. He answers the questions of the chorus and so evokes their songs. He answers with a long speech about his own situation or, when he enters as messenger, with a narrative of disastrous events; or else he submits to a catechism in stichomythia. Naturally, the transformation of the leader into an actor entailed a dramatization of the chorus, which was easy enough if a citizen-chorus became the spokesmen of a city. The process envisaged, if rather vague, is plausible enough. The problem, however, is complicated in several ways, all controversial.

Thespis was an Athenian, and tragedy was generally regarded as an Attic product. But Aristotle tells us that some of the Dorians in the Peloponnese laid claim to tragedy.[1] There is indeed elusive evidence bearing on tragedy from just those parts of the Peloponnese which were nearest to Attica: from Corinth, Sicyon and Phlius. At Corinth Arion was a notable figure in the days of Periander; that he helped to turn a primitive extemporized dithyramb into an elaborate form of art is beyond doubt. Herodotus tells us this, and only this, but a later writer gives Solon, in his elegies, as the authority for saying that Arion put on 'the first drama of tragedy'. Solon cannot have used the phrase but must have said something to evoke it. The Suda-lexicon mentions Arion's work on dithyramb (clearly following Herodotus), but also says that he was the discoverer of the tragic mode or style (*tropos*), whatever that may mean, and that he brought on the stage 'satyrs speaking verse'.[2] Obscure though this all is (the last words sound like a quotation from comedy),[3] the combination of dithyramb, tragedy and satyrs in one notice is bound to be suggestive. At neighbouring Sicyon, Herodotus tells us that the tyrant Cleisthenes, at war with Argos, wishing to suppress the worship of the Argive *heros* Adrastus whose sufferings were honoured with 'tragic choruses', gave them over to Dionysus.[4] What was it about these choruses that caused the friend of Sophocles to call them tragic? Finally, Pratinas of Phlius is said to have been the first to write satyr plays; and the presumption is that he introduced them from his native city to Athens, where he also practised as a tragedian in the early fifth century. One problem leads into another.

The evidence of Aristotle's *Poetics* is not lightly to be disregarded. Not only does he tell us that tragedy arose from the 'leaders of the dithyramb' but he also uses, mysteriously, the adjective 'satyric' (*satyrikos*): he says that tragedy, beginning with short 'myths' (plots or stories) and ridiculous language, was late in attaining dignity through a change out of a 'satyric' state (or performance), and he adds that the tetrameter was used first because the 'poetry' was 'satyric' and 'more danceable'.[5] Aristotle may, but need not, have meant that tragedy

---

[1] *Poetics* 1448a29–b2.
[2] Herodotus 1.23; Joannes Diaconus, *Comm. in Hermogenem*, ed. H. Rabe, *Rh.M.* 63 (1908) 150; Suda s.v. 'Arion'.
[3] An anapaestic tetrameter?　　[4] Herodotus 5.67.　　[5] *Poetics* 1449a20, 22.

developed out of a dithyramb sung and danced by a satyr chorus; if he did, he could have been right or wrong. There is little or no independent evidence for a satyric dithyramb, but naturally we think of the notice which associates Arion with dithyramb, tragedy and satyrs. At this point in the argument looms up the grotesque shadow of a goat. The members of a tragic chorus were 'goat-singers' (*tragoidoi*). Were they so called because they sang in goatskins or for a goat-prize or in connexion with a goat-sacrifice? Or because they were masquerading as goat-like demons? This sounds attractive but encounters the difficulty that Attic satyrs or *silenoi* had horses' tails. But they were conceived as shaggy and lustful; nor need we rule out this association simply because tragedy became sober and serious. Not only is the evidence on satyrs complex and disputed (see pp. 94ff.), but we are confronted with a basic dilemma. The fact that, in the competition, three tragedies were followed by a satyr play, that satyr plays were written by the same poets as tragedy, on stories drawn from the same fount, and were governed broadly by the same conventions, strongly suggests, if it does not prove, that there was a genetic connexion between the two forms. On the other hand, the members of a satyr chorus are already masked and 'dramatized' as satyrs – a serious obstacle to their re-dramatization as elders (or whatever it might be); and it can be argued that out of a satyr chorus no kind of drama could develop other than a satyr play, which did in fact so develop, perhaps at Phlius. *Non liquet*: neither the degree to which choral performances had approximated to drama in the Peloponnese nor the question whether dithyramb and tragedy shared a satyric background with satyr play can be determined on the evidence.

All three forms, along with comedy, were from the beginning, and remained, part of the cult of Dionysus. The myths sung in dithyramb and then acted in tragedy may originally have been taken from Dionysiac legend, but of these there was a limited supply. The proverbial expression 'nothing to do with Dionysus' (οὐδὲν πρὸς τὸν Διόνυσον) may suggest that the introduction of non-Dionysiac myths gave rise to protest, but this is likely to have happened fairly early in both contexts. In point of theme, tragedy moved away from Dionysus. But was its nature and character, its emotional impact, still in any degree determined by its Dionysiac associations? That there was a political factor is fairly clear. The cult of Dionysus was popular and may have been encouraged by tyrants seeking popular support, as a counterpoise perhaps to established cults under aristocratic control. We have seen some hint of this at Corinth and Sicyon; and at Athens the establishment of tragedy clearly owed much to Pisistratus and his sons (under whom Lasus of Hermione was active in the field of dithyramb). To suggest that their motives were purely political, that they had no concern to promote these new developments of that traditional choral art so intimately bound up with the cultural life of archaic Greece, might be unfair. It is likely, however, to have been under the Cleisthenic democracy that tragedy attained the greater dignity and seriousness of which Aristotle speaks; and one may speculate, if hazardously, about the effect on tragedy of a new social climate in which responsibility for grave decisions was placed upon the body of citizens meeting in the assembly – citizens who would then, at the festivals, meet in the theatre of Dionysus to hear and watch the tragedies.

Certainly, by 472 tragedy had become highly serious, political (in some sense) – and religious. Religious it had always been as part (like comedy) of a cult; and it was no doubt to cult that it owed those masks which became progressively less appropriate to the kind of plays which were written. It cannot be too strongly insisted, however, that tragedy was not itself a ritual,[1] having none of that rigid repetitive character by which ritual is marked, though tragedies did incorporate ritual features if the action so demanded (and choral odes often take the form of hymns and use hymn-language). Nor should we attribute to Dionysus both a hypothetical early grotesquerie and the later seriousness, which tragedy will have owed far more to the fact that it used and interpreted myths that were themselves impregnated with religion and had been treated lyrically in religious contexts, and to a tradition of thought upon great issues of human destiny and divine government which descended to the tragic poets from thinkers such as Hesiod and Solon. The tradition runs from them to Aeschylus.

How much tragedy owed to the sheer genius of Aeschylus, with what truth Murray called him 'the creator of tragedy', is not demonstrable, since we know so little of his predecessors and contemporaries.[2] It is just possible that four mythological play-titles (including *Pentheus*) attributed to Thespis are genuine, but nothing secure can be said about the character of his plays. Choerilus is little more than a name: he is said to have competed with Pratinas and Aeschylus in 499/496. Of Pratinas it is said that 32 of his 50 plays were satyric, which, if true, means that he cannot have operated entirely within the normal fifth-century Attic scheme. There is one substantial and very interesting fragment under his name, in which a chorus of satyrs protest that their words are being drowned by the *aulos*-accompaniment. That this comes from a satyr play rather than a lyric is pure surmise, and it has recently been suggested, with great plausibility, that the fragment really belongs to the late fifth century and has been wrongly attributed to this Pratinas.[3] Of Phrynichus, who won his first victory 511/508 and must have been senior to Aeschylus, we know a little more and get the impression of a considerable figure. In 493, during the archonship of Themistocles, he produced 'The capture of Miletus' (Μιλήτου ἅλωσις), as a result of which he was fined, says Herodotus, by the Athenians for 'having reminded the citizens of their own misfortunes'.[4] In 476 (probably), with

[1] Cf. Vickers (1973) 41f. [2] For bibliography see Appendix.
[3] Cf. Lloyd-Jones (1966) 15–18. [4] Herodotus 6.21.

Themistocles as *choregos*, he won a victory with *Phoenissae*, on the theme of Salamis. He also wrote on normal mythical subjects, about the Danaids, about Actaeon, and others. From Aristophanes we learn that his songs were still famous and sung in the late fifth century.[1] That is, however, no ground for asserting that his plays were more lyrical than dramatic. What kind of plays he wrote, and with what tragic content, we simply do not know,[2] except that he twice used contemporary themes and showed the way for Aeschylus' *Persae*.

2. TRAGEDY IN PERFORMANCE

Anyone who asks: What was Greek tragedy like? What was its effect, in performance? will find the business of answering these questions somewhat frustrating. For we are the prisoners of our evidence, which is everywhere slighter than we could wish, often much later than the period we are chiefly concerned with (the fifth century B.C.), and almost always difficult to interpret. There are all too many vital questions which we cannot answer without some measure of guesswork and speculation, nor without relying on *a priori* assumptions whose validity we can never adequately test. And yet it is essential that we do raise these questions, or else the texts of Greek tragedy must remain inert, like musical scores which we cannot and do not even try to perform. For the texts are essentially scripts for performance, and the style and context of that performance are fundamental to our understanding of the texts themselves.

We can roughly classify our evidence under three heads: the discoveries and conclusions of archaeological research, later tradition about the theatre, and the play texts themselves. Each kind of evidence has its own pitfalls. The evidence of archaeology is itself of two rather different kinds. The first depends on the conclusions to be drawn from the excavation of theatre sites, the second upon the interpretation of visual imagery drawing on the theatre which appears in the painted pottery of fifth-century Attica (and to a lesser extent in other pottery) and also in the relief sculpture and terracotta figures of the late fifth and fourth centuries.

The first stone-built theatre in Athens was the work of the late fourth century, in the decade which saw Athens fall under the domination of Macedon: the site was almost totally reworked in later centuries. Earlier performances, and thus all those in the period which most interests us, relied largely on temporary constructions in wood, which have left little or no trace in the archaeological record. Late tradition connected the earliest performances of tragedy at Athens

---

[1] *Wasps* 220; *Birds* 748ff.

[2] Unless we attribute to him a papyrus fragment containing part of a tragedy based on the story of Gyges (cf. Herodotus 1.8ff.). Scholars are not agreed whether this is a work of the early fifth century or of the Hellenistic period. For bibliography see Appendix.

with the *agora*: we have no reason to doubt the tradition, but the raised platforms for the performers and tiers of wooden seating for the audience have left no mark behind. For most of the fifth century the performances took place in the theatre of Dionysus at the foot of the southern cliff of the Acropolis, where an acting area had been terraced up with a stone retaining wall, but the theatre 'building', the *skene*, at the end of the century was still of wood on a stone foundation, and we can learn very little for certain from what is left of those foundations about the nature of the wooden building above. The evidence of vases and other representations is somewhat better, even if it is thin. Theatre scenes, which characteristically represent actors and chorus-men seen off-stage, before or after performance, occur as early as the first surviving plays of Aeschylus (perhaps earlier), and we have a number of such scenes covering most of the fifth century. But there is a problem of deciding what is relevant: it is never easy to distinguish between pictures of actors presenting roles from the heroic repertory of Greek tragedy and scenes showing the heroic figures themselves, with the artist influenced perhaps by dramatic performance in his imagining of the scene. Before we can be sure that what is being presented to us is a scene of actors and not of mythical figures, we have to have undeniably 'theatrical' features present (dressing scenes, unmistakable masks, or the figure of the *auletes*, the musician who played the double pipe that accompanied sung scenes in Greek tragedy). And even then we have always to reckon with the play of the artist's imagination and with the conventions within which he worked.

With the evidence of later tradition our problems are different again. Here, with the exception of Aristotle, we are dealing with antiquarians, men of the Hellenistic or Roman periods assembling a miscellany of information, almost entirely from their reading, in order to produce encyclopaedias and commentaries which would make intelligible a vanished past. For the most part we can assume that their first-hand knowledge, even of the contemporary theatre, is nil, and we cannot read their sources and assure ourselves of their reliability: often we do not even know to what period their information refers, and this last point is crucial since theatrical productions and indeed the actual pieces performed had changed radically by, say, the second century B.C., let alone by the second or third century A.D. Their evidence can never be used to contradict the evidence of archaeology; it can sometimes fill gaps in that evidence.

Our last category of evidence, that of the play texts themselves, raises problems that are like those we encounter when we try to interpret the painted scenes on pottery: how do we separate the theatrical experience presented solely through the playwright's imaginative use of language from what was there, in concrete fact, before the audience's eyes? In a masked drama, as Greek drama was, it is obvious enough that some things evoked in the play text, such as tears or smiles, existed only in language and in gesture, and did not, in the literal sense,

7

'happen'. But how are we to decide, for example, how much of the scene evoked by the chorus in the Parodos of Euripides' *Ion*, the temple sculpture of Delphi to whose detail they respond with such emotion, or of the complex cave setting in Sophocles' *Philoctetes*, was actually represented in the stage construction of the late fifth-century theatre? What of the presentation of dramatic events such as the earthquake in *Prometheus vinctus*, or Orestes' shooting his arrows at the Furies in the mad scene of Euripides' *Orestes*?[1] As we shall see, these are not easy questions to answer.

The first thing we have to take account of in trying to assess the impact of Greek tragedy as it was experienced in performance is the context of that experience, the place of tragic drama in the life of the Athenian community. Though it was not itself a liturgical, ritual act (see p. 5 above), it was nevertheless part of the worship of divinity, a sacred event with its place fixed in the religious calendar of Athens, and marked as sacred by the actual rituals which surrounded it (such as the torchlight procession in which Dionysus' statue was brought from the altar on the road to Eleutherae to his theatre in Athens, the great phallic procession on the first day of the Dionysia, and the sacrificial rites of purifying the theatre), as well as by the suspension of profane activities of the community during the festival. A second important aspect of the dramatic experience also derives from its social context: it is the analogy with the great religious contests of the Greek world, such as the Olympic and Pythian 'games'. In both, the endemic and potentially disruptive competitiveness of ancient Greek society was validated and sanctified by dedicating conspicuous display of competitive achievement to the worship of the gods. The dramatic performances of Athens, like the athletic contests, took much of their meaning for those who witnessed them from being contests in achievement before the eyes of the community. Playwrights, actors and *choregoi* (Athenians who displayed their wealth by paying lavishly for the costs of performance) were all taking part in competition with one another and the 'victories' of each were publicly proclaimed and attested in the records of the Athenian polis and in conspicuous private monuments alike. The role of the audience, thought of as both 'the Athenians' and 'the Greeks', is to give its recognition to the triumphant prowess of the victor, and, conversely, to deride unmercifully the humiliation of the defeated.

The very size of the audience at Athens (perhaps 15,000) made it natural and indeed accurate to think of the performances as an expression of the Athenian people's solidarity and as an act of the community, with two aspects; the first an act of celebration honouring the gods, and the second the provision of an arena for the acknowledgement of prestige and standing within the community.

[1] Eur. *Ion* 184ff.; Soph. *Phil.* 15ff.; Aesch. *P.V.* 1080ff.; Eur. *Orestes* 253ff.

Both aspects are reflected in the fact that, as we learn from Aristotle, the organization of the festival, the processions and the dramatic performances, was one of the major responsibilities of the archon, the chief magistrate of Athens.[1] The same two aspects of the dramatic performances also mean that, though they represented something radically new in form and presentation, the tragic competitions were rooted in tradition. The plays themselves not only draw heavily on traditional stories and on the traditions of religious imagery which gave those stories much of their significance, but also, in enacting heroic struggle both of man against man and of men against all that is alien to man, contribute to the reinforcing of the traditional values of ancient Greek society, even though the traditional values are at the same time subjected to scrutiny through the constant reshaping of myth. For the whole community, represented in the audience, the performances of tragedy constitute a fusion of the traditional past with a new, innovating present.

This is to put the double-sidedness of past and present, tradition and change, in sociological terms. We can see it equally clearly expressed in the concrete realities of the place and circumstances of performance. The centre of the performance space is the level circular area of the *orchestra*, the dancing-floor, now vanished at Athens in the re-ordering of the theatre of Dionysus for later styles of performance, but present and unaltered in the best preserved of Greek theatres, the theatre of Epidaurus (Pl. I*a* and Fig. 1). This was built probably no earlier than the third century B.C., to plans by an otherwise unknown architect, Polyclitus, but was already famous in later antiquity for the beauty and symmetry of its architectural composition.[2] The *orchestra* is the focal point of the whole design. It measures some twenty metres in diameter (the *orchestra* at Athens was probably a little larger), and is almost two-thirds enclosed by the rising tiers of the auditorium, in the shape of a cone, inverted and truncated. The origins of the *orchestra* are very much earlier than those of drama; in all probability they are to be found in the circular threshing-floors, often terraced out of the hillside, which are dotted in large numbers over the Greek landscape. As well as being the place for threshing grain or drying grapes and figs, such threshing-floors were a place for dancing. Dancing upon a circular floor, with a crowd of spectators surrounding it, is figured in the design of the shield of Achilles in the *Iliad*: 'a dancing-floor like the one Daedalus made in the wide town of Cnossus', on which the dancers circle effortlessly 'like the wheel of a potter when he crouches and works it with his hands to see if it will run' (18.590ff.). Upon such a floor the chorus of tragedy moves: it is the fixed and essential element in the construction of a theatre for dramatic performances. By contrast the ground for spectators might vary considerably in shape and siting. After the abandonment of temporary wooden stands, spectators were almost

---

[1] Aristotle, *Ath. Pol.* 56.2–5.   [2] Pausanias 2.27.5.

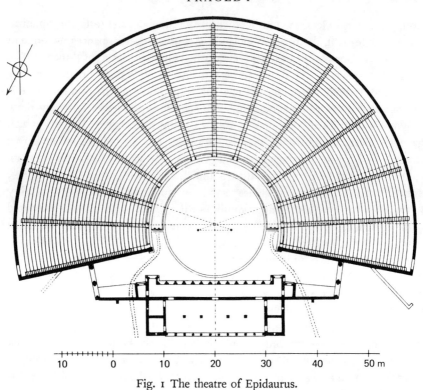

10 0 10 20 30 40 50 m

Fig. 1 The theatre of Epidaurus.

always placed on a hillside, usually curving but often far from the symmetrically graded and curving auditorium at Epidaurus: at Athens the curve is noticeably flatter, hardly more than half enclosing the *orchestra*, with acoustics that can never have been as good as those at Epidaurus, while local village theatres, such as the late sixth-century theatre at Thoricus in Attica, might be wholly lacking in symmetry.[1] Orientation also varied very widely: the theatre at Athens faced roughly south-south-east, while that at Epidaurus was almost diametrically opposed, facing north-north-west. In every case the orientation of the most appropriate hillside determined that of the theatre: at Athens the theatre overlooked the sacred precinct of Dionysus and his archaic temple, while at Epidaurus the sanctuary of Asclepius lay only some 500 metres away below the theatre.

The circular form of the *orchestra* is related to the ring-dances of early Greek folk celebration, and the traditional dance pattern was retained in the circling dance of the fifth-century dithyramb. Dithyrambic competitions for choruses of men and boys, each fifty strong, representing the ten tribes of Attica, also formed part of the celebrations in honour of Dionysus, and seem to have taken

[1] For the date of the theatre at Thoricus, see T. Hackens in Mussche et al. (1965) 75–96.

place in the theatre of Dionysus on the same days as performances of drama. But the chorus of tragedy characteristically moved in line, like a military unit parading, and did not, except rarely, reflect the traditional plan retained in the *orchestra* circle. It was also very much smaller (probably twelve in the plays of Aeschylus; fifteen in the later plays of Sophocles and Euripides), and had consequently a relatively much larger space in which to move.

The sense of openness of space pervades the performances of tragedy; open, not only to the light of the sky, with a total absence of walls or roof to give a feeling of enclosure, but also with open sight lines which converge from every angle on the huge, uncluttered *orchestra* and what lay beyond it. It is with the question of what lay beyond that our difficulties of interpretation begin. At a tangent to the *orchestra* circle but set back a little from its edge there was, by the time of the *Oresteia* at least (458 B.C.), the theatre building called the *skene*, and on either side of it, in the space between it and the forward edge of the half-circle of spectators, two open passage ways by which actors could enter the acting area from outside the theatre. These are the *eisodoi*, the entry passages, and at Epidaurus they pass through formal gateways of stone which stand at right-angles to the supporting wall of the auditorium. Since the late fifth-century *skene* at Athens was built of wood, there are questions we cannot very well answer as to its height and external appearance, the number of doors and other openings in it, and its painted decoration. It was a solid construction, of fairly substantial timbers, but could be taken down between festivals;[1] it seems to have had a flat roof, strong enough to support several actors upon it, and at least one double doorway facing the spectators. It is probable that from the first some such building served as a store-room for masks, costumes and props, and as a green room for actors preparing to make their entries. But we cannot be certain how early it came to be part of the fixed and accepted design of a theatre area or how it was at first interpreted. In Aeschylus' earliest surviving play, *Persae*, it has been convincingly argued that the action of the first part of the play is to be somewhat loosely imagined as taking place inside, not in front of, a building: this is certainly the most obvious and least strained interpretation of the words of the chorus of Persian elders in council with Xerxes' mother, Atossa: τόδ' ἐνεζόμενοι στέγος ἀρχαῖον 'sitting in (near? on?) this ancient building' (140f.). In that case, the *skene* was presumably either not yet in a position behind them as the spectators viewed the scene, or at least not thought of as part of the imagined scene of action, but rather as a non-dramatic piece of theatre equipment, like the banks of spotlights and floods in a modern theatre. But by the early 450s at least the *skene* is thought of as bounding the scene of action and in certain moments part of it. It may represent a building (commonly a palace or a temple) or the background of a scene of seashore or of mountainside. Entrances

---

[1] Xenophon, *Cyropaedia* 6.1.54.

are made from it and the scene of action is now clearly marked as being out of doors: interior scenes can be shown only in tableau.

It is convenient and natural to speak of the 'acting area', but as soon as we ask where it was, and how if at all it was distinguished from the *orchestra*, controversy intensifies. There is some slight evidence, partly in the plays themselves, partly in tenuous traces in the theatre of Dionysus and the fifth-century theatre at Eretria in Euboea, that the space in front of the *skene*, between it and the *orchestra*, was raised a little above the latter, at Athens probably on a low wooden platform with one or two steps down into the *orchestra*. We cannot be certain of this but it seems the most plausible interpretation of our slight evidence. What we can be confident of is that there was no high stage, lifting the actors a metre and a half or more above the level of the chorus, such as was imagined in the last century when reconstructions of the Greek theatre were attempted. Not only do the texts of the plays (such as the scene in Sophocles' *Oedipus at Colonus* (822ff., esp. 856–7) in which the chorus try physically to intervene as Oedipus and Antigone are carried off by the ruthless Creon and his armed men) tell strongly against it, but it is far more convincing to connect the high stage with the much later Hellenistic and above all Roman elaboration of the wooden *skene* into a stone-built façade of several stories. Such structures threatened to dwarf the actors and this effect was countered by raising them above the audience (the chorus having now effectively vanished from the theatre) and then, as we shall see, by elongating their figures with new kinds of mask and footwear which gave added height to suit the new perspective. For the fifth-century Athenian theatre we have to imagine the actors for the most part speaking and moving in front of the *skene* and close to it, on a low platform. One of the functions of the *skene* will thus have been to project the actor's voice forward towards the spectators and lessen the vocal demands made by the scale of the auditorium and theatre space.

The scene displayed before the spectators will thus have been one in which their eyes could travel across the breadth of the acting area and beyond it, into the side passages. The figures in that area will have been relatively few in relation to the space available and their movements therefore the more significant in spatial terms. There are important implications to this. The fact, for example, that entrances and exits, other than through the doorway of the *skene*, had measurable duration for the spectator and were made in full view, means that they had added dramatic weight. They were not instantaneous passages from the invisibility of the wings to the visibility of the stage, but extended happenings with considerable dramatic potential. It is only when we appreciate this that we can understand the dramatic strategy of the scene, for example, in *Oedipus at Colonus* in which Ismene enters. Her long approach is heralded and accompanied by an ecstatic account from Antigone, her sister, who describes to her blind father, in a controlled unfolding of detail, the appearance of the approaching figure, the mare she rides on, her broad Thessalian traveller's hat, until she is within the range of speech, and finally of touch (310ff.). Such moments of intense acceptance contrast with the silent, unacknowledged approach, equally visible, of characters whose arrival is, as it were, rejected and denied and who have to force themselves past the barrier of silence into the world of the play. An example of such entrances is given by the several arrivals of Jason in Euripides' *Medea*: he comes and goes in silence, addresses no greetings and receives no farewells. The dramatic weight of comings and goings is proportional to the openness of space that the Greek theatre presented to the playwright, who was also the producer, for exploitation.

In its function as part of the scene of imagined action, the *skene* is the place where those dramatic events which occur, as we should say, 'off-stage' are imagined as happening. Though it is not true that death is an event which, in Greek tragedy, can never occur in view of the spectators (the deaths of Alcestis and, more disputably perhaps, of Ajax in Sophocles' play are obviously exceptions),[1] nevertheless violent death characteristically occurs within, that is, inside the *skene*, and has its dramatic impact through the death-cries of the victim and the controlled passion of the messenger-speech. But there is another way also open to the playwright to give weight to violent death in his plays, through the use of the interior tableau. Late tradition provides evidence for the existence of a theatrical device known as the *ekkyklema*, most probably a low trolley which could be thrust forward towards the spectators through the doors of the *skene*, and several passages in Aristophanes, parodies in which its use is transferred to tableaux of the domestic interiors of tragic playwrights, make it certain that the device was used in the fifth-century theatre.[2] We can form some idea of its dramatic effect by looking at two scenes. In Aeschylus' *Agamemnon*, the death-cries of the king are followed almost at once by the opening of the *skene* doors and the first words of Clytemnestra's speech of triumph. At line 1379 she says 'I stand where I struck, over the work that I have done', and in the light of the other evidence, it is clear that we are to imagine Clytemnestra standing within the palace over the bodies of Agamemnon and Cassandra, the tableau revealed by the thrusting out of the *ekkyklema*. The scene is hauntingly repeated in the second play of the *Oresteia*, where (*Choephori* 973) the doors open again and this time Orestes stands over his mother's body and that of Aegisthus. In Euripides' *Heracles*, at line 1029, the doors of his palace open, revealing the scene of slaughter and havoc within, which the appearance of Iris and Lyssa (815ff.) had predicted and the messenger-speech (909ff.) described: Heracles is seen slumped unconscious over the bodies of his own children

---

[1] Eur. *Alc.* 387ff.; Soph. *Aj.* 815–65 with 891–9.
[2] Ar. *Ach.* 395–479; *Thesm.* 95–265.

whom he has murdered, then gradually returns to consciousness. In scenes such as these the device of the interior tableau is used to powerful effect.

Another piece of theatrical equipment is also best attested in use in the fifth-century theatre by Aristophanic parody. In *Peace* (154ff.) the hero Trygaeus flies up to heaven on an enormous dung-beetle to interview Zeus, and as with the *ekkyklema* dramatic illusion is suddenly abandoned with a panic-stricken address to the crane-operator (the *mechanopoios*). The *mechane* is a device also attested in later tradition about the theatre, and the scene in *Peace* looks like a parody of one in Euripides' lost play *Bellerophon*, in which Bellerophon flies to heaven on Pegasus. In extant tragedy it may have been used for the appearance of divinities who are described as winging their way through the air, as with Oceanus in *Prometheus vinctus* (284ff.), or Thetis in Euripides' *Andromache* (1228ff.), Athena in his *Ion* (1549ff.) and the Dioscuri in his *Electra* (1233f.): Euripides attained some notoriety for his use of the 'god from the machine'.

It was customary in the theatre of a generation ago, and in the West End commercial theatre of domestic comedies and farces still is customary, for the acting area to be occupied not only by actors but by a proliferation of objects, furniture, ornaments and the like, whose function is to give a naturalistic impression of lived-in space. By contrast the theatre space of Greek tragic drama was starkly bare: the actors were not lost in, nor their movements confined and determined by, a profusion of things defining and occupying space. Stage properties were certainly used, but for their dramatic quality, not to create an ambient illusion. Those of which we can be most certain are the focus of continuing and powerful dramatic emotion: thus, for example, the robe in which Agamemnon is killed in the *Oresteia*. Related to the purple cloths upon which Agamemnon walks to his death, it figures constantly as an image (often as a 'net') in the language of the first play, linking the death of Agamemnon to the fall and sack of Troy; and in the second it is displayed to the spectators by Orestes after the killing of his mother (*Choephori* 980–1020). It is spread out before their eyes ('stretch it out and standing in a circle display the thing that trapped a man') and insistently referred to in the sequel ('this robe', 'this fabric') as the visible symbol of Orestes' right action in killing his mother.[1] Sophocles has a particular inclination towards the use of such powerfully emotive properties: the sword of Ajax, the bow of Philoctetes, the urn in which the ashes of the supposedly dead Orestes are brought to his sister Electra. In Aeschylus stage properties have something of the uncanny force of an object with the power to cause of itself death and destruction, and are analogous in their use to the stage

---

[1] A recently published red-figure vase in Boston, without evident theatrical connexion but dating from the same period as the production of the *Oresteia*, gives a good idea of how Agamemnon's death-robe was imagined, as an almost transparent ankle-length garment without holes for neck or hands: cf. Vermeule (1966) 1–22 and plates 1–3; Davies (1969) 214–60.

events of an eerie strangeness, such as the ghost-raising scene in *Persae* or the Cassandra scene in *Agamemnon*, from which Aeschylus derives much of his theatricality. In Sophocles, on the other hand, they are felt more as the focus of powerful human attachments and feelings, and around these feelings much of the stage action revolves. Their use in Euripides seems more attenuated, even ironical (the shield of Hector in *Troades* 1136ff. or Apollo's bow in *Orestes* 268ff. are slight instances beside the Sophoclean examples: the latter even may be imaginary, the product of Orestes' insane hallucinations), but in all three dramatists their effect in the theatre derives from the spareness of the use of properties in general.

Another kind of property, the appurtenances of splendour and power, seems also to have been used. Such are the chariot in which Agamemnon returns with Cassandra from Troy (*Agamemnon* 906), or that in which Clytemnestra visits her daughter, supposedly in childbirth, at the peasant cottage to which she has been exiled (Euripides, *Electra* 966, 998ff., 1135ff.). They too have a dramatic point to make and underline the ironies of splendour in a context of violent death: they are very different from the illusionistic properties of later theatres. It is much more difficult to be sure about the use of properties, and of painted scenery generally, whose function is largely or solely to create a specific sense of place, the illusion of a scene designated by objects. How, for example, was the raising of Darius' ghost in *Persae* actually staged? Our difficulties in interpreting the contemporary archaeological evidence are well illustrated by a fifth-century Attic vase-painting which has, unconvincingly, been used to answer this particular question. Fragments of a hydria found in Corinth (Pl. I*b*) show a scene which is seemingly marked as theatrical by the presence of the *auletes* playing his double pipe; five or more Oriental, probably Persian, figures are depicted in trousered costume with a flapped headdress, and in attitudes of horror or amazement, but without any attempt to suggest that they are wearing masks. The central figure is a king, to judge from a wooden pyre, constructed of logs with each row laid at right angles to the one below. The pyre is alight and flames are licking about it. What are we to make of this? It seems unlikely, though on purely *a priori* grounds, that burning pyres formed part of the stage properties of a fifth-century tragedy: perhaps the combination of the *auletes* and the horrific scene presented was meant to evoke a dramatic moment described in a messenger-speech or even in a dithyramb. Perhaps, though, our assumptions are false and such a scene could have been staged literally as depicted. The question is an open one.

The problem of such properties and of scenery inevitably brings in the evidence of later tradition: our earliest source is Aristotle who records laconically that Sophocles introduced *skenographia* ('painting the *skene*') into performances of tragedy (*Poet.* 1449a18f.). A much later source, the Roman architect

Vitruvius, asserts that Aeschylus adopted the idea from the painter Agatharchus of Samos.[1] Like the introduction of a third actor, this development seems to have been attributed to the decade in which the theatrical careers of Aeschylus and Sophocles overlapped, with some uncertainty about which of the two was responsible. But how are we to interpret the assertion? Tragedies were performed at the Athenian City Dionysia in sequences of three, followed by a satyr play, and it was normal for the three tragedies to have no continuity of setting: even Aeschylus, who alone seems frequently to have written connected sequences of three plays presenting different stages in the unfolding of a single story, did not seek to place his plays within a single setting. Indeed the third play of the *Oresteia* itself involves a change of setting, from before the temple of Apollo at Delphi to the Areopagus at Athens. Another of Aeschylus' plays, the *Women of Aetna*, seems to have had a setting which was imagined to shift five times within the play.[2] But here (the play is lost and the assertion occurs in the ancient *hypothesis*) the inference must be from the language of the play and we may be dealing with an action very loosely anchored in spatial terms, as we are in *Persae*, where the relationship between the 'ancient building' of line 141 and the tomb of Darius later in the play is left entirely open and the setting almost freely variable. There is a world of difference between this and the opening, for example, of Sophocles' *Electra*, where the evocative landmarks of Argos are pointed out one after another by the *paidagogos* to Orestes on his return as a young man from exile since childhood. The introduction of 'painting the *skene*' almost certainly falls between these two plays. Indeed we have already seen that in the earliest plays there may have been no *skene*-building placed so as to focus the acting area immediately in front of it. In the early plays of Aeschylus (*Persae, Septem contra Thebas, Supplices*) it is noticeable that the setting is either left without precise locality or imagined as an open space: there are several references to a rocky crag or mound (*Persae* 659f., the tomb-mound of Darius; *Supplices* 189; the crag recurs in the probably somewhat later *Prometheus vinctus*, lines 20, 130, 272 etc.); moreover in the theatre of Dionysus at Athens the ground beyond the *orchestra* from the spectators was almost two metres lower than the *orchestra* terrace itself. Thus the placing of a *skene* in that area may have been a development of the middle or late 460s and 'painting the *skene*' may have occurred very shortly after the building itself was first constructed so as to close the spectators' view.

As to what was painted we have no contemporary evidence and are left to guess: the most plausible guess is that it represented a building or buildings or a landscape-setting painted in a kind of primitive perspective with multiple

[1] Vitruvius, *De architectura* 7.1.11; cf. 1.2.2. For Agatharchus' date, which is disputed, see also Plutarch, *Alcibiades* 16.5; *Pericles* 13.3 and the discussion in Pollitt (1974) 236–47.
[2] Aesch. fr. 287 Lloyd-Jones.

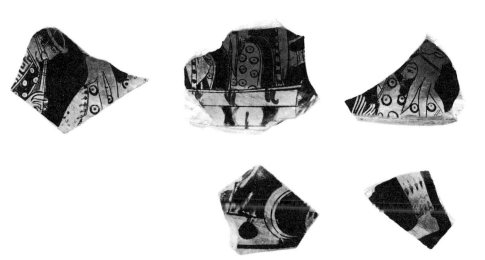

Ia Epidaurus: the theatre from the air.
Ib Fragments of a hydria found in Corinth, showing an *auletes* and figures in oriental costume.

17

IIa Red-figure pelike from Cervetri showing actors dressing and rehearsing, *c.* 430 B.C.
IIb Red-figure bell-krater showing actors dressing and rehearsing, *c.* 460 B.C.

IIIa Vase-painting in several colours, *c.* 350 B.C., from Tarentum. This seems to show a painted backdrop for a play, rather than a stage building.

IIIb Wall-painting from Herculaneum, probably a copy of a Greek model of *c.* 300 B.C., showing an actor and his mask.

IVa Red-figure jug from Athens, *c.* 470–460 B.C., showing the mask of a tragic heroine.
IVb Red-figure vase-painting from Athens, *c.* 400 B.C., showing a female tragic mask.
IVc Vase-painting in several colours, *c.* 340 B.C., from Tarentum, showing an actor holding his mask.

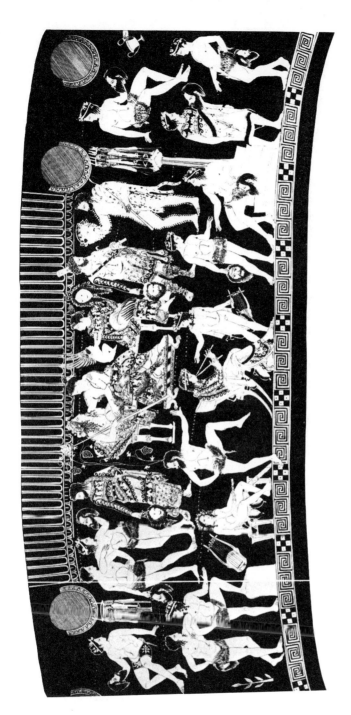

▽ The Pronomos Vase: red-figure volute-krater from Athens, c. 400 B.C., showing actors, a satyr chorus, an *auletes*, the play-wright and a lyre-player.

vanishing points. This tradition of painting was connected with Agatharchus and found its fullest expression considerably later, in the Hellenistic wall-paintings which were the source for the painted 'theatrical sets' used to decorate the houses of southern Italy, at Pompeii, Herculaneum and Boscoreale. Our earliest evidence for this tradition comes from a vase of the mid-fourth century from Tarentum in southern Italy which shows (on Erika Simon's interpretation),[1] not a stage-building, but a painted theatre set of a building, with projecting porticoes at either end, each crowned by a pediment with gilded *akroteria* and ceiling panels, and with two double doors, one at the end of each portico (Pl. III*a*). But the relevance of this painting to the fifth-century Athenian theatre is highly uncertain.

When we turn to the question of actors and acting styles, we are to begin with on firmer ground. The first, essential fact is that all actors and chorus-men in Greek tragedy were male: that is, that female parts were acted, not by boys as in the Shakespearian theatre, but by adult men, often of middle age or older. For acting careers in the tragic theatre seem to have been long.

The actor Mynniscus who acted for Aeschylus (that is before 456 B.C.) won first prize in a play by Menecrates in the competition of 422 and in the late fourth century the actor Polus was still performing eight tragedies in four days at the age of seventy.[2] It is tempting to suggest that the part of Clytemnestra in the *Oresteia* was played by Aeschylus himself, then in his late sixties: tradition recorded that it was Sophocles who was the first playwright to abandon acting the leading part in his own plays, and that was not at the beginning of his career (he almost certainly acted in his early plays *Thamyras* and *Plyntriai*). Thus we have to imagine not merely female roles that convey an almost aggressively masculine feeling, such as that of Clytemnestra or of Euripides' Medea, played by men, but also highly 'feminine' roles such as those of Io in *Prometheus*, Deianira in *Trachiniae* or Euripides' Creusa (in *Ion*), Iphigenia or Helen: the only comparable theatrical experience available to us is perhaps the same tradition in the Japanese No and Kabuki theatres. The parts of children were indeed played on stage by children, but as silent mimes: children are never given spoken lines in Greek tragedy, and it is noticeable that the brief snatches of sung lamentation, which is all the utterance that they are given, are always so placed that there is a male actor available to sing them off-stage.

In his account of the development of tragedy, Aristotle records the introduction of a second actor by Aeschylus, and of a third by Sophocles: at this point, in Aristotle's view, tragedy had 'attained its natural form' and no further changes took place (*Poet.* 1449a14f.). Correspondingly, the series of nouns 'protagonist', 'deuteragonist', 'tritagonist' does not continue beyond its third member. It follows that, down to Aristotle's time, only three actors were avail-

[1] Simon (1972) 35.   [2] Plutarch, *Moralia* 785b.

able to the playwright in writing and casting his plays. Silent walking-on parts might be used: hence the unspeaking figures such as Pylades in the Electra plays of Sophocles and Euripides. The explanation for this limitation may have been financial but is more likely to have been aesthetic and practical. It will not have been easy to find large numbers of trained voices capable of meeting the vocal demands of text and theatre. In addition, masked drama makes it difficult to identify the source of speech, so that if a considerable number of speakers are all engaged together in dialogue the audience may become confused: it is very noticeable that even with three actors a genuinely free-flowing three-cornered dialogue is extremely rare in Attic tragedy. Usually, if two speakers are engaged in dialogue, the third is silent until one or other has fallen out of the exchange: a carefully patterned sequence of utterances is the norm, as in the scene between Oedipus, Creon, Jocasta and the chorus in *Oedipus tyrannus* (512ff.). An important consequence of the limitation, of course, is the doubling of parts by a single actor; occasionally, even, the splitting of a single part between two actors. We cannot in the nature of things be certain which actor played which parts in a given play (a subject on which we have no direct evidence), but sequences of entrances and exits, speech and silence, often suggest inferences, and the likely doubling of parts is sometimes striking in its histrionic possibilities. The probability that the parts of Deianira and Heracles (in *Trachiniae*), of Phaedra and Theseus (in *Hippolytus*) or of Pentheus and Agave (in *Bacchae*) were played by the same male actor gives an idea of the challenge to an actor's technical skills, and a messenger-speech will often have been delivered by an actor who in the same play also acts the part of one of the central figures in the scene he is describing: again *Bacchae* produces an example, since the messenger is likely to be the same actor as he who played the part of Dionysus.

The extreme case of doubling and splitting parts is that of Sophocles' *Oedipus at Colonus*, where on a strict interpretation of the three-actor limit the role of Theseus must be played by two, perhaps even three, actors and Ismene is present but silent for almost a third of the play, played by an 'extra' (in the technical language of the theatre a *kophon prosopon*, a silent mask), because no fourth actor was available. The story of Oedipus' death, involving his two daughters, his son, Creon and Theseus in a shifting pattern of conflict and loyalty, presented a fifth-century dramatist with major problems of dramatic construction.

Soon after the introduction of the third actor, acting as such, as a skill distinct from that of play-writing, became a sphere of achievement in its own right, and from 449 B.C. actors, as well as playwrights, were ranked in competition and awarded prizes. The entry into the theatre of the new specialism is perhaps reflected in the extent to which sung passages (not unlike operatic recitatives and arias) are given to actors of the later fifth century: already in the *Oresteia* such sung passages are important (the Cassandra scene of *Agamemnon* is the most striking example: the part of Cassandra was perhaps played by Mynniscus, the recently introduced third actor), and in Euripides actor-arias figure from the first and play a steadily increasing and important part in his later productions. The actor's apprenticeship in the chorus may be one of the factors lying behind this development.

Before we turn to the question of acting techniques, we must look at the evidence for the actor's theatrical appearance, his costume and mask. All actors, whether playing speaking or silent parts, and the members of the chorus, were masked: indeed the word *prosopon* means not only 'face' and 'mask', but also 'character' in the theatrical sense. Only the *auletes* (who played throughout in view of the spectators) was unmasked. Masks were full face and covered the whole of the front half of the head, including the ears, with wigs attached. Fifth-century masks seem to have been made of linen or other flexible material, stuccoed over with plaster and painted: none has survived. Vase paintings are our best evidence. The earliest certain example of a theatrical mask appears depicted on fragments of a red-figure jug found in the *agora* at Athens and dating from 470/460 B.C. (Pl. IV*a*). It is the mask of a female character, painted white in the conventional way in which female skin colour was shown in all Greek art, with hair cropped short and held in with a head-band; the eyes are fairly wide-set, almond-shaped not circular, and the mouth is small in proportion to the breadth of the face and the lips only slightly parted. There is no striving after intense emotional expression in the painting of forehead, eyebrows or mouth; rather a certain openness of regard. The style is reminiscent, as has been pointed out, of the so-called 'severe style' of the temple sculptures of Olympia, which date from around 460 B.C., and there seems to be nothing specifically 'theatrical' in its presentation. The general impression of clarity and simplicity of expressive means is confirmed by other paintings of masks on Attic pottery in the decades from 460 to 430 or a little later, such as the dressing scenes on a bell-krater in Ferrara (Pl. II*b*) and on a pelike in Boston (Pl. II*a*), and a more imaginatively treated scene of a chorus-man who has become the maenad whose role he is playing, with theatrical reality retained only in the mask and in the figure of the *auletes* who faces him: in the last two, the mask is shown in profile and we can form a clear impression of its relationship to the actor's own head and hair, which is commonly cut short and held in by a sweat-band. To the last decade of the fifth century probably belong two vases (Pl. IV*b* illustrates one of them), perhaps by the same painter, and a relief from the Piraeus. From all three we can see that the mask mouth is now somewhat larger and more widely open, though still very far from the gaping, almost trumpet-like mouths of Hellenistic and Roman masks: the effect of emotional strain in the painting of the face is also rather more marked, with the forehead and the area of the mouth heavily lined.

One of the two vases, the so-called Pronomos vase in Naples (Pl. V), is our most detailed and magnificent depiction of a scene of actors: it figures three, perhaps four actors carrying masks and in costume, and a complete satyr chorus, as well as the *auletes* (the central figure, who must have commissioned the painting), the playwright and a lyre-player, all three named on the vase. One of the actors is dressed to play the part of Papposilenus, the stock old man who accompanies the satyr chorus, wearing neck-to-ankle tights of white fleece flocked with tufts of wool, with a leopard-skin over his left shoulder and carrying a mask of grotesque and sad old age: his role in extant satyr plays makes it clear that he is not the chorus-leader. This is presumably the figure to the right of the altar bearing the victory tripod, who holds a satyr mask (indicated by its snub nose, wrinkled forehead and animal ears) but wears an elaborately decorated *chiton*. The other satyr chorus-men wear only bathing-trunk shaped tights of animal skin with a large, erect phallus and animal tail attached: they too have their human names on the vase. There is continuing argument over the three figures dressed as actors and carrying masks, two of whom flank the central couch in the upper bank while the third is perched on its foot: are they actors from the cast of a tragedy or from a satyr play? Happily there is no need to pursue the argument here, since the silence of all our sources makes it virtually certain that, apart from Papposilenus, the actors in a satyr play (as distinct from the chorus) were not distinguished by mask or dress from those in a tragedy. The actor who faces Papposilenus is playing Heracles, as his club and lion-skin (worn with a breastplate over it) make clear, while the figure who balances him at the other end of the couch has a mask with an oriental tiara attached: his part is not that of a Greek. The third figure with a mask (also with tiara) has the face of a woman, not a male actor: we are perhaps to think of her as the image of an abstraction, perhaps Tragedy or *Paidia*, the burlesque personification of the satyr play, dressed as though an actor. Interpretation is difficult, since in the artist's eye these last three figures have become fused with their parts and have taken on a heroic and distant dignity: none is named on the vase. The latest (and persuasive) suggestion of a subject for the play in which these actors appeared is the story of Heracles and Omphale.[1]

Two other representations of actors come from later centuries and from outside Athens, but are still of interest. The first is a fragment from Tarentum (Pl. IVc), like the *skиngraphia* painting we have already discussed, and is of much the same date in the second half of the fourth century. The mask, again seen in profile, is not very different from those on the Pronomos vase of half a century earlier, the eyebrows and forehead perhaps more strongly marked but the mouth-opening no greater, the forehead no higher: it suggests that there had been little change in masking designs. The piece is particularly interesting for a new, sociological point that it makes in the eloquent contrast between actor and

[1] Simon (1971) and (1972) 30.

part: the actor is stocky, balding and greying, square-faced and flat-nosed, with the stubble of a beard strongly marked on his chin and jaws; beside his mask he is palpably ordinary. Conversely, on a wall painting from Herculaneum but drawing probably on a Hellenistic picture of around 300 B.C. (Pl. III*b*), the actor appears as matinée idol, handsome, tall and slim with delicate hands and hair elegantly ruffled. The painting of his mask is in equally striking contrast with its vast, staring sunken eyes, mouth hugely open and towering pointed forehead and peak of hair, the *onkos* of theatre handbooks. It belongs to the new theatre of the Hellenistic world, in which as we have seen the actor has to compete with the towering stone façade behind him, and will serve as a classic reminder of what the fifth-century mask was *not* like.

Besides giving us, at least in general terms, a fair idea of the look of fifth-century masks, the pottery scenes we have considered also remove another widespread misunderstanding about the actor's appearance. In the Hellenistic and Roman theatres actors wore shoes and boots with blocked soles and heels to give them extra stature by perhaps as much as six inches. The pottery scenes make it absolutely clear that footwear of this kind was never worn in the fifth-century theatre. What we find on the vases is actors either barefoot or wearing shoes or boots (it is not always possible to tell which, but in some cases certainly they are calf-length) made of soft, pliable leather with a thin sole and a marked turning up of the toes. Such shoes appear on the pottery scenes from the 460s right through to the end of the century, sometimes elaborately decorated, sometimes plain: they seem to be early established as the traditional actor's footwear. If the actor's boot was, in the fifth century, called a *kothornos* (and there is no contemporary evidence that it was), then passages in Herodotus, Aristophanes and Xenophon make it clear that its associations were not with added stature but with women (Dionysus in actor's gear is even more effeminate than usual) and with a degree of looseness of fit that ruled out distinctions of left and right.[1] The tradition that connects Aeschylus with the platform-soled boots of the Hellenistic theatre is certainly the result of some misunderstanding, which goes back at least to Horace, probably to the third century B.C., and presumably arose when the word *kothornos* had come only to refer to what was by then the characteristic footwear of the actor.[2]

Our evidence for costume is somewhat confusing. If we take the pottery scenes as our guide, the picture is of a dress that becomes markedly more elaborate and stylized as the century proceeds, though interpretation is complicated by the fragmentary state of some of the pots and the fact that while some of the scenes can be firmly identified as representations of chorus-men and others

---

[1] Herodotus 1.155.4; 6.125.3–4; Ar. *Frogs* 47; *Lys.* 657; *Eccl.* 313ff.; Xenophon, *Hellenica* 2.3.30f.

[2] Horace, *Ars poetica* 280.

of actors, some remain uncertain. The earlier scenes show actors or chorus-men generally in a long, ankle-length *chiton* with a heavier *himation* over it: decoration consists largely of borders and there are no sleeves, any more than there were in contemporary dress outside the theatre. But by the end of the century, on the Pronomos vase, for example, and on other scenes that seem to have at least heavily theatrical overtones, the actor appears wearing costumes of elaborately decorated and heavy material, with sleeves that stretch to the wrist: an example is an Attic krater found at Capua showing the captive Andromeda surrounded by figures some of whom have a distinctly theatrical air. From now on, sleeves seem to be an unchanging and characteristic feature of costume in the theatre as they never were in the world outside. At all periods, of course, distinctive costume can be used to identify characters (such as Heracles, Hermes or Dionysus) or groups (the Persians on the pyre scene from Corinth (Pl. I*b*) wear trousers, like the Ethiopian girl on the Andromeda krater). But rich and elaborately patterned fabrics made up into sleeved garments are the mark of the actor dressed to play a part. It seems likely enough that the sleeved *chiton* came into the theatre through being worn by the *auletes*, who is shown wearing it from the first, in a garment of almost standardized patterning of black circles with a central dot and a long stripe running from shoulder to ankle. We could be fairly confident of recognizing the late fifth-century actor by the richness and stylization of his costume if it were not for a string of jokes in Aristophanes about Euripides' repeated use of actors dressed in rags (*Acharnians* 412ff.).

Aristophanes' jokes seem to suggest that we are wrong, about Euripides at least, but perhaps a simple inference as to theatrical fact would be a mistake: Aristophanes has a habit of making comic capital out of treating the metaphors of tragic language as statements of literal fact (for example, the stage business with the chopping-block in *Acharnians* when Dicaeopolis offers his head as guarantee of his words, 355ff.) and this may be merely another example. Certainly Euripidean characters do talk of themselves as tattered, dishevelled and sometimes filthy (his Electra or the shipwrecked Menelaus of *Helen* are good examples), but already in Aeschylus' *Persae* the defeated Xerxes is described as returning with his clothing torn to shreds.[1] Faced with this contradiction between the evidence of the pottery and that of comedy, we can only back a hunch: it seems most likely that the vases show what the spectators actually saw in the theatre, and that Aristophanes' jokes do no more than exploit Euripides' intensification of the language of degradation in his plays. The nearest we get to 'rags' in the pottery evidence is the rather muted brown fringed *chiton* of the actor on the Tarentum fragment (Pl. IV*c*).

From the evidence we have been discussing we can form a good impression of an actor's visual impact in the theatre. But what of his acting? We have to

---

[1] Eur. *El.* 184ff., 304ff.; *Hel.* 415ff., 554; Aesch. *Pers.* 834ff., 1017ff.

make do here with generalized accounts of the emotional effect that acting could have on an audience, with scrappy references to voice production and to gesture, and with what we can infer from the play texts and from the actor's costume and mask. Descriptions of an actor's performance in terms of the emotional experience involved are certainly important, but they can tell us almost nothing of the technique that produced that experience. Descriptions of Japanese actors in the No and Kabuki theatres, of actors in the Shakespearian theatre from those of his own day through to Garrick, Kean and Irving are all evidence for the sense of 'life' displayed and for the emotions aroused in the audience, but where we can compare these accounts with more technical descriptions or with present-day representations of the same tradition, we can readily perceive the stylization involved and the extent to which it is the audience's acceptance of a particular stylization which leads to the experience of 'naturalness' and to a strong, direct emotional response. That there was such a response to the performance of Greek tragedy is clear enough: it is attested in stories such as that of the great fourth-century actor Polus moving an entire audience to tears by his playing, under the impact of his own son's death, the part of Electra in the recognition scene of Sophocles' *Electra* (Aulus Gellius 6.5). That is a late story: other similar stories refer to fifth- and fourth-century actors such as Callippides, Theodorus and Satyrus. A near-contemporary analogy is Ion's account in Plato (*Ion* 535c–e) of his solo performances of the Homeric poems: the audience weep, their faces filled with anger, while his own eyes well with tears and his heart pounds. But references to the actor's technique are more often concerned with qualities of voice, and many of them refer to dieting and to vocal training and exercises that suggest the world of opera rather than the spoken theatre. Actors, of course, might have to sing, but it is clear that vocal control, the capacity to vary tone and colour as well as dynamic range, was a prime requirement for delivery of the spoken as well as the lyric portions of the complex texts of Greek tragedy in a large, open-air theatre space.

As for style in movement and gesture, there are traces of changes in the fifth century. Aeschylus' third actor Mynniscus is reported by Aristotle (*Poet.* 1461b26ff.) as having described his younger contemporary Callippides as an 'ape' for his excessively emotional and extravagant style of gesture and move ment: Callippides won a victory at the Lenaea of 418 B.C. It is a reasonable guess that the development of sleeves in the actor's costume and the increasingly striking decoration was partly at least a response to the need to make gesture more expressive and more clearly visible, so that an actor's 'line' (to use a ballet term) was more marked. On the other hand, both the thin soled shoe and what we hear in later tradition about the movements of the chorus suggest that a smooth and gliding movement of the body was more typical of tragedy than angularity and muscular tension, a sinuous continuity rather than explosive staccato movements. The construction of the plays themselves, the formality of long speeches on the one hand, and of such exchanges as stichomythia on the other, must have inhibited the development of a wholly naturalistic delivery and movement. It would be contrary to what we know of theatre history elsewhere to assume a divorce between styles of writing and styles of acting since the playwright was himself very much of the theatre, and it is not until the fourth century, when revivals become a feature of the dramatic festivals, that the question of 'interpreting' in the theatre an existing body of classic plays can have arisen. An increasingly 'expressive' use of voice and gesture in the last quarter of the fifth century would be exactly what we should expect from changes in the writing of plays, particularly in the later theatre of Euripides. In his plays, along with a spoken line that becomes steadily freer and more flexible in its metrical patterning goes a rapid adoption of the new possibilities of expressiveness offered by developments in music. In the hands of composer-poets such as Melanippides and Timotheus, the tight structuring of sung passages by the demands of symmetrical responsion of stanzas and the harmonic discipline of modal composition gives way to a new astrophic use of long, highly flexible stanzas and to the abandonment of the strict demands of the musical mode. Euripides adopts these features as early as *Troades*, and late plays such as *Ion*, *Helen* and *Orestes* are marked by a quite new style of writing in which long, elaborate arias are given to actors as well as by increasing experimentation in the use of new versions of old forms, such as immensely extended passages of stichomythia and of whole scenes written in trochaic tetrameters. It is likely enough that all of this goes closely with developments in acting style aimed at a greater range of expressive possibilities. If we imagine Callippides in the role of the Phrygian slave in *Orestes* (1369ff.), we can well understand the reaction of an older generation of actors whose style had been moulded by the far more severely controlled writing of Aeschylean theatre.

3. AESCHYLUS

Aeschylus won his first victory in 484, which will be a firm date based on records, and it could throw some slight suspicion on 525/524 as the date of his birth (*floruit*-dating?), though, if he competed as early as 499/496, it may not be too far out. He was born to Euphorion, a eupatrid, at Eleusis. The known facts of his life are few. He fought at Marathon, where his brother Cynegeirus fell; doubtless at Salamis, which he describes; and perhaps also at Plataea. When he wrote of war, he wrote as one who knew its glory and its misery. He visited Sicily at least twice. Some time between 472 and 468 he was at the court of Hieron I at Syracuse, where he is said to have revived *Persae* and, in honour of the newly-founded city of Aetna, produced a play called *Aetnaeae* (part of the argument to which may be preserved on a papyrus).[1] In 458 or later, after the fall of the Sicilian tyrants, he went to Gela, where he died in 456. What part, if any, he played in Athenian politics is debated, but there is reason to suppose he was sympathetic towards Themistocles, who was in trouble when Aeschylus wrote his *Persae*; and it seems clear from *Eumenides* that he accepted the radical reforms of the Areopagus by Ephialtes, but scholars are not agreed whether it was with enthusiasm as an extreme democrat or with reserve as a 'moderate'. His importance to us is that he wrote plays. He wrote, acted and produced, devising new dance-movements for the chorus. His mastery of stage-effect is obvious.

The number of his victories is given both as 13 and as 28.[2] The latter figure must include victories won after his death, since we are told he was granted the unique honour that his plays might be entered in subsequent competitions; the lower figure in itself suggests a considerable pre-eminence. Some 80 of his titles are known to us, but only seven of his plays survive entire, three of which constitute the trilogy of the *Oresteia*. The trilogy was a striking feature of his dramatic art. It had become a rule of the competition (we cannot say when) that each poet should put on three tragedies followed by a satyr play. These plays could be, and after Aeschylus generally were, unconnected with one another, but it was clearly his practice, at least during his later career, to write three tragedies dealing with successive phases of the same myth, followed by a satyr play on a closely related story.[3] (It is to these linked plays that the terms trilogy and tetralogy are alone properly applied.) We have the rare good fortune that a complete Aeschylean trilogy has survived, since without it we could hardly have understood how he used this form to explore human destiny upon an extended time-scale or how he imposed architectonic unity so as to create, virtually, a single work of art. It follows that, where, as with *Septem contra Thebas*, *Supplices* and (probably) *Prometheus*, we possess only one play out of three, interpretation labours under a grave disability. Of the lost plays some can with certainty, and others with fair probability, be grouped in trilogies.[4] It is quite likely that Aeschylus invented the form (though others are known to have used it), but how early we cannot tell. Some titles are known, and others conjectured, to be satyric, about 15 in all, but, since we do not know when the rule of three tragedies and a satyr play came in, we have no idea how many

[1] Cf. Lloyd-Jones (1957) 593.

[2] Works: for references and bibliography see Appendix.

[3] E.g. the satyr play of *Oresteia* was *Proteus* (Menelaus and Helen in Egypt, cf. Homer, *Od.* 4.351ff.); of the Theban trilogy *Sphinx*; of the Danaid trilogy *Amymone*.

[4] A *Lycurgeia* is certain, cf. schol. *ad* Ar. *Thesm.* 134 (*Edoni, Bassarides, Neaniskoi*, satyr play *Lycurgus*), and an *Achilleis* virtually certain (*Myrmidones, Nereides, Phryges* or *Ransom of Hector*). A second Dionysiac trilogy (including *Semele* and *Pentheus*) is highly probable; also a trilogy on the Ajax-story (*Judgement of the arms, Threïssae, Salaminiae*); possibly trilogies on the Argonauts and on Odysseus. In some cases there may have been only two related plays. Cf. Mette (1959) and Lloyd-Jones (1957).

satyr plays Aeschylus had been required to write, though we know that his reputation in this line was great. His early career is thus quite obscure, and it is not until 472 that we reach firm ground, and that with a play which differs from the other extant plays in two respects.

Between *Persae* and the lost plays produced with it (*Phineus, Glaucus Potnieus,* and the satyric *Prometheus pyrkaeus*) there is no discernible link; it is the only extant tragedy on a subject taken from contemporary history. It might seem surprising that a tragedian could move from, say, Achilles to Xerxes, from Xerxes back to Agamemnon, but this is to misunderstand the twin facts that the Greeks regarded myth as history and that Aeschylus treated history as myth. If the emotions of a recent threat and triumph were vividly evoked (if Themistocles, and perhaps Aristides, were not forgotten), the Persians are not mocked, and patriotic exultation takes second place to a religious interpretation of events which has, to a degree, determined the form of the play. Stiff and archaic the form may seem. The play opens with the chorus of Persian counsellors: concerned that no news has come from the great expedition, they declaim and sing for 150 lines before the first character appears. It is the mother of Xerxes, who tells them of an ominous dream that the great king's chariot had been wrecked, when he tried to yoke two women, one in Persian dress, one in Greek. Then enters the second actor, a messenger, giving the news of Salamis to queen and chorus. Messenger-speeches are a staple feature of Greek tragedy: so also are *kommoi* or lyric-scenes between chorus and actor (or actors); and *Persae* ends with a long and tense lamentation between Xerxes and the elders. But the return of a humiliated Xerxes is postponed, while the ghost of Darius is raised from his tomb. Spectacular effects are found elsewhere in Aeschylus, who was held by ancient critics to aim at 'astonishment'; and this apparition, prepared by an incantation, must have been sensational enough. But Darius was introduced not merely to amaze but to instruct; not merely because he has foreknowledge of that other great disaster at Plataea, but because he alone (though a Persian) understands the significance of events and the moral order upheld by Zeus who 'is set as the chastener of minds that are over-proud, and heavy is the account which he exacts' (827f.). Earlier in the play the divine power is seen as cruel, fickle and unpredictable; so it is seen by Xerxes on his return. The final *kommos* – a ritual dirge with its music and dance-movements – may be the emotional climax of the piece, but by reverting to the religious notions and superstitious tone of the earlier phase it highlights the advanced morality of the Darius-scene, which is thematically and structurally the central feature.

In *Septem contra Thebas* five years later (467), if we find once more an austere simplicity of structure, we are confronted with far more complex problems of interpretation, and that not only because the plays which preceded it in the trilogy (*Laius, Oedipus*) are lost. In *Persae* the moral and religious issue is straightforward: Xerxes and his Persians offend and are punished. The Theban trilogy is, like *Oresteia*, the story of a doomed house; and *Septem* came at the end of a series of disasters – and doubtless crimes – in the royal house of Thebes, initiated by Laius and affecting the destinies of Oedipus and his sons. How the earlier events were distributed and handled in the lost plays we do not know with any certainty. The third play opens after the death of Oedipus and the quarrel of his sons; Polynices, in exile, has brought a foreign army against Thebes, and Eteocles leads the defenders. It opens with a speech by Eteocles, who is virtually the sole character in the play. That a play should be so dominated by a character is something new, and we shall not find it again except in *Agamemnon* and *Prometheus vinctus*. A word should be said at this point about characterization in Aeschylus.

It is austere and limited and in keeping with the archaic simplicity of the dramatic action. The extent to which Aeschylus was interested in character for its own sake is not easily defined. It has been said, with much truth, that the Aeschylean character is his role in the play and nothing more. What complicates the case of Eteocles is the fact that his role is twofold: he is at once 'lord of the Cadmeans', leading the defence of his native-city, and 'son of Oedipus', lying under his father's curse which he is bound to fulfil in the mutual fratricide; and he is thus the focus of a twofold issue, since the fates of family and city are both involved. When, at the climax of the play, he decides to fight his brother at the seventh gate, this has been seen as the instantaneous transformation of conscientious patriot into demon-haunted fratricide. It is less simple than that. The motivation of Eteocles is specifically explored, and a complex fabric is woven out of patriotic duty, personal honour, brotherly hatred, and paternal curse. If Aeschylus has not created a 'character' in the modern sense, he has imposed a notable figure on the stage, but how, exactly, we are meant to understand the relationship of the curse-Erinys to the human motives of Eteocles is hard to determine in the absence of the earlier plays.

We are left with a strangely gripping, if elusive, play. Once again, there is a big central scene, in which a spy describes the foreign champions at each gate and Eteocles posts a defender against each. The sombre rhetoric is magnificent; but what could be more static? Yet a tension is built up towards the moment of decision, when Eteocles finds his brother at the seventh gate. At the end of the play we are confronted with one of those textual problems which dog the study of Aeschylus. Enter Antigone and Ismene and a herald who forbids the burial of Polynices. But many scholars believe that all this was interpolated subsequent to the *Antigone* of Sophocles, that the authentic play ended with the young women of Thebes who form the chorus lamenting over the brothers.

If there is an archaic stiffness about *Persae* and *Septem*, what could be more archaic than *Supplices*? The play opens, like *Persae*, with the entry of the chorus, to which well over half the lines belong. There are still only two actors, and little use is made of the second; there is no dominant figure, but as it were a collective heroine; the dramatic interest is in their fate, the dramatic tension is generated by their songs. It is not surprising that this was long regarded as the earliest play, datable perhaps to the 490s. Perhaps scholars should have been more cautious, reflecting, among other things, on the leading role played by the chorus in *Eumenides*, on the function of choral odes in *Agamemnon*, and in general on that deep concern of the Aeschylean chorus with the action, and the interpretation of action, which is nowhere more evident than in *Oresteia*. In 1952, however, there was published a fragmentary didascalic notice on papyrus which indicates that the Danaid trilogy was victorious in competition with Sophocles, who first competed in 468 (or at the earliest 470); the plausible restoration of an archon-name would date the production to 463.[1] Rearguard actions have failed, and there is now general recognition that the early dating must be given up.

The story of the fifty daughters of Danaus, living in Egypt but descended from Argive Io, who fled to avoid marriage with their cousins, the fifty sons of Aegyptus, was a myth of great antiquity which had already been treated in tragedy (see pp. 5f. on Phrynichus). The surviving play was first in the trilogy. It opens with the Danaids newly arrived in Argos, their cousins in hot pursuit. They appeal to the king Pelasgus, who needs 'deep salutary thought that plunges, like a diver, into the depths, with seeing sober eye' (407–9). He is confronted with a dilemma between war with the Egyptians, if he protects the suppliants, and the wrath of Zeus Hikesios, if he rejects them; to which is added the prospect of pollution, if they carry out their threat to hang themselves from the images of the gods. Pelasgus decides that he will commend their case to the people of Argos, who have the final word. This word is favourable, but a herald lands from the Egyptian fleet and with barbarous violence seeks to drag the Danaids from the altars. They are saved by the king, but war seems inevitable.

The king's dilemma and decision are clearly a factor of dramatic importance, and his reference to the people adds to the play a political dimension which was doubtless taken up in the sequel. But Pelasgus does not emerge as an individual, while Danaus is merely characterized as the planner and plotter behind his daughters. Not even a tormented Pelasgus really takes the stage from the Danaids. It is their play and remains their trilogy – a trilogy of remarkable unity in point of place, time and theme, the events of the three plays following in quick succession at Argos, concerned with the fate of the same set of persons, who formed the chorus of two – and perhaps of all three – plays. *Aegyptii* and *Danaides* are lost, but, if we cannot work out their economies in detail, we know

[1] Cf. Lloyd-Jones (1957) 595ff. and *A.C.* 1964 (see App.).

33

some of the things that happened.[1] We know that the Danaids did marry their cousins and, on the instigation of their father, killed them on the wedding-night, the victims (and threatened suicides) of the first play becoming murderers in the sequel; that one Danaid, Hypermestra, spared her husband and so created the dramatic situation of the final play; that Aphrodite appeared and proclaimed her universal power in nature. There may or may not have been a trial, on stage or off stage, of somebody. There must have been a solution: but of what problem?

It is a remarkable fact that the whole trilogy seems to have been focused upon the relations between men and women and the place of marriage in the structure of society. The Danaids have an abhorrence of marriage which may have stemmed less from the cousinship than from the violence of their suitors. Yet women must marry, as their handmaidens (who are introduced as a subsidiary chorus at the end of *Supplices*) knew, and as Hypermestra accepted, and as Aphrodite will have proclaimed. How the trilogy ended we cannot be sure, but it may well have ended with a 'conversion' of the Danaids. If this is a social issue (becoming political through the involvement of the Argive democracy), it is also religious, not merely because of Aphrodite, but because Zeus presides, with his mysterious purposes, the protector of suppliants, who nevertheless are wedded against their will, and of strangers, whom nevertheless they kill, the god who, with Hera, presides over marriage.

With the Oresteian trilogy, produced in 458, we can at last survey an Aeschylean drama in all its sweep and intricacy. It consists of three plays (*Agamemnon*, *Choephori*, *Eumenides*), each with its own action, its own tone and character, but constituting a single dramatic exploration of a single tremendous theme. *Agamemnon* is the longest, as it is the most complex; yet in some ways its dramatic technique is the oldest. The action could not be simpler: Agamemnon returns from Troy and is killed by his wife. It receives, however, an elaborate preparation through the exposition of past events and an accumulation of foreboding, to both of which the chorus (of Argive elders) contributes. The choral odes, particularly the entrance-song, are long and highly elaborated. Though Aeschylus now has three actors at his disposal, scenes tend to be played between one actor and the chorus; genuine dialogue is rare: the more impressive, therefore, when Clytemnestra persuades her husband to enter the palace treading on scarlet draperies. The third actor provides a Cassandra who is silent, until, left alone with the chorus, the prophetess weaves past, present and future into a single fabric, in an astonishing scene of song and speech. But the play is dominated by the figure of Clytemnestra, the injured mother and wife, but also the man-woman who threatens the principle of male domination.[2]

[1] Cf. Garvie (1969) 163–233 for a careful examination of the problem.
[2] Cf. Winnington-Ingram (1948).

If the dramatic technique of *Agamemnon* is in several ways archaic, the play is full of colour and variety; its horizons are wide, since they embrace the earlier events in Argos and at Aulis and the Trojan War itself, all leading in their different ways to the fall of Agamemnon, the quality of whose vengeance upon Troy is revealed by chorus, Clytemnestra and Herald. By contrast, *Choephori* is sombre, narrowly concentrated upon the theme of vengeance through matricide: Orestes – a relatively colourless figure – has returned to avenge his father and restore male domination in Argos. Now we meet for the first time two more staple features of Greek tragedy: a recognition, when Electra recognizes her brother returned from exile, and an intrigue, when together they plot the killing of Aegisthus – and of their mother. In the second half of the play, the action moves rapidly, and the old nurse of Orestes plays her part, but perhaps the most striking feature of all is lyrical, a great *kommos* in the centre of the play, when son and daughter join with the chorus of palace-slaves to pay respect to the dead Agamemnon within the earth and invoke his aid. A tensely moving ritual, it is also a preparation (of Orestes and of the audience itself) for the bloody acts to come.[1]

Eumenides is a play of gods, even the chorus is divine; it is a play of brilliant variety and scenic effect. Orestes is pursued by the Erinyes – to Delphi, where he is disclosed in the shrine of Apollo surrounded by sleeping demons, and then (a change of scene rare in Greek tragedy) to Athens, where they dance round him singing their Binding Song. Athena empanels the Areopagus; Apollo enters to oversee the defence of Orestes; there is a trial and a ceremony of voting. Orestes goes free, and Athena persuades the Erinyes to accept his acquittal and a cult in Athens. The play ends with a procession: singing songs of good will, the Erinyes, now Eumenides, are escorted by torchlight to their new home in the rock.

The three plays are forged into a unity not only by the causal sequence of events but by the carrying through from play to play of themes – and above all of one paramount theme, which is justice, the justice of men and the Justice of Zeus; indeed the trilogy can well be seen as a vast dramatic exploration of the nature of justice human and divine. Which raises a problem, since at both levels justice first appears to be a matter of retaliation, of *talio*. It is characteristic of the earlier stages of the trilogy that, at every point, the issue is complicated. In *Agamemnon*, the just punishment of Troy involves, mysteriously, the sacrifice of Iphigenia, the dilemma – and the guilt – of Agamemnon. The stage is held far more, however, by Clytemnestra the avenger, who is studied and presented (so it has been held) as herself involved in a tragic situation, being a woman with the will and power to dominate within a man-dominated world; and if as an avenger she has her case, her menace lies within the context of a social situation.

[1] Cf. Lesky, *TDH* 125 and Appendix bibliography.

This social theme runs, like a counter-subject, throughout the trilogy. In *Choephori*, the dilemma is obvious: justice must be done, but it can only be done by Orestes and through an act of matricide, by a crime parallel to that of Clytemnestra, the parallelism being brought out in many ways. Orestes acts at the command of Apollo, but under threat of persecution by Erinyes, and he is pursued by Erinyes. In *Eumenides*, Apollo and Erinyes are in dispute before the court of the Areopagus; and a human jury is in its turn confronted with an apparently insoluble dilemma. The human votes are equal:[1] it is Athena who resolves the situation, giving her vote on preference for the male; and the arbitrary fiat of a prejudiced divinity may well convey what Aeschylus saw as a social necessity. But Athena does more than decide the case: she persuades the menacing Erinyes to accept a home and worship in Athens. To what extent the close of the trilogy can be said to resolve the complications of its earlier phases is a question to which we must return.

Prometheus vinctus raises special problems: even its authenticity has been impugned.[2] This hypothesis, based upon real peculiarities of language and technique (if not also of thought), needs to be taken very seriously. If a majority of scholars do not accept it, this is partly because some of the linguistic arguments have little cogency when so few Aeschylean plays have survived, more because of an unlikelihood that there were two poets alive, one of them anonymous, capable not only of the grand dramatic conception but of such an Aeschylean effect as the entry of Io. Perhaps the strongest argument for authenticity is the fact that the play demands a sequel and what we know of *Prometheus lyomenos* ('The loosing of Prometheus'), which is more than we had any right to expect, provides the kind of sequel required: in fact the *Prometheus vinctus* and the *Prometheus lyomenos* would seem to stand or fall together, and both were accepted as Aeschylean by Hellenistic scholarship. Since there is a good deal of linguistic evidence to associate the play more closely with *Oresteia* than either with earlier plays, it is likely, if Aeschylus wrote it, to be late and there are reasons for supposing that it could have been written in Sicily during the last years of his life. A third title remains to be considered: *Prometheus pyrphoros*, which may have been the third play of a Promethean trilogy. If so, it is more likely to have been the last play than the first, the title referring, not

[1] Some scholars believe that Athena cast a vote for Orestes as a member of the jury, so that a majority of human jurors found against Orestes. It depends on the interpretation of *Eum.* 734–41, which is controversial.

[2] The case for authenticity is well put by Herington (1970) but Griffith in a careful study (1977) suggests the opposite conclusion. (See also Taplin (1975) 184–6.) The present writer must confess that his faith in the traditional authorship has been severely shaken, but it seemed right in all the circumstances to discuss the play here as Aeschylean, not least because, if another wrote it, he did so under strong Aeschylean influence. Perhaps we assume too readily, thanks to Aristophanes and Aristotle, that there were three great tragedians only and the rest were indifferent performers.

to the bringing of fire to men, but to a torch-race cult of Prometheus at Athens. We cannot be quite sure, however, that there were more than two plays or that a trilogy, if planned, was ever carried to completion. We have to make what we can of the extant play, helped by some knowledge of the *Lyomenos*.

One of the puzzles of *Prometheus* has always been its presentation of Zeus, whose character, as seen by the hero and his friends, corresponds at every point to the traditional Greek picture of the tyrant. Prometheus is the persecuted friend of man. Taking the trickster-god of folk-lore (and Hesiod), who also bore a significant name ('Forethought') and had become the patron of Athenian potters, Aeschylus made of him a great symbol at once of goodwill to mankind and of practical intelligence. In a long speech which is an astonishing feat of historical imagination, Prometheus tells how he not only gave men fire but brought them out of a Hobbesian state of nature into the semblance of civilized life by teaching them the practical arts (*technai*). For this he is punished by that Zeus who, in *Oresteia*, 'set mortals upon the path of wisdom' (*Ag.* 176f.).

The shape of the play is determined by the situation: other heroes come and go, but Prometheus, crucified upon a rock in the Caucasus, abides and is visited. He is visited by the chorus of Oceanids and by their father Oceanus; he is visited – the entry is sensational and unprepared – by another victim of Zeus, the 'cow-horned virgin' Io, whose sufferings match his own but whose ultimate destiny foreshadows his own release. The hero remains for a brief span of dramatic time at a remote point in space, yet no play has broader horizons. The whole world is embraced, when Prometheus tells us of the journeyings past and future of Io (matched, apparently, by the journeys of Heracles in *Lyomenos*); and, brief though the traffic of the stage may be, the dramatist conveys the long process of development from the bestial state of primitive man to that settled community in which the story of Io is placed. Much of the play is taken up with long expository speeches. Where, then, does drama reside? It resides in the conflict between Prometheus and Zeus, the intensification of his obstinate resistance, and the fact that he holds a weapon against his oppressor, a secret. Zeus, whose lust appears to be victimizing Io, will one day lust after a goddess destined to have a son greater than his father, and so Zeus may fall from power.

Our knowledge of the sequel is limited. We know that Heracles, in *Lyomenos*, killed the eagle which came to devour the liver of Prometheus and, ultimately, released him from those bonds that Hephaestus had made so firm. Somehow the quarrel between Zeus and Prometheus must have been resolved. The secret was revealed, because Zeus did not marry Thetis; there was reconciliation, but on what terms, and at what level, we cannot easily judge. It has been suggested, with plausibility, that Zeus not only accepted the survival of the human race but to the material and intellectual gifts of Prometheus added his own gift of justice necessary to human society. To say that Zeus has 'developed' may go beyond the evidence; and perhaps the question we should ask ourselves is this: Under what other mode could the government of the world present itself to primitive man, as depicted by Aeschylus, than that of harshness and force?

This review of the extant plays may have given some impression of the power – and the range – of Aeschylean tragedy. To sum up the character of Aeschylus as dramatist and as religious thinker – the two roles are indissociable – is no easy task, and the difficulty resides partly in a combination of all but contradictory qualities. There is a traditional picture of Aeschylus – the stern moralist, prophet of a Zeus who is concerned with the inexorable punishment of offenders; master of a grand style, with an imagination so lofty as to set him apart from common humanity. The picture is both true and false.

His style is indeed grand, though not grandiloquent, since it is strikingly free of ornament applied for its own sake. Rich but disciplined, if at times it appears lavish, it is lavish with a density of meanings. Style cannot profitably be discussed without a degree of illustration which is impossible here, but some points can be made. If the wide vocabulary of Aeschylus owes a debt to his epic and lyric predecessors – a debt which, with the loss of most of the early poetry, cannot be particularized – he was doubtless a bold innovator in his own right, particularly perhaps in the coinage of those compound epithets which are so characteristic of his diction; and, like many great poets ancient and modern, he had a bold way with language. Not only in smaller matters of semantics and syntax did he strain normal usage but in metaphor, where he has no peer except Pindar, his combination of images seems sometimes to strain figurative language almost to breaking-point; when he wished, however, he could elaborate a single image with amazing skill. Of the Greeks who died before Troy, the Chorus of *Agamemnon* sing:

> ὁ χρυσαμοιβὸς δ' Ἄρης σωμάτων
> καὶ ταλαντοῦχος ἐν μάχηι δορὸς
> πυρωθὲν ἐξ Ἰλίου
> φίλοισι πέμπει βαρὺ
> ψῆγμα δυσδάκρυτον ἀντ-
> ήνορος σποδοῦ γεμί-
> ζων λέβηιτας εὐθέτους.   (437–44)

But the money-changer War, changer of bodies,
Holding his balance in the battle
Home from Troy refined by fire
Sends back to friends the dust
That is heavy with tears, stowing
A man's worth of ashes
In an easily handled jar. (tr. Louis MacNeice)

The style is grand, in dialogue as well as in lyric, but he could also write very simply and give colloquial turns of speech to humbler personages.

For his minor characters are not to be forgotten or else we shall miss the wide range of his sympathies. In *Agamemnon*, for instance, alongside Clytemnestra (and her beacon speech) and a cold triumphant Agamemnon, we have the Watchman and the Herald, with their wry peasant humour and that concern for their own affairs which reveals the effects of high tragic events upon common people. These are 'character-parts'; and it could well be that it was through such figures that a degree of naturalness in characterization first found its way into Greek tragedy. The Nurse in *Choephori* harks back to the incontinence of the infant Orestes and to his dirty linen. Perhaps we should not have been surprised, when extensive fragments of some Aeschylean satyr plays came to light, to discover with what a light touch he could handle the traditional obscenities, what a charming song (in *Dictyulci*) Silenus sings to the infant Perseus, as the child plays with the monstrous phallus.[1]

Aeschylus combines with an intricate detailed art a mastery of overwhelming emotional effects, which are often produced by the sheer force – or poignancy – of language. All three tragedians, however, in their different ways, used spectacle as well as language for dramatic ends; and the visual effects of Aeschylus are particularly striking. Reference has already been made to the raising of Darius, the unprepared entry of the cow-horned Io, and to the whole sequence of spectacles in *Eumenides*; to these could be added the irruption of the terrified female chorus in *Septem*, not marching sedately but dancing in to the dochmiac metre, or the cries and contortions of Cassandra when, after her long silence, she enters into trance. This is the *ekplexis* 'astonishment' ancient critics spoke of. In *Agamemnon* Clytemnestra is disclosed standing over the bodies of her victims; in *Choephori* Orestes stands over his. The effect is visual and powerful, but the aim is different, since a comparison is invited between the two pictures and a question is thereby raised about the relationship of the two actions. There is a pattern; and such structural patterning is not rare in the art of Aeschylus.

A certain formality is characteristic of Greek art, literary as well as visual. Much has been written recently about ring-composition, which is found in Homer and may have originated as a convenient device of the oral bard, which we can observe in Pindar and infer from him for his lyric predecessors. A section, long or short, is concluded by returning to a word or theme with which it began. With a great artist, this is not a mere formal device for its own sake, but the word or theme when it reappears may carry more meaning than it had before: 'release from troubles' means more at the end of the first half of the Watchman's speech than it meant at the beginning (*Ag.* 1; 20); the words and

[1] Cf. Lloyd-Jones (1957) 531ff.

themes, images and symbols, picked up at the end of *Oresteia* mean more and other than they meant early in the trilogy. Ring-composition on every scale is all-pervasive in Aeschylus. Another device of emphasis concerns his imagery. It is characteristic of him to sustain an image or images throughout a play: in *Septem* the ship of state, in *Supplices* birds of prey, in *Oresteia* nets and snares, indeed a whole complex of metaphors from hunting and fishing. But these are only special cases of a much wider phenomenon. Words, or groups of words, carrying an important theme are repeated, often at points of emphasis. For instance, in *Oresteia* we find words of mastery and victory associated with the theme of male/female domination; words of heredity; words of justice and legal process. The polarities of good and evil, light and darkness, joy and sorrow, paeans and dirges, force and persuasion, run right through the trilogy. Scholars may dispute this or that interpretation, but there would be wide agreement that the texture *is* dense, that repetitions *are* deliberate, that themes *are* carried through. Similarly with those ambiguities which Aeschylus uses as a kind of compressed metaphor, often looking backwards or forwards to link the superficially disparate. Some scholars are more cautious than others in identifying ambiguity, but few would deny that the language of Aeschylus is often deliberately ambiguous, that references to parents and children in *Agamemnon* are made with thought of the matricide in *Choephori*, that references to legal process in the earlier plays look forward to a trial in *Eumenides*.

These are some of the resources of the art of Aeschylus, ranging from overwhelming, and often spectacular, effects to the intricate working-out of themes. To what dramatic ends are they applied? How did Aeschylus see the world, and see it as tragic? And here perhaps we come up against the most remarkable combination of all. The thought and art and language of Aeschylus are deeply rooted in an archaic past, in a world haunted by terrors and superstitions; and yet many have found in his drama a rational control, a power of general thought, a profound insight into fundamental problems of the human condition, a movement out of darkness into the light.[1] Disagreement is, however, fairly wide within this field, and no coherent statement can fail to be in some degree personal.

Aeschylean tragedy is concerned with human destiny, with the individual fate of an Eteocles or an Agamemnon. But the individual is part of a family, a cohesive kinship-group: Eteocles suffers under his father's curse, Agamemnon for the sins of his father. And the family is part of a wider kinship-group, the *polis*. All are closely bound together, as they still were in the contemporary Greek world: the relationship of *oikos* to *polis* is a fundamental theme in *Septem* and hardly less important in *Oresteia*. All the great issues are social, and they

---

[1] Cf. e.g. Dodds (1951) 40. Contrast the Introduction to Denniston–Page (1957). See also Lloyd-Jones (1956) and (1971).

touch the social life of the poet's own time. If, in the heroic context, the polis is rudimentary, neither could he speak nor his audience hear of the polis without thought of their own political experience; and it is indeed an essential feature of *Oresteia* that the action moves from the heroic monarchy of Argos to Athens and the Areopagus, to a court and a trial; and the Eumenides pray for blessings on an Athens that Aeschylus and his hearers knew. He wrote for his own time and for his fellow-citizens.

Individual, family and state, all are dependent on the gods, so that there is an integration of personal, social and religious issues. But what were these gods, and how did they operate in the world of men? It is generally, and rightly, held that Aeschylus, his thought centred upon Zeus, was greatly concerned with what is sometimes called theodicy, with the justice and the justification of the gods. But theodicy was not an invention of Aeschylus or of the fifth century. The more the Greeks felt gods about them (and within them) and the more dependent they felt, then the more concerned they were to understand how the gods worked. Were they jealous of human greatness and prosperity? Were they, as men wished to believe, just? Or were they themselves, by sending infatuation, the ultimate cause of the offences they punished? Was this the way offenders were punished through their descendants? Aeschylus had inherited these questions and, from Hesiod and Solon, some answers. To questions and answers he had given his own thought.

One does not look to a poet for the strict formulation and solution of philosophical and theological problems. On one issue, however, Aeschylus formulates clearly, when he makes the chorus of *Agamemnon* sing (*Ag.* 750ff.) that it is not wealth and prosperity in themselves that cause woe, but impiety and outrage which breed after their kind. They breed, in this case, within the family; and we discover that Agamemnon dies not for his own offences only but for those of his father; and Clytemnestra claims to embody the avenging spirit which haunts the house. Here we get another formulation: because the *daimon* has lent its aid, she cannot therefore disclaim her own responsibility.

Κλ. αὐχεῖς εἶναι τόδε τοὔργον ἐμόν,
μὴ δ' ἐπιλεχθῆις,
'Αγαμεμνονίαν εἶναί μ' ἄλοχον·
φαντιαζόμενος δὲ γυναικὶ νεκροῦ
τοῦδ' ὁ παλαιὸς δριμὺς ἀλάστωρ
'Ατρέως χαλεποῦ θοινατῆρος
τόνδ' ἀπέτεισεν
τέλεον νεαροῖς ἐπιθύσας.

Χο. ὡς μὲν ἀναίτιος εἶ
τοῦδε φόνου τίς ὁ μαρτυρήσων;
πῶ πῶ; πατρόθεν δὲ συλλή-
πτωρ γένοιτ' ἂν ἀλάστωρ.   (1497–1508)

41

CLYT.   You say this is *my* work – mine?
        Do not cozen yourself that I am Agamemnon's wife.
        Masquerading as the wife
        Of the corpse there the old sharp-witted Genius
        Of Atreus who gave the cruel banquet
        Has paid with a grown man's life
        The due for children dead.
CHORUS That you are not guilty of
        This murder who will attest?
        No, but you may have been abetted
        By some ancestral Spirit of Revenge. (tr. Louis MacNeice)

It seems to be generally true that, in Aeschylus, while divine and human causes operate simultaneously, the divine justice accomplishes itself through human motivation; that, whatever the pressures of hereditary guilt and delayed vengeance, a responsibility does lie upon the human agents.

In the background there is a problem of freedom and compulsion of which the Greeks, who had slaves and oxen, were well aware. The metaphor of the yoke is common in tragedy, and so is the notion of *ananke*. Passionate for freedom, conscious at all points of the constraints put upon them by the gods, they may well have asked themselves how free in fact they were. When our own philosophers and theologians have got these matters straight, then will be the time to criticize the mental competence of ancient writers, but meanwhile there is perhaps something to be learnt from a poet who faced the questions of divine government and human responsibility with so much honesty. We shall not learn it, until we realize that, for Aeschylus, Zeus was not so much the solution of a problem as the problem itself (which is why he could present it through myths as disparate as those of *Oresteia* and the Prometheus-plays).

It is only in *Oresteia* that we can observe the full development of Aeschylean trains of thought. The main theme is justice in the mode of *talio*, human and divine. Human beings resent their wrongs and retaliate, but in doing so they are ministering to a divine justice. They are not wrong – neither the Atridae going against Troy nor Clytemnestra and Aegisthus – to claim this function, yet the result is a sequence of horrific events. Again and again there is a reference to Erinyes, those demons in whom Aeschylus found – or created – a symbol of rigid punitive justice, of an inflexible past. In the last two plays the issue is firmly focused on the case of Orestes, who commits matricide, at the command of Apollo but also in furtherance of a law cited by the chorus in the great *kommos*, which had already been proclaimed as an ordinance of Zeus by the chorus of *Agamemnon* – the law that doers must suffer for their actions.[1] Must Orestes suffer for his? He is pursued by the Erinyes of his mother; he is acquitted

[1] *Cho.* 306–14, 400–4; *Ag.* 1560–6.

at Athens, thanks to the vote of Athena, who endorses that preference for the male which had been part of Apollo's defence of Orestes. If the sociological problem admits an answer, the votes of the human jury were divided, and the Erinyes fume and threaten. There is still a problem to be solved; and the play – and the trilogy – end not with the acquittal of Orestes but with the persuasion of the Erinyes. Angry demons could not be left threatening Athens. If they acquire benevolence (without losing their punitive role), it could be said that Aeschylus has invoked, in the interests of Athens, another aspect of chthonian powers, as givers of fertility. One may doubt, however, whether this exhausts the significance of the closing scene.

No poet has presented tragic evil with less mitigation than Aeschylus. Yet *Oresteia* – and so far as we can judge both the Danaid and Promethean plays – end with reconciliation and the prospect of harmony, which is a kind of tragedy that has found few imitators. Clearly Aeschylus was no sentimental optimist. What, then, is it that makes reconciliation possible? Among the tools of Greek thought was a polar opposition between force (or violence) and persuasion. There is no more insistent theme in the later Aeschylus. In the Danaid trilogy force and persuasion are contrasted modes of sexual approach and Aphrodite will have come to persuade. The ministers of Zeus in *Prometheus* are Mastery and Violence, evoking an answering stubbornness in the hero, but already there are hints of that persuasion which must have brought about the ultimate reconciliation. The earlier stages of *Oresteia* are a story of recurrent violence, as the justice of Zeus is carried forward by Erinyes, making a mystery, if not a mockery, of the Hymn to Zeus in the Parodos of *Agamemnon*, in which the Chorus sings, in one breath, of the favour (χάρις) and the violence of the gods (*Ag.* 182f.). Apollo commands the matricide and, when it has been committed, threatens the Erinyes with his bow; Athena persuades them. In a context of democratic Athens, she brings persuasion to bear upon the very exemplifications of violent revenge. If this is a notion which dominates the last phase of Aeschylus, then perhaps it was his supreme religious insight that the Greek gods of power could also be seen to work persuasively.

4. SOPHOCLES

Sophocles' long life almost spans the fifth century B.C.: he was born c. 496 before the first Persian invasion and died c. 406 in the last years of the Peloponnesian War. He has often seemed to symbolize all that is Attic and classical: dignity, formal perfection, idealism. At the same time critics have found him in some ways the most elusive of the three great tragedians. No one disputes that he is a dramatist of the first rank; and in the surviving plays at any rate – a mere seven out of 123 – it is hard to find any trace of the 'unevenness' criticized by Plutarch;[1] but beyond this there is no critical consensus: now serene, pious and conventional, now passionately humanist or despairingly pessimistic, Sophocles undergoes transformations with every new book that is written about him. Paradoxically, the impact of his work on reader, actors, or audience, is one of striking lucidity, even of simplicity, but it is a lucidity like Virgil's, which gives expression to deep complexities of meaning, difficult to discuss except in the poet's own terms.

Interpretation is made all the harder because so few plays have survived and most of these cannot be securely dated. Thus it is impossible to give a reliable account of Sophocles' development; four plays and some fragments are all that is left to represent the first fifty years of his extremely productive career. 468 is the date given for his first contest, which was also a victory over Aeschylus, but none of the extant plays seems likely to be earlier than the 450s. Most scholars would put *Ajax* before *Antigone* (probably late 440s: see Appendix), though the evidence is not conclusive. *Trachiniae* is often placed next after *Antigone* and before *Oedipus tyrannus* (in the 420s), again on very insecure evidence. With *Electra* (between 418 and 410), *Philoctetes* (409) and *Oedipus at Colonus* (c. 406) we are at last on firmer ground, and some characteristics of 'late' Sophocles can be identified, but in general we simply lack the materials for a literary biography.

There is some record of what the ancients thought of his merits and of his place in the history of drama: this can help to fill some at least of the gaps in our knowledge, provided that it is treated with great caution and pruned of the more fanciful growths of anecdote. The biographical tradition is overwhelmingly enthusiastic: Sophocles was well born, handsome, accomplished, patriotic, outstandingly pious. The picture looks suspiciously roseate, but the warmth of contemporary references must count for something. Sophocles was treated very favourably by the comic poets, who normally missed no opportunity of making fun of tragedians, and his friend Ion of Chios told stories illustrating his gaiety and wit which give credibility to the picture drawn in the ancient *Life* of his magnetic charm of personality. He was by far the most successful, and therefore presumably the most popular, of the tragedians of his time: he won the first prize with about two thirds of his plays and was never placed lower than second. Moreover he was a well known public figure, and if our authorities are to be even partially believed he was entrusted with responsible public offices. He was certainly elected *strategos* at least once (441/0), and it was probably he and not a namesake who was *hellenotamias* in 443/2 and one of the *probouloi* after the Sicilian disaster; according to the ancient *Life* (1) he also served on embassies. He was deeply involved in the city's religious life: the role he played in establishing the cult of Asclepius at Athens

---

[1] *De recta ratione audiendi* 13; cf. 'Longinus', *Subl.* 33.5.

44

was so important that he himself received heroic honours after his death under the cult name of Dexion. Like Aeschylus, he founded a family of dramatists: his son Iophon and grandson Sophocles were both tragedians of some note.

The ancient sources have a good deal to say about Sophocles' place in the history of tragedy. Aristotle (*Poet.* 1449a18) gives him credit for introducing the third actor, presumably sometime between 468, the date of his first contest, and 458, when Aeschylus used a third actor in the *Oresteia*. It is easy to see how this gave scope for sophisticated dramatic effects (see p. 63), but it is harder to deduce what lay behind another Sophoclean innovation, the raising of the number of chorus men from twelve to fifteen. The same source (*Life* 4) says that he gave up the habit of acting in his own plays owing to the weakness of his voice, but changes in the organization of the Dionysia may in any case have discouraged dramatists from doubling as actors. According to the Suda it was he who began the practice of presenting plays on different subjects at the same contest rather than writing connected trilogies (or tetralogies, count-ing the satyr plays).[1] This cannot be quite true, since we know that Aeschylus presented unconnected plays at least once (*Phineus*, *Persae*, *Glaucus Potnieus* in 472), but it is likely that Sophocles deliberately broke with what had latterly become a regular Aeschylean habit. So he established the norm – the single play – that has prevailed throughout the entire European dramatic tradition.

Aristotle refers cryptically to Sophocles' introduction of *skenographia* (*Poet.* 1449a18). We know too little about the fifth-century theatre to be able to say for certain what this implies; probably *skenographia* refers to perspective painting of panels for the wall of the stage-building, which perhaps to begin with represented an architectural façade rather than anything more closely connected with a particular play (see pp. 16–22). Evidently there was still plenty of scope for pioneering work in the theatre, at any rate in the earlier part of Sophocles' career, and he must have influenced Aeschylus as well as following in his footsteps. We must certainly also allow for close interdependence between Sophocles and Euripides, as many parallel passages testify;[2] for nearly fifty years the two playwrights were in active competition at the Athenian festivals.

Sophocles appears to have been a highly self-conscious writer. The Suda records that he wrote a book *On the chorus*, but despite all the speculation this has prompted nothing is known for certain about it (even the title may mean something more like 'On tragedy'). The literary pronouncements attributed to him in various ancient sources could possibly be quotations from this book, but they are more likely to have been *bons mots* recorded in the memoirs of friends and contemporaries. He said of Aeschylus that he did the right thing

---

[1] This seems to be the correct interpretation of the Suda's confused text, cf. *DFA* 80–1.
[2] E.g. Soph. *Trach.* 899ff. and Eur. *Alc.* 157ff.

without knowing what he was doing, which has been taken to suggest a strong interest in technique on Sophocles' part (though the remark occurs in a gossipy passage in Athenaeus about Aeschylus' drunkenness, 1.22a–b). Euripides occasioned the famous dictum, preserved in the *Poetics* (1460b35), 'I portray men as they ought to be, Euripides as they are'. On his own development Sophocles is recorded as making a more detailed comment, which turns out to be extraordinarily difficult to interpret: 'Sophocles used to say that after practising to the limit the pomp of Aeschylus and then the harsh artificiality of his own manner of elaboration, he turned finally to the kind of style which was best and most expressive of character' (Plutarch, *De prof. in virt.* 7). With only seven surviving plays it is impossible to identify these three stages convincingly. Many scholars think that the early 'Aeschylean' stage is not represented, but whether we have an extant example of the second stage is less clear. All that the passage actually proves is Sophocles' literary self-awareness and his interest in character.

Portrayal of character is indeed singled out by the ancient critics as one of Sophocles' chief merits. One of the most interesting comments in the *Life* (21) runs as follows:

οἶδε δὲ καιρὸν συμμετρῆσαι καὶ πράγματα, ὥστ' ἐκ μικροῦ ἡμιστιχίου ἢ λέξεως μιᾶς ὅλον ἠθοποιεῖν πρόσωπον. ἔστι δὲ τοῦτο μέγιστον ἐν τῆι ποιητικῆι, δηλοῦν ἦθος ἢ πάθος.

> He knows how to arrange the action with such a sense of timing that he creates an entire character out of a mere half-line or a single expression. This is the essential in poetry, to delineate character or feelings.

Elsewhere (6, citing Istrus) the *Life* records that Sophocles composed his plays with the talents of his actors and chorus-men in mind. This may be further evidence of a special interest in character portrayal, but there is no certainty that it refers to acting rather than to musical talent: it could mean that Sophocles varied the proportion of lyric for solo performance according to the musical capabilities of his cast.[1]

Unanimously the ancient sources praise Sophocles, nicknamed 'the Bee' for his 'honeyed' style, the highest compliment that could be paid to poet or speaker. 'Sweetness' (γλυκύτης), which to the Greeks suggested flowing eloquence as well as charm, is noted in the *Life* (20) as one of Sophocles' prime qualities; the others are a sense of appropriateness and timing (εὐκαιρία), boldness (τόλμα), and intricacy of ornament (ποικιλία). This is praise of the kind that the ancients gave to Homer himself; and when they called Sophocles 'the tragic Homer' (Polemo, cited by Diogenes Laertius 4.20) or 'the only disciple of Homer' (*Life* 20) they were making a qualitative judgement, not just alluding to the strongly Homeric colouring of his style.

[1] Owen (1936) 148.

For Aristotle, whose work lies behind most of the ancient critical tradition, Sophocles plainly exemplified what was most to be admired in tragedy. This is clear from his repeated use of *Oedipus tyrannus* as a model example and from his generally very favourable comments on Sophocles, as at 1456a25 on the superiority of his handling of the chorus. It is no doubt the overwhelming influence of the *Poetics* as much as Sophocles' midway historical position that has led critics to treat him almost as the norm of Greek tragedy, by comparison with whom Aeschylus has often been judged primitive and Euripides decadent.

In one important respect there has been a marked shift away from the critical emphasis of Aristotle. For modern interpreters from the nineteenth century onwards the question of meaning, which was traditionally either ignored or taken for granted, has been a major concern. In its cruder forms, as the search for an explicit 'moral' or 'message' or 'philosophy', it is bound to lead to distortion and bafflement: the focus of Sophocles' plays is not on ideas, but on the doing and suffering of men and women, and although he shows his characters facing the fundamental problems of life the plays never offer unambiguous solutions. It would be simplistic to expect anything more clear-cut; but at least a remarkable consistency of attitude can be detected in the seven extant plays, despite the fact that they must span a period of forty years or more, and it is not misleading to speak of a distinctively Sophoclean treatment of certain tragic issues.

Fundamental to all the plays is the same two-sided view of man, in which his heroic splendour is matched by his utter vulnerability to circumstance. Of course this had traditionally been the way the Greeks looked at the human condition, as we can tell from Homer, the early elegists, and the lyric poets, but Sophocles gives it new expression in dramatic form. Like all these poets Sophocles seems to require an assumption that the human spirit has an ultimate dignity and value: man *can* be brave, clever, morally strong, humane (though filled at the same time with what Bernard Knox calls 'passionate self-esteem'),[1] and most of all he can face suffering with endurance, not the mere uncomprehending submission of an animal. These qualities are not negated and their value is not nullified by the presence of misfortune, suffering and wrong-doing in the world, what the Greeks called *to kakon* and we translate, for want of a better word, as 'evil'. This is always recognized by the poet as part of the way things are: alongside man's potentiality for greatness are set his helplessness and mortality. He may indeed be 'godlike' in his endowments or his achievements, but he is caught in the infinite web of circumstances outside his control, limited by time, by ignorance of past, present and future, by his passions which impede his judgement or undermine his will, always liable to

[1] Knox (1964) 57.

47

destroy himself and others through failure – or unwillingness – to understand.

This is the consistent Sophoclean background, though the emphases vary from play to play. In *Ajax* the dualism in man's condition is brought sharply into relief, particularly through the contrast between two different ethics, the heroic code and the fifth-century ideal of *sophrosyne*, though (as always) the centre of the play's interest is not a conceptual problem but human action and suffering: the disgrace, death and burial of Ajax. A great military hero, believing himself to have been grossly insulted because he did not receive the highest mark of honour, plans to take bloodthirsty revenge on his former associates, but he suffers from a delusion which causes him to butcher animals instead of his intended victims. The action of the play centres on his return to his senses, his shame and regret at finding that he has not after all killed his enemies, and his subsequent suicide. What is the meaning of these events, particularly of his self-chosen death? What kind of significance is there in this portrait of Ajax? Is it a case-study in abnormal psychology, a celebration of heroic ideals coupled with a recognition of their unsuitability in the modern world, an edifying example of the punishment of arrogance, or (more simply but also more subtly) an insight into a universal human predicament?

In bare outline Ajax's behaviour seems psychopathic, yet the play ends not with his dying curses but with his rehabilitation through burial accompanied by full heroic honours. Indeed, the audience's sympathy is so much directed towards Ajax (following the cue of Odysseus in the Prologue, then of the Chorus and Tecmessa) that critics have tended to overlook his brutality and to stress the heroism of the great man who refuses to compromise, choosing to sacrifice his life rather than abandon his view of what a hero should be. 'The well-born man should either nobly live or nobly die' (479–80). But this approach, too, is open to objection on the ground that it could not be honourable to intend the treacherous murder of the Atridae and the torture of Odysseus. Besides, Ajax has twice boasted that he does not need divine help in battle (774ff.): his behaviour has been either savage or inspired by the more-than-human thought that he is too special and too strong to need the gods' favour. One way of reconciling revulsion at his deeds and intentions with the strong sympathy generated for Ajax is to see him in historical rather than universal terms as representing the old heroic code which must make way for the new 'quiet' ethos of the fifth century typified by the *sophrosyne* of Odysseus. The trouble with this view is that the dramatic focus is not on Odysseus, who though admirable and sympathetic cannot command our attention in the way that Ajax does: it is Ajax who is the tragic figure, and we look for an interpretation which will not confine him so narrowly to a particular set of historical circumstances.

Ajax, superficially an improbable paradigm of humanity, acquires a universal significance by virtue of his suffering, which is caused by the sense of total disgrace and shame following a disastrously mistaken action. He has enjoyed a fantasy of revenge only to discover that his victims were simply animals. His first reaction is the deepest possible dismay that he should be the object of society's derision; all he wants is that the sailors should kill him (361). His relations with his crew and with his wife and son (towards whom he is tender and brutal by turns), and his thoughts about his parents are all part of his tragic situation: Ajax can only be fully himself if he is surrounded by his family and dependants, filling his place in society. But now he is hated by the gods (as he knows from the fact of his madness, which he can interpret only as a divine visitation), by the Greeks, and by the Trojans, and he cannot go home to face his glorious father in disgrace. The only escape from shame is by a 'noble' death, but it is hard to find room for nobility when a man is so humiliated. Then something happens to lift Ajax out of this state of despair, though not to deflect him from his intention to commit suicide. Hitherto he has seen only one side of the dual picture of man, the capacity for great achievement of the talented individual, with a corresponding sense of that individual's unique importance and of the total unacceptability of insult. Now in his great speech at 646ff. he sets himself in the context of unending time and sees that all men have to accept the reality of change; he too will learn to behave with a proper sense of his human limitations (*sophronein* 677).

This speech makes his wife and followers think he has given up his plan to kill himself, but the terms he uses are ambiguous, and the audience must at least fear that he is still intent on suicide. It is less important to answer the question how far Ajax is deliberately deceiving his hearers; what matters is our sense of the intensity of his insight. He is not recognizing that he has been wrong to hate the Atridae and Odysseus, or feeling sorry for it: a simple moral interpretation would be very wide of the mark. He is using his newly found awareness (which he says has been prompted by pity for Tecmessa, a new emotion for Ajax, 652) in order to come to terms with himself, instead of allowing his overwhelming shame to take possession of him and make his suicide another senseless killing. The suicide speech (835ff.) confirms that he still hates his enemies, even to the point of calling down curses on the entire army, and it is clear that the only gesture he can make towards change is through death, but there is no longer any word of his shame.

The end of the play after 973 is an emotional anticlimax until the final tableau of the funeral procession, but the issue on which the action turns – the burial and rehabilitation of Ajax – is important for the audience's response to his story. His last two speeches in particular have given us reason for believing that despite all his savagery he deserves honourable burial, no longer just in memory of his great achievements in the past, or because (as at the beginning of the play) he is an object of pity; and this feeling is confirmed by the final success of Odysseus in persuading the Atridae. *Their* meanness and lack of dignity confirm all the more strongly our sense of the grandeur of Ajax.

This play's appeal for an audience derives both from the reality of Ajax's suffering – as a man most acutely susceptible to feelings of shame – and from the moments of self-knowledge which he seems to experience: out of his despair he finally recognizes (though he cannot will himself to accept) that his view of himself has been mistaken. He has succumbed to the temptation, ever present to the competitive Greek mind, of thinking more-than-mortal thoughts; he has behaved in a way that has been more bestial than heroic and has been brought low, yet his fall itself is not what matters: it is his response to the fall that the play explores. *Ajax* tells us little about the gods and their purposes or the working of divine justice, but it profoundly illuminates the value and the fragility of man.

Ajax's speech at 646ff. says much about time and the rhythm of change. Sophocles often returns to the theme of time, as one of the great limiting and therefore tragic factors in human life. Time must be taken into account because it brings death, but even more because it brings change: how can a man ever be sure that what he believes is worth dying for will not be transformed or swept away? Is there anything permanent in this mortal world?

Both Ajax and Oedipus in the *Coloneus* (607ff.) emphasize that in the course of time friends become enemies and enemies friends. This might seem to suggest a relativist or cynical attitude, an assertion that there are *no* absolute values, but Sophocles is offering a deeper insight. The imagery in both these speeches is drawn from the natural rhythms of the universe: winter alternating with summer and night with day, the endless reciprocal relation of winds and sea, sleep and waking, decay and growth, death and life. One is reminded of the language in which he describes the mutability of human fortune, another aspect of the process of time and change. In the Parodos of *Trachiniae* the cycle of good and bad fortune is compared to 'the circling paths of the Bear' (131), the constellation which for the Greeks of antiquity never set, but was always visible in its rhythmic movement round the Pole. Similarly, Heracles experiences successes and reversals like a swimmer raised and thrown back by a succession of waves (112ff.). Tossing on the sea is a more violent image than the movement of the stars, but Sophocles makes the two essentially comparable: like the rhythms of the seasons and of natural life they suggest permanence in change. In every instance the stress is on regular alternation rather than on chaotic and unpredictable diversity. Hence time is a principle of order as well as an inescapable destructive force.

This sense of time and mutability is important in Sophoclean tragedy because it gives the essential context for man's endeavour. He must do and suffer in the awareness that nothing remains as it is, except the gods and their eternal laws; Knox was right to insist that Sophoclean man is heroic precisely because he resists 'time and its imperative of change'.[1] But there is an important gloss that needs to be added: the hero may defy time, but he can never ignore it; his defiance is made in full knowledge that he is bound to lose. Time's tragic lesson is that mortal creatures never win. For the advantage is always on the side of time, which is linear as well as circular: as it draws each man and woman nearer to death it makes them what they are. 'Accompanying time' (*O.C.* 7) may damage or embitter the sufferer's mind as irreversibly as old age affects his body. So Electra sees her chances of marriage and childbearing fading as she lives enslaved by her mother and stepfather, dedicated to keeping alive the memory of Agamemnon whom they murdered: '... the best part of my life is already gone leaving me without hope, and I have no strength left; I, who am pining away without children' (185–7). What the audience see is the tragic effect of this dedication on her personality, an effect which cannot be reversed when the vengeance is at last achieved. The Chorus in this play may call Time a 'soothing god' (179), but the action of *Electra* does not bear them out.

The process of arriving at an understanding of time and its power over man, and the ordeal of facing and enduring it, are central preoccupations of Sophoclean thought. A great part of all men's lives is lived in ignorance or rejection or evasion of the truth, particularly about their own natures and their mortality. Sophocles, like all great tragedians, is concerned with the attainment of knowledge; his characteristic emphases are on the ironic contrast between appearance and reality, on the climactic moment of revelation, and on how men come to terms with the truth about themselves. Two plays which give particular prominence to this theme are *Trachiniae* and *Oedipus tyrannus*, both of which explore the irony of human ignorance and show their characters arriving, through extremes of suffering, at knowledge which totally alters their lives.

Oedipus tyrannus makes a more explicit and insistent contrast between appearance and reality, most of all through its sustained use of the imagery of sight and blindness: Oedipus who has physical sight is blind to the truth about himself and puts out his eyes when he learns it; Tiresias who is physically blind is the true seer. In *Trachiniae* the stress is on the irony of finding out too late: Deianira, Hyllus and Heracles all discover too late the true nature of their situations, and Sophocles so designs the structure of the play that each discovery is given great prominence. Deianira tries to win back the love of her unfaithful husband with what she supposes to be a benign love charm; only when she has taken the risk and sent Heracles a robe anointed with it does she find out that it is a deadly poison. Their son Hyllus sees Heracles tortured in the robe and rushes home to denounce his mother as a murderess; but she kills herself

---

[1] Knox (1964) 27.

before he discovers her innocence. Heracles understands only when he is on the point of death the meaning of an oracle told him long before, that he would be killed by the hand of the dead: the poison that Deianira unwittingly adminis- tered came from the centaur Nessus, who was killed by Heracles himself. Almost everything the characters say has an ironic import for the audience, who know – or guess – better than they. But this use of irony is not easy sensationalism; for Sophocles irony is a means of conveying profound insights into the nature of man and his world.

Similarly, the climax of revelation is not a mere melodramatic thrill of horror, but what John Jones has called 'the flash of perfect clarity' which comes at 'the moment when a man perceives the operation of the powers that are destroying him'.[1] At such moments there is a very strong sense that things are as it were swinging into place: now at last the oracles are seen to be intel- ligible and true. ἰοὺ ἰού, cries Oedipus when the truth is out at last, 'every- thing comes out clearly!' (1182). So Heracles, who utters the same great cry (*Trach.* 1143ff.), 'Now I understand ...' Knowledge is combined with a strong sense of inevitability.

Acceptance of the revelation is the mark of the great human being, who unlike the ordinary unheroic person, the average member of any audience, does not evade or deny or seek to shift the blame. Jocasta's reaction in *Oedipus tyrannus* to the discovery that her husband is also her son is to stifle the truth and allow Oedipus to live on in ignorance. This is deeply understandable, but for Sophocles the extreme of endurance is only met when like Oedipus a man faces and accepts that truth, with whatever appalling implications it may have. In effect this acceptance may be identical with the hero's 'defiance' discussed above; when he refuses to ignore the implications of the truth he does so because of the need to retain his integrity. The ordinary person runs away and tries to forget, or patches up some compromise, but for the heroic individual no such evasion is possible. Thus Ajax does not try to save himself, as Tecmessa and the Chorus hope he may, and Oedipus both persists against advice in making his discovery and when he has made it finds ways of coming to terms with his new identity.

If knowledge of reality is endurable only through intense suffering, what of the authors of this reality, the gods? Is it right, critics have asked, that men should have to suffer these things, men like Oedipus, who committed his terrible deeds without knowing what he was doing? In other words, are Sophocles' characters justified in worshipping the gods and trying to live by their laws, and does Sophocles himself endorse their attitudes, or present them with ironic detachment?

Like almost all Greeks before them, Sophocles' men and women believe in

[1] Jones (1962) 170.

gods who are the source of everything in life, evil as well as good. The universe controlled by these gods is involved in a constant process of rhythmic change, but they themselves are outside time. 'Only to the gods comes neither old age nor death . . .' (*O.C.* 607f.); Zeus is 'unaged by time' (*Ant.* 608). Worship them as they must, men cannot expect unmixed blessing from the gods: it is the condition of mortals to experience pain as well as happiness (*Trach.* 126f.). The only sure event in any human future is death; 'tomorrow does not exist until today is safely past' (*Trach.* 943ff.). But men who are *eusebeis* should expect more divine favour than the *asebeis*, who are unfailingly punished, either in their own lifetimes or through their descendants. 'Pious' and 'impious' are inadequate translations of these terms: being *eusebes* means respecting the divine laws that are the foundations of human society, and hence it includes right behaviour towards others as well as proper worship of the gods. These are the 'unwritten and unfailing statutes' invoked by Antigone (*Ant.* 454f.) when she defends her burial of Polynices in defiance of Creon's decree; in *Electra* it is clear that for the Chorus as well as for Electra herself loyalty to Agamemnon's memory is in harmony with the eternal laws (1095f.). It is an affront to the gods to allow a corpse to remain unburied or to fail to respect parents; and if a man is guilty of this sort of insulting behaviour he is forgetting his place as a mortal and courting divine disfavour.

It used to be claimed that Sophocles' purpose was to justify the ways of these gods to men. 'Undeserved suffering', wrote S. H. Butcher in a sensitive essay published in 1891, 'while it is exhibited in Sophocles under various lights, always appears as part of the permitted evil which is a condition of a just and harmoniously ordered universe. It is foreseen in the counsels of the gods . . .'[1] Much was made of Sophocles' known personal piety to corroborate this reassuring view, and so to create the stereotype of the serene, conventional poet untroubled by the more disturbing aspects of life around him and of the stories he chose to tell. Many modern critics, reacting against what they see as wishful thinking in this approach, have preferred a Sophocles who is more humanist, more Euripidean, vastly more pessimistic. But there is a danger here, too, that a misleading stereotype will impose itself.

'Pessimism' after all seems to be a misplaced term for the traditional Greek attitude to human life. Men may be creatures of a day, but they are not abject, unworthy, valueless unless redeemed by god. And the gods are objects of worship, not of mere brute fear: Dodds was right to speak of the beauty as well as the terror of the old beliefs.[2] If human achievement at its greatest is thought to be 'godlike' and the humane virtues are believed to be enjoined by divine law, that is, to have absolute value, then there is a sense in which traditional Greek thinking is not pessimistic. The cosmos may be cruel, but it cannot be

---

[1] Butcher (1891) 127.   [2] Dodds (1951) 49.

simply meaningless. Against this background Sophocles creates a drama that explores unmerited suffering, without protest on the one hand or justification on the other, but with pity and respect. When he chooses Oedipus as the paradigm of human blindness – and human intelligence – he uses him as a *consolatio*, not to question why these horrors should happen to a man. They do happen, the play says, but we with our imperfect understanding cannot tell why; all we can do is try to come to terms with the strange necessities of being human. Even the most perceptive and intelligent of our kind, Oedipus, was hopelessly wrong, even about his own identity; but he endured the revelation of the truth.

It can of course be argued that *Oedipus tyrannus* shows the work of malicious gods playing with men's sufferings for their sport. But that is not how it is seen by Oedipus himself, or by the Chorus watching his ordeal. When all is revealed they reflect not on the unfairness of the gods but on the fragility of human success and the inexorable revelatory process of time: ἐφηῦρέ σ' ἄκονθ' ὁ πάνθ' ὁρῶν χρόνος 'time the all-seeing has found you out against your will' (1213). Even so, one might ask, are *we*, the audience, not to recoil with disgust at the cruelty of Apollo, who did not give Oedipus a straight answer to the question 'Who are my parents?' but simply told him that he would kill the one and marry the other? This no more undermines Apollo than the story of the oracle he gave to Croesus, told by Herodotus (1.53, 91): 'If you invade Persia you will destroy a great empire'. Men do not always know what are the important questions to ask, and when told the truth they are prevented by their human limitations from understanding it. As guardian of the truth Apollo is actively concerned to see it fulfilled and revealed, but he has no ultimate responsibility for what happens to Oedipus.

If Apollo, the play's presiding deity, cannot be made to carry the responsibility, what of the will of the gods generally? Sophocles nowhere illuminates the divine purpose by explaining why it had to be that Oedipus would kill his father and marry his mother, but he does lay stress on the idea that such was his destiny. How important, then, is the idea of fate in this play, or for that matter elsewhere in Sophocles? It would be anachronistic to think of fate as a detailed predestined programme of each man's life, an idea which only makes its appearance in Hellenistic thought.[1] Sophocles treats the notion of fate in a way much more appropriate to tragedy; in his plays fate is simply being mortal and being the person one is. A man's freedom to act is at every point limited by his circumstances and temperament, which are an inheritance from the past; about the future the only thing he knows for certain is that he will die; for the present he is compelled to act as if he knew all the things of which he is ignorant.

[1] Reinhardt (1947) 108.

Oedipus' act of parricide was freely chosen: it was his decision to take the road to Thebes, his choice to retaliate when Laius insulted him. But if we ask what lay behind these decisions we see the limitations of human knowledge and the complexity of human action. Oedipus' avoidance of Corinth and choice of the road to Thebes were prompted by the commendable wish to avoid harming his parents, but since he did not know who his parents were this was a misconstruction of the oracle and in fact he was leaving Corinth unnecessarily. Once on the road to Thebes he was more likely to meet Laius, though the timing of their meeting was a matter of coincidence – the coincidence that he and Laius should have chosen to travel when they did. The actual killing was provoked by Oedipus' natural resentment at the high-handed behaviour of Laius; this vigorous self-defence was characteristic of Oedipus' royal temperament, and of course the deed was done in ignorance of his own and Laius' identity. If Laius had been more gracious ... or Oedipus had been a milder man ... or if he had for a moment suspected that there could be any kinship between them ... then things might have turned out differently. But for the audience listening to the story of these events there is a strong feeling of inevitability, just as the actions of Oedipus within the play itself seem inevitable, though each is freely chosen and fully motivated. Thus the poet achieves that 'tension between freedom and necessity which seems essential to the tragic paradox'.[1] And the importance of the idea of fate lies in its power to convey the compulsions of the human condition.

Sophocles' characters and choruses describe these compulsions as supernatural forces, *daimones* like Ate and the Erinyes; this was traditional in Greek religious thought and may well have been part of the poet's own belief. But the question of what he personally believed is only marginally important; it is more interesting to study the use he makes of the traditional religious language. It is through this language that he expresses the mysterious, non-rational, frightening and awe-inspiring aspects of life, both the 'dark underpit' (to use Lattimore's phrase)[2] and the inscrutable orderliness of the cosmic design.

Antigone and *Oedipus at Colonus* illustrate very well how Sophocles uses the ambiguities of religious language to express his deepest insights. A crude analysis of the two plays might lead one to posit an historical development in his attitudes: in *Antigone*, one might say, he protests at the gods' arbitrariness; in *Oedipus at Colonus* he celebrates their making amends to one of their most notable victims. But it would be hard to find a more misleading formulation. In both plays Sophocles creates a powerful sense of the forces outside man's control and the emotions that they inspire; in neither does he take up attitudes or sit in judgement or find answers.

---

[1] Winnington-Ingram (1965) 50.   [2] Lattimore (1958) 102.

For many modern critics *Antigone* is one of Sophocles' darkest plays: 'the *Antigone* conceals vast potentialities of unreason and chaos';[1] 'the message of the Chorus in their odes is one of helpless bewilderment and dark despair; but it is fully consonant with the evils that we have witnessed on the stage'.[2] Creon the new ruler of Thebes issues an edict forbidding the burial of Polynices, who has committed treason by attacking his native city. Antigone disobeys the prohibition, claiming that she has a sacred and overriding duty to bury her brother; for this Creon punishes her with imprisonment in a rocky tomb and leaves her to die. But when the seer reports that Polynices' corpse is polluting the city Creon goes to release her, only to find that she has already hanged herself. A question that is often raised is why the gods allow Antigone to die if she is really upholding their laws. They show their displeasure quickly enough when Creon leaves Polynices unburied; why do they not intervene to keep Antigone alive so that she can be released when Creon changes his mind? Sophocles almost encourages his audience to expect – or hope for – a miracle by lavishing so much detail (998ff.) on the signs of divine displeasure at the unburied corpse, but no miracle happens: Antigone is dead by the time Creon arrives. She had freely chosen to risk death in order to bury her brother; when that death actually comes it tells us nothing about the gods, only about life as it really is in which actions have their consequences and the consequences have to be faced. The task of a tragedian is to confront the worst facts of life; in such contexts miracles can too easily seem like evasion or fantasy.

But a more subtle question can be raised about our view of Antigone's action. She belives that she is right to bury Polynices because this is in accordance with the eternal laws, a god-given and permanent moral order, whose validity she never doubts until her last pathetic scene in which she confronts the fact of death. 'Nor did I think', she says to Creon at 453ff., 'that your decrees were so compelling that a mortal could override the unwritten and unfailing statutes of the gods. For they endure not just today and yesterday, but eternally, and no one knows when they were ordained.' It is natural for an audience to approve Antigone's generous act of loyalty to her brother and her courage in dying for her beliefs; but for some critics there is only pathetic self-delusion in her claim that these beliefs are divinely sanctioned. How then are we to interpret the language used by the Chorus at the end of the episode in which Antigone makes her great speech?

τεάν, Ζεῦ, δύνασιν τίς ἀν-
δρῶν ὑπερβασία κατάσχοι;
τὰν οὔθ' ὕπνος αἱρεῖ ποθ' ὁ παντογήρως
οὔτ' ἀκάματοι θεῶν
μῆνες, ἀγήρως δὲ χρόνωι δυνάστας

---

[1] Torrance (1965) 300.   [2] Coleman (1972) 27.

κατέχεις Ὀλύμπου
μαρμαρόεσσαν αἴγλαν.
τό τ' ἔπειτα καὶ τὸ μέλλον
καὶ τὸ πρὶν ἐπαρκέσει
νόμος ὅδ'· οὐδὲν ἕρπει
θνατῶν βιότωι πάμπολύ γ' ἐκτὸς ἄτας.   (604–14)

Your power, O Zeus, what human transgression can limit? That power neither
Sleep the all-aging nor the gods' tireless months can master, but you dwell, a
ruler unaged by time, in the dazzling radiance of Olympus. And for the future,
near and distant, as for the past this law will be found true: nothing that is vast
comes to the life of mortals without ruin.[1]

It is true that this stasimon is full of irony: the Chorus are trying to explain
the frightful situation of Antigone in terms of the family curse of the Labdacids,
yet in doing so they use language of sin and punishment which is much closer
to Creon's case and foreshadows his fall. But these ironies do not reduce the
power of the lines on the unchanging certainty of Zeus's laws. If the poetry of
this passage carries conviction it is hard to feel so sure that Sophocles is denying
the existence of a suprahuman order.

But if protest is not a characteristic Sophoclean mode neither is the positive
assertion of divine benevolence. The nearest he comes to this is in the sense
of holiness and blessing which he evokes in *Oedipus at Colonus*, for instance
in his description of the sanctity of Colonus and the grove of the Eumenides
(16ff., 36ff., 54ff., 466ff., 668ff.), or in the intimacy with which the divine voice
summons Oedipus (ὦ οὗτος οὗτος Οἰδίπους, τί μέλλομεν | χωρεῖν; 'Oedipus,
Oedipus, why are we delaying to go?' 1627f.), most of all in the mystery of
Oedipus' favoured passing, which only Theseus was allowed to witness.
'... and we could no longer see Oedipus anywhere, but the king alone and
holding his hand over his face to shade his eyes, as if he had seen some terrible
sight that no one could bear to look upon' (1648ff.). In this play, indeed,
Sophocles places a miracle at the centre of the action, but even here he is so
reticent that we are given no illumination of the gods' purposes. Certainly
it would be wrong to interpret what happens to Oedipus as a sign of divine
recompense for his sufferings; perhaps even the view that the gods rejoice in
human heroism goes further than Sophocles suggests (though it is a natural
Greek idea). The most that can be claimed is that the sense of holiness conveyed
in this play implies something more than a purely humanist vision of the world.

The question of crime and punishment is not central to Sophoclean tragedy.
His characters are caught in complex destructive situations which – being
human – they have helped to create for themselves, but the issue never turns

---

[1] The text of 614 is not certain, but most editors interpret the passage in the sense given here.
Cf. Easterling (1978).

on the precise degree of their guilt: in tragedy as in life it is common for a man's suffering to go far beyond what he morally deserves. Even in *Ajax*, where some stress is laid on the hero's hubris, the sequence of pride and punishment is plainly not the main subject of the play. The function of the Messenger's report at 748ff., in which we are told of Ajax's arrogant behaviour and Athena's anger, is partly to create a sense of crisis (if only Ajax can be kept safe for one day the danger will pass), partly to give a fateful pattern to his story, not to spell out the moral 'message' of the play. In *Trachiniae* some critics treat the sins and punishment of Heracles as the real issue; but Heracles is more convincingly interpreted as a paradigm of man's helplessness. Even the greatest of Greek heroes 'the best of men' (177, 811) – the strongest, bravest, most successful – is a slave to his sexual passion (Sophocles makes much of the idea of 'slave' in this play) and no better able than anyone else to escape the limitations of his ignorance.

What matters, evidently, is the way the characters respond to their appalling predicaments; and here we meet the question of Sophocles' idealism. He notoriously represents men 'as they ought to be'; but in what sense can idealized characters exemplify the realities of human experience? If we compare the Electra plays of Sophocles and Euripides we find Euripides forcing us to see the implications that such a situation would have in real life; the social embarrassments and the jealousy of his Electra compel us to believe in the continuing and urgent reality of the old heroic tale. But the Sophoclean heroine, though more elevated, has no less power to convince; and particularly in her total commitment to the mother-murder and her absence of regret at the end of the play she is a more frightening example of man's capacity for self-destruction in the cause of preserving moral integrity. In Euripides the horror is to some extent mitigated by Orestes' hesitation before he does the deed and by the remorse of brother and sister after it. In Sophocles there is no irresolution; no regret; Electra from the stage calls out to the unseen Orestes as he kills their mother: 'Strike again if you have the strength!' (1415). After the tender scene of her reunion with Orestes the starkness and cruelty of the end of the play are almost unbearable, but they grow out of the earlier action of the play in a way which forces the audience to accept them as real.

This impression of reality is achieved because Sophocles presents the action with extreme psychological nicety and sureness of touch. It is only in a very limited and individual way that he can be said to idealize: he is quite ready to portray evil characters when the plot demands them, like the villainous Creon in *Oedipus at Colonus*, and he certainly does not sentimentalize his heroes (though many critics have written as if he did). Antigone's harshness towards Ismene, the brutal way Ajax treats Tecmessa, the virulence of Philoctetes' hatred of Odysseus, are all uncomfortable features which ought to warn us against taking a romantic view of Sophoclean heroism. And yet his characters do make a distinctively different impression from those of Euripides. It is partly a matter of style. Sophocles prefers to maintain the distance of the world of the epic stories, whereas Euripides is more insistent in his reminders of contemporary humdrum reality. But there is also a difference in the way they appeal to the audience's sympathy. In Sophocles' extant plays we are not asked to transfer our sympathies or make a fundamental reappraisal of a character in mid-action: there is nothing comparable to the shifts in response that we are required to make in *Medea* or *Bacchae*. Sophocles seems often to have been interested in exploring the limits of human endurance: man's capacity for asserting his belief in himself against all external pressures, including the promptings of good sense and the pull of ordinary emotional ties. The conversion or moral collapse of one of these intransigent heroes would profoundly alter the character of his drama.

But the term 'hero' must be used with caution, in case it leads us to adopt a formula too rigid for the fluidity of Sophoclean drama. The intransigent, isolated, suffering figure is clearly the most important of his symbols of mankind, but it is not the only one. Neither Deianira nor Heracles can be forced into such a mould, but this does not reduce their claim to be regarded as tragic characters; Creon in *Antigone*, too, who finally changes his mind, and Neoptolemus in *Philoctetes*, who undergoes a process of moral transformation, are also central figures who demand as much attention in their respective plays as Antigone and Philoctetes themselves. We should be rash to call *Trachiniae* an 'odd' play because it does not have the more familiar kind of hero: we have no reason for thinking that the limits of the poet's range coincide with what is offered in seven plays out of 123. Who would have thought that he made bold use of changes of scene if *Ajax* had not happened to survive?

There is another respect, too, in which the image of the isolated hero is liable to mislead. This is in its associations with specifically modern, post-romantic ideas of the outsider, the individual who rejects society or is permanently and profoundly alienated from it. Sophocles' men and women, it is true, reject the norms of ordinary behaviour, the safe compromises, the comfortable or corrupt evasions familiar in everyday life, which the dramatist illustrates in vividly contemporary detail, but they do not reject society as such, and they define themselves in relation to society.

Ajax cannot be truly Ajax without his *philoi* – his kin and dependants – to defend and his enemies to fight; Antigone dies as much for her brother as for her principles; Electra, who cuts herself off from all the normal life of the household, still values that life as the only meaningful context in which to exist. This is what gives pathos to the picture she draws for Chrysothemis of the rewards they will win if they murder Aegisthus singlehanded:

'Do you not see what fame you will win for yourself and me if you do as I say? Everyone who sees us – citizen or stranger – will greet us with praises like these: "See these two sisters, friends, who saved their father's house...all must love them, all must reverence them; at festivals and wherever the people are gathered all must honour them for their bravery."' (973 ff.)

Oedipus in *Oedipus at Colonus*, first an outcast from his own city, then himself rejecting it, comes to find new citizenship in Athens; most of all Philoctetes, who to the modern reader seems so clearly an archetypal outsider, set apart by his wound and his bow from the rest of the world, in Sophocles is only truly fulfilled when he consents to go to Troy as the comrade of Neoptolemus, to be healed and win glory. Sophocles has not made his story sentimental by suggesting that the world Philoctetes will rejoin is perfect, or glory something worth having at any price: much of the play is concerned precisely with the evaluation of ends and means; but it is so designed that although the world (represented by the Greeks at Troy) is decadent, Philoctetes' going to Troy is also the reintegration of the wild man into society and something which the audience must endorse.

Sophocles' greatest strength is his mastery of the dramatic medium. Everything in his plays, plot structure, character drawing, language, spectacle, is fully exploited to achieve that 'imitation of action and life' which Aristotle sees as the essence of tragedy. The intense aesthetic pleasure given by Sophocles' plays has been well compared to the effect of Mozart's music, the exhilaration felt by an audience when the artist is superbly in control of his material. This aesthetic impression demands to be taken into account when we try to grasp the poet's meaning: it makes a significant difference to the way we respond to his terrifying stories.

A major principle of Sophoclean composition is the use of contrast. This is seen at all levels: contrasting themes, as in *Oedipus at Colonus* where the behaviour of Oedipus' sons is repeatedly set against that of his daughters; contrasting moods, as when a song of joy and hope is at once followed by the climactic revelation of disaster (e.g. *Ajax* 693ff.); juxtaposition of contrasting characters, as in *Antigone* and *Trachiniae*, where the central pairs are both opposed and intimately interconnected. It is relevant to mention the use of irony here, for irony draws attention to the fundamental contrast between appearance and reality, to the distance between what the characters think and what we the audience know to be true, and between what they intend and what actually happens: *peripeteia* itself is dependent on the principle of contrast. Thus Sophocles finds essentially dramatic means of expressing his sense of the ambiguity of all experience, the two sides of the human picture and the corresponding antinomies in nature.

His language is less exuberant than Aeschylus', his imagery comparatively 'ordinary' and unobtrusive. This however is art that conceals art. His seemingly effortless verse depends on bold extensions of syntax and meaning and on great metrical virtuosity, and his imagery is often all the more effective for being understated. Stylistic reserve does not imply lack of inventiveness or complexity: themes are developed and interwoven, and the language shades from literal to metaphorical, with an intricacy which belongs only to the very greatest poets. At one of the high points in *Trachiniae*, when the Nurse has just burst in to tell the Chorus of Deianira's suicide (893ff.), they cry out ἔτεκ' ἔτεκε μεγάλαν ἁ | νέορτος ἅδε νύμφα | δόμοισι τοῖσδ' 'Ερινύν 'This new bride has given birth, given birth to a great Erinys for the house', meaning Iole, the girl for whom Heracles sacked Oechalia, the girl who is now ruining his family. It is natural to think of the bride bearing a child – Heracles' child – and the image gains weight from its literal appropriateness in the context. More than this, it specifically recalls the ironic scene where Deianira asks of Iole whether she is 'unmarried, or a mother' (308), and concludes that she must be 'without experience of all these things'. But the child is no human child; it is a 'great Erinys', a great avenging spirit: the Chorus recognize that the death of Deianira is the inevitable consequence of Heracles' bringing home Iole. The image thus advances one of the play's dominant themes, the inescapable power of sexual passion, and in representing a death in terms of giving birth it restates a connexion made twice before in the play. In the Parodos (94f.) night is said both to give birth to the Sun and to put him to death (imagery which is related in complex ways to Deianira and Heracles) and in the Third Stasimon (834) the poison of the Hydra, with which Heracles killed Nessus and which Deianira used as a love charm, is said to have been 'generated by death' (the Greek uses the same verb τίκτειν each time).

Because Sophocles (particularly by contrast with Euripides) is neither a theoretician nor an apologist, the intellectual content of his plays has often been minimized. But it is hard to see how he could have used language of such finesse, variety and sophistication if he had not been in touch with the important movements of thought of his time as well as deeply read in the poetry of his predecessors. As A. A. Long has emphasized, we find evidence in his plays of interest in Presocratic thought and sophistic argument, of medical knowledge, of concern with politics and political ideology, all exemplifying 'a mind which was completely involved in the intellectual life of fifth-century Athens'.[1] The terminology of the ethical debates in *Electra*, the sophistic attitudes of Odysseus in *Philoctetes*, the political programme of Menelaus in *Ajax* or of Creon in *Antigone* all have precise relevance to contemporary ways

---

[1] Long (1968) 167.

of thought, suggesting that 'remote' and 'detached' are not terms too readily to be used of Sophocles.

Boldness, intelligence, resourcefulness are all characteristics of his dramatic technique as much as of his use of language. He is daring in his manipulation of inconsistency, which gives him some marvellously concentrated and dramatic moments, though its purpose is subtler than just the creation of isolated brilliant effects. In *Philoctetes*, for example, there is notorious inconsistency in the treatment of Neoptolemus' knowledge of the prophecy that he and Philoctetes are destined together to take Troy: in the Prologue he knows hardly anything about it, but by the end of the play he can give Philoctetes a circumstantially detailed account. There is no satisfactory way of explaining this logically, as if we were dealing with the facts of history, but there are good dramatic reasons for releasing the crucial information piecemeal and for presenting Neoptolemus at the outset as wholly dependent on Odysseus, while the deeper significance of the inconsistency seems to be that it enables the audience to share with Neoptolemus a growing awareness of the true meaning of the prophecy.

Sophocles pays more attention than Aeschylus to the interaction of his characters. This is particularly a feature of his latest plays and may have been what he had in mind when he used the term ἠθικώτατον 'most expressive of character' to describe his mature manner (see p. 46). The effect of one person's words or actions on another's feelings is brought out in all kinds of ways: in *Trachiniae* the enigmatic Iole stands in silence while Lichas lies to Deianira about her and the Messenger challenges his lies; in *Electra* the false messenger speech on the death of Orestes, which was designed to disarm Clytemnestra, has a devastating effect on Electra, who is also there to listen; in *Philoctetes* the silences and ambiguous language of Neoptolemus make the audience suspect that he is under increasing strain as he comes to know and pity Philoctetes. Often the use of visual effects deepens this study of the relations between characters, as when Electra cannot be convinced that Orestes is alive and standing before her until she has been forced to put down the urn in which she thought she held his ashes (*El.* 1205ff.), or when Neoptolemus' action in supporting Philoctetes physically is at once followed by his own emotional breakdown (*Phil.* 889ff.).

It is easy to overlook the visual side of Sophocles' dramaturgy because we have only the text on the page without explicit stage directions; but readers who attempt to act the plays or imagine them in performance soon become aware of the unerring theatrical instinct that created them. His use of props – the sword of Ajax, the casket in *Trachiniae* that carried the poisoned robe, Philoctetes' bow – is both simple and sophisticated: each represents a fundamental theme in its play and is closely related to the verbal imagery, but there is nothing contrived in the prominence given to it. The stage action, too, often makes a strong visual impact, as in *Ajax* when the door of the stage building is opened and the hero is seen surrounded by the butchered animals (346f.), or later in the searching scene (866ff.) when the Chorus agitatedly look for the missing Ajax, and Tecmessa finds him where he fell on his sword. In *Oed'pus at Colonus* there is a remarkably violent scene (818ff.) when Creon seizes Antigone and very nearly comes to blows with the Chorus. Even more gripping is the final scene of *Electra* (1466ff.): Aegisthus lifts the cover from the corpse he believes to be the dead Orestes, sees with horror that it is Clytemnestra, and at once finds himself in a trap, facing the drawn swords of Orestes and Pylades. The same sense of theatre is evident in Sophocles' use of entrances and exits, such as the unexpected reappearances of Odysseus (*Phil.* 974, 1293), or the slow silent departure of Deianira after Hyllus has denounced her (*Trach.* 813ff.), or the great moment in *Oedipus at Colonus* (1540ff.) when the blind Oedipus leaves the stage, leading the way to the place where he is to die. Many scenes show how resourcefully he made use of the third actor, scenes like *El.* 66off. when Electra and Clytemnestra listen to the story of Orestes' death, or *Phil.* 542ff. when the False Merchant purports to talk to Neoptolemus without letting Philoctetes overhear, or *O.T.* 1110ff., the brilliant scene in which Oedipus and the messenger from Corinth cross-question the Theban herdsman and elicit the truth he is trying to hide.

These effects ought not, of course, to be considered in isolation from their contexts, as if they were mere virtuoso displays: in each play they are part of the distinctive shape and emotional movement of the whole, a complex unity which can hardly be described without oversimplification. How, for example, can the critic, particularly the modern critic, who has no knowledge of Sophocles' music, do justice to the effects created by his handling of the different modes of delivery – speech, lyric dialogue and choral song? Some of the most exciting and intense sequences are formally very elaborate, with a symmetry which can more easily be paralleled in opera than in modern spoken drama. So Ajax' first appearance after the killing of the animals is marked by an elaborate exchange (348ff.) between him, the Chorus and Tecmessa. Ajax sings three pairs of agitated lyrics, each pair metrically different and each punctuated by responses, now by the Chorus, now by Tecmessa, in the iambic trimeters of spoken dialogue. The contrast strongly emphasizes their different emotional states: Ajax in a wild frenzy of despair, Tecmessa and the sailors begging him to be calm. Much of the power of this *kommos* comes from the words, but the formal patterning plays a significant and subtle part in conveying the emotional quality of the scene.

The plays of Sophocles strikingly confirm the truth of Eliot's claim that 'in genuine drama the form is determined by the point on the line at which a tension between liturgy and realism takes place'.[1] In the search to understand Sophocles we need to be sensitive not only to his realism – both in universal terms and in the context of fifth-century Greek life – but also to the 'liturgical' aspect of his language, rhythms and structures, for it is this in combination with his realism that gives his plays their particular distinction.

5. EURIPIDES

The relative abundance of surviving Euripidean drama (we have eighteen tragedies which have come down to us as his work) is not wholly a result of his continuing popularity in antiquity; like the other great dramatists, Euripides survived the early centuries of Byzantium in a selected edition, in his case one of ten plays. By some fortunate accident, however, part of what seems to have been a complete edition arranged in alphabetical order by title survived the later centuries in which so many classical texts vanished; it was available for reproduction in the revival of classical learning which marked the Byzantine recovery from the disaster of the Fourth Crusade. In addition, the papyrological finds of the last hundred years have given us extensive fragments of lost plays, which, combined with quotations found in ancient authors, often enable us to form a clear idea of the play as a whole.

Not only do we possess a large body of material, we also have a fair idea of the chronology of Euripidean production. Many of the plays are dated in ancient records; for many of them we have a *terminus ante quem* in the shape of an Aristophanic parody. For others an approximate date (or rather period) is suggested by the frequency of metrical resolution in the trimeter,[2] since this phenomenon shows a steady progression from the earliest dated plays to the latest. Of the extant plays, the earliest we possess is *Alcestis* (438). *Medea* is securely dated in 431; *Hippolytus* in 428. The decade 427–417 probably saw the staging of *Heraclidae, Hecuba, Electra, Andromache* and *Supplices. Troades,* with *Alexander,* is firmly dated in 415, and *Helen* in 412; *Phoenissae, Antiope, Heracles, Ion* and *Iphigenia in Tauris* belong to the next six years. *Orestes* was staged in 408 and *Bacchae* and *Iphigenia in Aulide* were produced at Athens after the poet's death in Macedon in 406 B.C.

When news of Euripides' death reached Athens, Sophocles had still some months to live, but Euripides was by far the younger man. His first production (which earned him a third prize) took place in 455 B.C., three years after the staging of Aeschylus' *Oresteia;* Sophocles' debut (a first prize) had preceded the *Oresteia* by ten years. This disparity in age was of great importance for the intellectual formation of the younger poet, for during the middle decades of the century sophistic teaching explored new critical attitudes towards politics and

---

[1] Eliot (1926) x. [2] See below, p. 85.

morality, expressed in new rhetorical forms. Sophoclean drama shows familiarity
with the rhetoric and a sharply critical awareness of the ideas; but they are
viewed from a distance, as it were – the reaction of an older man whose vision
of the world is already formed. Euripides, though his critique of the ideas may
be just as incisive, is very much a man of the sophistic age; the language and
techniques of the new rhetoric come naturally to him and his plays fully reflect
the intellectual controversies of the time.

He is an intellectual dramatist and his career has a curiously modern look.
His unpopularity during his lifetime is clear from the rarity of his victories at
the Dionysia, the frequency of jibes at his tragedies and travesties of his person
on the comic stage, and his eventual withdrawal from Athens to Macedonia;
it was followed by overwhelming popularity with succeeding generations. In
the fourth and later centuries his plays, both in reading and performance,
eclipsed and almost extinguished the reputations of his competitor and predeces-
sor. The late tradition that he composed his plays in a cave on Salamis is
certainly apocryphal but the story does symbolize a real situation – the isolation
which we have come to recognize as the usual fate of the intellectually advanced
artist in democratic society. And there are passages in his dramas which seem
to derive from consciousness of such a situation. Medea, for example, in
her attempt to reassure Creon sounds a contemporary, possibly a personal
note.

> 'This is not the first time...that my great reputation has injured me...No
> man of intelligence and judgement should ever have his sons educated so that
> they become excessively clever...If you introduce new, intelligent ideas to
> fools, you will be thought frivolous, not intelligent. On the other hand, if you do
> get a reputation for surpassing those who are supposed to be intellectually
> sophisticated, you will seem to be a thorn in the city's flesh. This is what has
> happened to me. I am a clever woman, and some feel envious spite toward me,
> others count me their adversary...' (292–305)

The dramatist's engagement with the intellectual, political and moral controversies of the day did not however result in a clear position on one side or
the other. Dramatists, who speak through the masks of their creations, are notoriously difficult to pin down, and Euripides more so than most. He was a
problem to his contemporaries and he is one still; over the course of centuries
since his plays were first produced he has been hailed or indicted under a
bewildering variety of labels. He has been described as 'the poet of the Greek
enlightenment'[1] and also as 'Euripides the irrationalist';[2] as a religious sceptic
if not an atheist, but on the other hand, as a believer in divine providence and
the ultimate justice of divine dispensation. He has been seen as a profound
explorer of human psychology and also a rhetorical poet who subordinated

---

[1] Nestle (1901).   [2] Dodds (1929).

consistency of character to verbal effect; as a misogynist and a feminist; as a realist who brought tragic action down to the level of everyday life and as a romantic poet who chose unusual myths and exotic settings. He wrote plays which have been widely understood as patriotic pieces supporting Athens' war against Sparta and others which many have taken as the work of the anti-war dramatist *par excellence*, even as attacks on Athenian imperialism. He has been recognized as the precursor of New Comedy and also as what Aristotle called him – 'the most tragic of the poets' (*Poetics* 1453a30). And not one of these descriptions is entirely false.

There have been attempts to frame these contradictions in schemes of artistic and intellectual development. A persuasive spiritual biography has been drafted along the following lines: an early period of what might be called high tragedy (*Medea*, *Hippolytus*), followed by the patriotic plays of the opening years of the Peloponnesian War (*Heraclidae*, *Supplices*); plays expressing disgust with the war as the fighting went on and became more senseless (*Hecuba*, *Troades*); a turning away from tragedy to romantic intrigue plays (*Ion*, *Iphigenia in Tauris*, *Helen*) and a final return to the tragic mood, more despairing and violent than before (*Orestes*, *Phoenissae*, *Bacchae*). But of course the procedure is hazardous if only because so many plays are missing and, although sometimes we can guess at their contents, we have no idea of their mood. And the last set of his plays included both *Bacchae* and *Iphigenia in Aulide* – one of the most violently tragic and one which contains scenes whose tone and technique seem to foreshadow New Comedy.

That there was development in Euripidean technique is undeniable, but if there was a similar development in his thought we do not have sufficient evidence to chart its course. And in any case some basic themes and attitudes are common to the latest and the earliest plays. The merciless Dionysus of *Bacchae* is cast in the same mould as the vindictive Aphrodite of *Hippolytus* and the revengeful Athena of *Troades*: all three gods wreak havoc to punish human disrespect for their divinity. Medea's ferocious revenge is very like that of Hecuba and Electra, not to mention the vicious reprisals planned by Orestes, Electra and Pylades in *Orestes*. The disturbance of the heroic atmosphere by realistic scenes which may even verge on the comic is constant throughout, from the degrading quarrel of father and son in *Alcestis*, through the burlesque arming of Iolaus in *Heraclidae*, all the way to the spectacle of two old men, one of them blind, dressed in fawn skins and trying to dance like Maenads, in *Bacchae*. Even the most harrowing of the tragic plays, *Troades*, has an incongruously comic line (Menelaus is advised not to take Helen home aboard his own ship and asks: 'Why? Has she got any heavier?' 1050) and the play which is the closest Euripidean approach to Menandrian comedy, *Ion*, contains Creusa's lament for her lost child (859ff.), one of Euripides' most poignant and bitter solo arias. The pattern of the extant work suggests not so much changing views as variation on persistent themes.

The characterization of Euripides as a spokesman for the new ideas and his responsibility for what were thought of as their destructive effects were first given pungent and exaggerated expression in his own lifetime by Aristophanes, the comic poet who was both fascinated and repelled by his work. A recurrent tactic of his assault is to identify Euripides with many of the subversive ideas which were felt to be typical of sophistic teaching, prominent among them a destructive scepticism about the Olympian gods. The widow of *Thesmophoriazusae* whose husband was killed on Cyprus and who feeds her five children by making wreaths for worshippers, complains that her business has been cut by more than half since Euripides 'in his tragedies, has persuaded men that the gods do not exist' (450–1) and in *Frogs*, while Aeschylus prays to Demeter, Euripides addresses his prayer to 'other gods' (889) among them 'upper air, my nourishment' and 'intelligence' (892–3). The result of such teaching, the comic poet claimed, was moral degeneration. Euripidean drama is blamed by 'Aeschylus' in the *Frogs* for converting noble, warlike Athenians into 'marketplace loungers, tricksters and scoundrels' (1015), for teaching 'ranting and blather which has emptied the wrestling schools' (1069–70). In modern times the case has been put seriously: Nestle's *Euripides, the poet of the Greek enlightenment* attempts to construct a Euripidean philosophical outlook – the poet's message 'of enlightenment about the real state of things as against the traditional belief, blindly accepted by the mass of mankind'.[1] Quite apart from the fact that Euripides is a dramatist, not a philosopher, the argument is insecurely based, for the passages used to support it are cited with little regard to context (many of the most important, in fact, are isolated quotations from lost plays). But in drama, context can modify or even contradict the surface meaning of a particular passage. Hippolytus' line ('My tongue has sworn an oath but my mind is free', 612) was often used against Euripides by his comic critic, and if the play had not survived we would never have known that in fact Hippolytus goes to his death precisely because he will not break his oath. Nevertheless Nestle's title can serve as a reminder that Euripidean drama gives us the clearest reflection of the intellectual ferment of fifth-century Athens, and unlike the Platonic retrospective (and partisan) reconstruction it is the reaction of a contemporary.

The plays reflect, more literally than those of Sophocles, the intellectual controversies of the time, sometimes in a manner incongruous with the mythical setting. One recurrent theme is the problem of education for civic life, the problem to which the sophists proposed a solution. In *Antiope*, a play with a

[1] Nestle (1901) 50.

violent revenge action, two sons, Amphion and Zethus, stage a celebrated debate about the value of the active as opposed to the artistic life.[1] Amphion champions the intellectual and artistic life, Zethus the military, agricultural and political. It is remarkable that Zethus' speech echoes many of the criticisms levelled at Euripides himself by the comic poets. Zethus reproaches his brother for his lack of manliness and inability to stand by his friends in war and council.

'Where is the cleverness in this, an art which receives a noble nature and makes it inferior?...A man who...lets his household affairs go to waste and pursues delight in song, will become remiss in both private and public duty...Put an end to your singing, practise the fair art of practical affairs. Sing its praises and you will be thought a sensible man, digging, ploughing the earth, watching the flocks. Leave to others these elegant, intellectual pursuits...' (frs. 186, 187, 188)

Amphion's reply rejects the active life.

'The quiet man is a source of safety for his friends and of great benefit to the city. Do not sing the praise of dangerous action. I have no love for excessive boldness in a ship's captain, nor in a statesman either...Your contempt for my lack of physical strength is misplaced. If I can think straight, that is better than a powerful right arm...It is by a man's brains that cities are well governed and households too, and therein lies great strength for war...' (frs. 194, 199, 200)

Education is not the only controversial issue of the day reflected in the plays; political theory, another speciality of the sophistic teachers, also bulks large. In a long scene early in *Phoenissae*, the brothers Eteocles and Polynices dispute their rights to the throne of Thebes; their mother Jocasta tries to mediate between them. To Polynices' reasonable offer of a return to the *status quo* Eteocles replies with an unashamed proclamation of his will to rule – words which are echoed in the Athenian speeches of the Melian dialogue and the arguments of Thrasymachus and Callicles in Plato.[2]

'Mother, I will speak out...I would go to the place where the stars rise or below the earth, if that were possible, so as to hold Absolute Power, greatest of the gods. This is a prized possession I have no wish to let pass to another; I will keep it for myself.' (503–8)

Jocasta rebukes them both equally but counters Eteocles' argument with democratic theory.

'Why do you pursue, my son, the most evil of divinities, Ambition? She is an unjust goddess. She comes into prosperous homes and cities and when she goes out leaves destruction for those who entertained her...It is better to honour Equality, who firmly links friends to friends, city to city, ally to ally...For it is

[1] Cf. Plato, *Gorgias* 485eff.
[2] Thuc. 5.105, Plato, *Rep.* 343bff., *Gorg.* 482cff.

Equality which has fixed for mankind its divisions of measures and weights, has defined number. The rayless eye of night shares the cycle of the year equally with the blaze of the sun and neither one feels hateful envy for the other as it gives way . . .' (531–45)

But Euripides reflects the negative as well as the positive aspects of sophistic thought; in particular the plays cast scorn on those prophecies which played so important a part in Greek life and which in Sophoclean drama are always, in the end, vindicated. The most explicit condemnation of prophecy is put in the mouth of the messenger in *Helen*; he has just learned that the woman the Greeks fought and died for at Troy was merely an image made of cloud – the real Helen was in Egypt all the time.

> 'I realize how contemptible. . . are all the words of the prophets. So there was nothing sound in the voices of the fire oracle or the birds. Birds indeed – it was simple-minded to think that they were any use to men. For Calchas gave no word or sign to the army as he saw his friends dying for a cloud, nor Helenus either – but his city was sacked, and all for nothing.' (744–51)

This is not the only radical opinion on religious matters to surface in Euripidean drama. Tiresias in *Bacchae* explains that the goddess Demeter is the earth – 'call her by either name' (276) – and similarly Dionysus, besides being the inventor of wine, *is* the wine, 'a god poured out in libation to the gods' (284). Similar theories of the nature of divinities are attributed to the sophist Prodicus. But Euripidean characters propose even more unusual religious formulas, such as those of Hecuba in *Troades*. 'O You who are the earth's support and have your throne upon it, whoever you may be, beyond our knowledge or conjecture, Zeus, whether you are natural necessity or human intelligence, hear my plea . . .' (884–7). It is no wonder that Menelaus remarks on her 'innovative prayers' (889).

Some Euripidean characters go beyond philosophical reformulations of religious belief, they indulge in harsh criticism of the Olympian gods. Amphitryon in *Heracles* condemns Zeus for abandoning the family of Heracles, his own son, in scathing terms.

> 'So you were not the friend you seemed to be. You are a great god but I, a mortal man, surpass you in excellence: I did not betray the sons of Heracles. But you, you knew how to steal secretly into women's beds, to take another's bride . . . what you do not know is how to save your children. You are a callous, ignorant god (ἀμαθής τις εἶ θεός) – or else there is no justice in your nature.' (341–7)

A common motif in Euripidean plays is an appeal to a god for mercy, coupled with a reminder that gods should have higher standards of morality than men. So Cadmus in *Bacchae* appeals to Dionysus for forgiveness: 'Gods should not be like mortals in their passions' (1348). And the old servant of Hippolytus addresses Aphrodite in almost the same words. Both prayers are rejected; both gods merciless. These passages seem to suggest that gods are no better than men; in the case of Hippolytus, who does forgive the father who unjustly engineered his death, that they are perhaps worse. Such criticism may culminate in rejection of the whole mythological tradition. In *Heracles*, the hero is urged by Theseus to reject suicide and live with the consequences of his murderous action, just as the gods live on Olympus, though they have committed adultery and violence against each other. But he replies (1341–6): 'For my part I do not believe the gods have forbidden loves; that one of them could chain the other's hands I never accepted and will never believe. For a god, if he is rightly a god, needs nothing. These are the wretched tales of poets' (ἀοιδῶν οἵδε δύστηνοι λόγοι). This comes close to denying the existence of the Olympian gods altogether, for the adulteries of Zeus, to take only one example, were the genesis of Dionysus, Perseus, Helen and many another. It is true that Euripides seems never to neglect an opportunity to bring the gods on stage, but modern critics have found it easy to dismiss the divine appearances at the end of so many of the plays as a device to reassure the pious or a merely technical solution for the problems raised by the radical treatment of the myth. The juxtaposition of amoral gods and human beings who vainly expect justice or mercy is taken as an ironic denial of the existence of such gods; Euripides was 'attempting to show citizens bred on traditional views . . . that such conceptions of the gods *should* offend them'.[1] Such gods cannot exist: they must be 'the wretched tales of poets'.

Yet such dramatic statements must be seen in context. Heracles' famous repudiation of divine wrongdoing, for example, refers specifically to adultery as unthinkable for a god. Yet he is himself the offspring of divine adultery, and the madness which has ruined his life is the vindictive reaction of Hera, the divine jealous wife. The audience has seen Iris and Madness, the ministers of Hera, at work, experienced the shock of their sudden appearance and sensed in the rhythm of the racing trochaics the pulse of the insane fit which before their eyes descends into the house to seize its innocent victim. Heracles can talk in the way he does because he has not seen Iris and Madness at work; but the audience has. And since in the theatre everyone who appears on stage is equally real, Heracles is quite surely wrong.

This qualification by context obtains for all manifestations of the new intellectual views in Euripides: they are the words of dramatic fictional characters and parts of an overall design. It is usually thought (and may very well be true) that in the argument between the brothers in *Antiope*, the case put by Amphion must have been dearer to Euripides' heart, but Amphion seems to have conceded defeat in the argument, and it is certainly Amphion who at the

[1] Conacher (1967) 51.

end of the play is about to kill the tyrant Lycus when Hermes arrives to stop him.[1] In *Phoenissae* Jocasta's eloquent praise of Equality falls on deaf ears; before the play is over the mother and the two sons lie together in the equality of death. In one play after another the 'rationalist' point of view is repudiated by the outcome of events.

On the other hand, Euripides shows concern with and knowledge of religious phenomena which many would regard as 'irrational'. His presentation of Hippolytus, for example, is an understanding and sympathetic picture of a religious abstention from the sexual life which must have been extremely rare in the ancient world. An almost monastic obsession with purity can be sensed in Hippolytus' first speech, his dedication of a crown of flowers to Artemis. It came from 'a meadow undefiled ... where no shepherd dares to pasture his flocks, no blade of iron ever came; only the bee in springtime haunts this untouched meadow, and Modesty tends its garden with the river waters' (73-8). A similarly moving picture of piety in a young man appears in *Ion*; the monody with which the acolyte greets the dawn (82ff.) suggests what the religious atmosphere of Delphi must have been in its great days. In fact it is remarkable how often Euripides chooses a religious, ritual background for his great scenes: the death of Neoptolemus in the shrine at Delphi (*Andromache*), the temple of Artemis among the Taurians (*Iphigenia in Tauris*), the sacrifice Aegisthus offers in the grove of the nymphs (*Electra*), the sacrifice of Polyxena on the tomb of Achilles (*Hecuba*). And of course *Bacchae*, in its ferocious action and in the ecstasies of its choral odes, is the greatest portrayal of the Dionysiac spirit in all literature.

Whether this play is a celebration of the blessings of Dionysiac religion or a condemnation of its violence, one thing is sure: the poet who created this passion play was no 'rationalist'. It is the only Attic tragedy we know of which features a god as the protagonist; Dionysus, who in the prologue announces his assumption of human form as a votary of his own worship, dominates the central scenes and appears at the end in divine majesty. The play presents us with different reactions to his divinity: the mockery of Pentheus, the cynical adhesion of Cadmus, the political conversion of Tiresias; the ecstatic visions of the chorus alternating with their vengeful imprecations against the king who resists the new cult; the total possession of the women of Thebes, their paradisal peace and communion with nature, their ferocious reaction to interference and finally their frenzied dismemberment of Pentheus.

The dramatic centre of the play consists of three scenes in which man and god confront each other. In the first, the god, in the person of his votary, is bound, jeered at for his effeminate appearance, told he will be shorn of his hair, and imprisoned; he defends Dionysus with mock humility (the actor wore a

[1] Cf. Page (1942) 66-8.

smiling mask in this scene).[1] In the central scene, after an earthquake that wrecks the palace and releases Dionysus, the god begins to dominate the mind of Pentheus, persuading him to go and spy on the Maenads at what he imagines are their obscene revels. In the last scene the reversal is complete: Pentheus, his senses deranged, appears dressed as a woman, a Maenad with long hair. Now it is the god's turn to mock his victim; he congratulates him on his appearance, rearranges his wig, readjusts his waistline and skirt length before he sends him off to his hideous death. These scenes have a bizarre, deadly magic which has never been surpassed; Euripides here drew on some deep vein of primitive feeling which made his play unique in the annals of the theatre.

To the objection that the gods who end so many of the plays seem mechanical and lifeless, a dramatic convenience or a bow to convention rather than a religious epiphany, the obvious answer is that Euripides did not have to end his plays in this way, that, in fact, as far as our evidence goes, he is the inventor of this particular kind of ending. And not all of these gods are unimpressive figures; Dionysus at the end is the same terrifying relentless deity he has been all through the play, and Artemis at the end of *Hippolytus* is as credible in her pride and anger as her opposite number Aphrodite, who spoke the prologue. Further, these divine figures usually have specifically religious functions: instructions for the founding of a cult or a city, for the burial of the dead, for the administration of an oath and the attendant sacrifices. They also regularly predict the future, and these prophecies are evidently meant to be taken seriously; they range from confirmation of the further development of the legend through legitimization of contemporary dynasties to fully-fledged panegyrics of Athenian expansion or promises of protection for Athenian soil.

The passages which demand a higher standard of morality from gods than from men, and the portrayal of the Olympian gods as jealous, vindictive, merciless, unjust, do not necessarily imply a rationalistic viewpoint. These are Homeric gods; it is hard to imagine gods more unforgiving than Athena and Hera in the *Iliad*, Poseidon in the *Odyssey*. The centuries since Homer had seen incessant questioning of this pessimistic view, even attempts to reshape it along more moral lines, but Euripides recreates in all their fierce passions the gods of Homer's poems. The gods who rule the Euripidean universe are not like the Zeus of the *Oresteia*, who imposes suffering that is a step to wisdom, nor are they like the Sophoclean gods who seem to represent an assurance of divine order though it is one which can only be accepted not understood. Euripides' gods, Aphrodite, Artemis, Athena, Hera, Dionysus, are just like Homer's – which is to say, just like us. Torn by the same passions, pride and the vindictiveness of pride insulted, revengeful anger, jealousy and desire, they

[1] Dodds (1960) on l. 439.

are huge and awesome images of everything that is violent and uncontrollable in man, and they order the universe according to their conflicting and changing wills, bargaining for the fates of human beings as Athena does in *Troades* or promising to take a life for a life as Artemis does in *Hippolytus*.

These are the gods to whom mortals, despairing of human nature, appeal as representatives of something higher and better. 'You should be wiser than mortals, you are gods', says the old servant in *Hippolytus* (σοφωτέρους γὰρ χρὴ βροτῶν εἶναι θεούς, 120). The goddess he is addressing is Aphrodite, the personification of Eros, the most capricious and irrational of all human emotions. The Euripidean gods are naked passion unrestrained by any sense of moderation. Aphrodite engineers the deaths of two mortals to pay for Hippolytus' neglect of her worship (and cynically admits that one of them is innocent); Athena in *Troades* organizes the destruction of the Greek fleet because one Greek hero insulted her divinity; Hera, acting from jealousy, sends the spirit of Madness to wreck Heracles' life the moment he has finished his great labours for mankind; Dionysus demands as payment for the denial of his divinity not only the dismemberment of Pentheus but the exile of Cadmus and Agave as well. The gods, in Euripidean tragedy, project on to the enormous scale of the divine those passions which human beings struggle vainly to control in themselves; these passions, in the shape of Olympian gods, self-absorbed, unrelenting, rule the life of men and women.

It is not likely that Euripides believed in these gods with the literal acceptance and religious awe of the archaic time which gave them their shape. They serve him as dramatic incarnations of the capricious, irrational forces which his tragic vision saw as the determinants of the fate of mankind. They may sometimes be replaced in the prayers of his characters by abstractions such as those formulas of Hecuba which so surprised Menelaus, or by the all-embracing concept of *Tyche*, blind chance. Yet they are more than symbolic figures; they have a terrifying vitality which betrays a religious imagination at work under the sophisticated surface. Whatever else they are, they are not the creation of a 'rationalist'; rather, they are the dramatic expression of that bewilderment the poet puts in the mouth of the chorus in *Hippolytus*.

> ἦ μέγα μοι τὰ θεῶν μελεδήμαθ' ὅταν φρένας ἔλθηι
> λύπας παραιρεῖ. ξύνεσιν δέ τιν' ἐλπίδι κεύθων
> λείπομαι ἔν τε τύχαις θνατῶν καὶ ἐν ἔργμασι λεύσσων. (1104–6)

When I think of the care the gods have for men, my heart is greatly relieved of its sorrow. But though deep within me I hope to attain understanding, I fail to reach it, as my eyes see what happens to men and what they do.

This haunted vision of irrational forces at work in the universe has its counterpart in Euripides' exploration of the irrational in individual human beings; he is the first of the dramatists for whose work the modern term 'psychology' does not seem out of place. This is not to deny (as some have done) consistency of character and subtlety of motivation to the dramaturgy of Aeschylus,[1] still less to that of Sophocles; it is merely to assert that Euripidean characters are less linear and monumental, more complicated, more changeable. They run the gamut of human emotions, change direction suddenly, reveal what seem to be contradictions which, though they violate the canons of Sophoclean classic art, make them more recognizably and compellingly human.

Such psychological reversals are a Euripidean trade-mark from the earliest plays on. In the *Alcestis*, Admetus, who has never for a moment questioned the propriety of accepting his wife's sacrifice, who over her dead body has abused his father Pheres for not taking his place and angrily rejected the old man's cruel (but justified) reply, mourns her death in terms which still emphasize nothing but his own loss and then suddenly realizes how he will appear to others. His wife's death is glorious 'while I, who was supposed to die, but eluded my fate, will live out a sorry life. ἄρτι μανθάνω. Now I realize the truth' (939–40). The realization is not prepared by any hint in the speeches of Admetus or the chorus, and yet it is not unexpected. For the home truths his ignoble father told him in the earlier scene are so forcibly expressed ('You enjoy living: do you think your father doesn't?' 691), so scandalous but irrefutable, that even Admetus must eventually look them in the face and see his real situation – from which however he is rescued by the fairy-tale restoration of Alcestis from the kingdom of death.

The action of *Iphigenia in Aulide* turns on a change of mind so sudden that Aristotle cites it as an example of failure to maintain consistency of character; it is Iphigenia's decision to offer herself as a sacrifice to ensure the Greek departure for Troy after previously begging her father to spare her life. Aristotle's criticism – 'the girl who makes the speech of supplication here bears no resemblance to the later one ...' (*Poetics* 1454a32) – overlooks the fact that the audience has been subliminally prepared for this volte-face by the whole of the play's action so far; a series of swift and sudden changes of decision which is unparalleled in ancient drama. Agamemnon opens the play by sending a letter to Clytemnestra countermanding the instructions previously sent her to bring Iphigenia to the camp in Aulis. Menelaus intercepts this letter and taunts Agamemnon with his instability; but when Agamemnon expresses despair at the news that Iphigenia has arrived, Menelaus changes his mind and urges Agamemnon to disband the army and abandon the expedition rather than sacrifice his daughter. 'You will say I have changed, my words no longer fierce. This is true. But what has happened to me is natural. I have changed over to feel love for my brother. And such shifts are by no means the mark of an evil man' (500–3). But Agamemnon has changed his mind again: he now sees no way out; the army will demand his daughter's sacrifice.

An even more striking change, which is in fact something of a psychological puzzle, is the eerie process by which Dionysus, in *Bacchae*, transforms the menacing tyrant Pentheus into a crazed victim. It is of course a presentation of Dionysiac possession but it is also rooted in a Euripidean perception of the obscure depths in the human soul. Dionysus persuades Pentheus not to lead his troops against the wild women on the hills; he appeals to Pentheus' fevered vision of their orgies, and Pentheus reveals the strength of his obsessive desire to see them with his own eyes. There is only one way to fulfil it, Dionysus tells him: disguised as a maenad. Pentheus goes into the palace to decide what to do, but he is now the prey of dark forces in motion in his own soul. The god-priest on stage calls on Dionysus to 'derange his wits, set loose a giddy madness' (850–1) and the god's full power, exerted from outside, now combines with the forces released inside Pentheus' mind by his surrender to temptation, to produce the macabre figure who comes on stage, 'a giggling, leering creature, more helpless than a child, nastier than an idiot . . .'.[1]

This scene is unique, but everywhere in Euripides a preoccupation with individual psychology and its irrational aspects is evident: Hermione's emotional breakdown and suicidal mood after the failure of her attempt to kill Andromache's child; Medea's soliloquy in which, after deciding to kill her sons, she alternately yields to and masters her maternal instincts; Electra's exultant speech over the corpse of Aegisthus, shot through with perverted sexual jealousy; Phaedra's delirium as she tries to conceal her guilty love and the account she later gives of the stages of her struggle to conceal her passion – these situations and reactions are characteristically Euripidean. In his hands tragedy for the first time probed the inner recesses of the human soul and let 'passions spin the plot'.

The originality of Euripidean psychological characterization has in recent years been given less than its due in the justified reaction against interpretations which, in nineteenth-century style, tried to reach behind the surfaces of the characters displayed by the action and construct a fully rounded personality, its past as well as its present. Against such probing below the surface, other critics urged consideration of the action and its demands and also of the rhetorical possibilities open to exploitation. We may get much nearer to Euripides' thinking, it has been suggested, if instead of asking ourselves in any dramatic situation 'What would . . . such a man be likely to say . . .?' we asked ourselves: 'How should he . . . best acquit himself? How gain his point? Move his hearers? Prove his thesis? . . .'[2]

[1] Dodds (1960) 192.   [2] Dale (1954) xxviii.

There is much truth in this observation; rhetoric was the principal offering of the sophistic teachers and Athenian audiences were expert judges of the oratorical skills demanded by assembly and law-court.[1] Aristophanes was not slow to seize on this aspect of Euripidean style; his Euripides in the *Frogs* claims that he taught the Athenians to 'chatter' by means of 'introductions of subtle regulations and angle measurements of verses' (956). And it is true that Euripides' characters all seem to have had at least an elementary course in public speaking; their speeches are sometimes self-consciously rhetorical. Electra, for instance, begins her arraignment of the dead Aegisthus with what sounds like textbook language:

εἶεν. τίν' ἀρχὴν πρῶτά σ' ἐξείπω κακῶν,
ποίας τελευτάς; τίνα μέσον τάξω λόγον;   (907–8)

'Let me see. What shall I express first as the beginning of the wrongs you have done, what as the end? And what discourse shall I arrange in the middle?'

Other Euripidean characters are less naively technical but they are just as anxious to put their case well; the characteristic Euripidean dialogue is a debate, with long speeches of more or less equal length, one on each side, followed by the cut and thrust of one-line exchanges. And they can make out a case for anything. In a fragment of the lost *Cretans* (Page (1942)), Pasiphae, haled before an outraged Minos after she has given birth to the Minotaur, pleads her case with virtuoso skill. Denial, she says, would be useless. But she is no adulteress, giving her body to a man in secret lust. It was madness sent from heaven; what else could explain her action? 'What could I see in a bull to sting my heart with shameful passion? Was he handsome? Well dressed? Was it the gleam from his tawny hair, his flashing eyes ...?' (11–15). She goes on to put the blame on her husband: he had sworn to sacrifice the bull to Poseidon but failed to do so. 'The fault is yours, you are the cause of my sickness ...' (34–5). It is no wonder Minos begins his reply by asking his guards: 'Has she been muzzled yet?' (44).

Pasiphae is pleading for her life before a judge, and this courtroom atmosphere, so familiar to the Athenian audience, is typically Euripidean. Hecuba and Polymestor plead their case in contrasted speeches before Agamemnon in *Hecuba*, as Hecuba and Helen do before Menelaus in *Troades*, Orestes and Tyndareus before Menelaus in *Orestes*; so Hippolytus defends himself against Phaedra's accusation before Theseus.

Yet though they use rhetorical techniques in formal debate the effect is not monotonous; the speeches are fully expressive of individual character and also designed for dramatic effect. Hippolytus, for example, proves the truth of his earlier assertion that he is not at home in a public assembly (986) by using

[1] Cf. Thuc. 3.38.7.

arguments which infuriate the father he is trying to convince; he even tries to prove lack of motive (a standard sophistic approach) by asking: 'Was her body pre-eminent in beauty over all other women?' (1009–10). It was not exactly the best thing to say to a sorrowing husband in the presence of his wife's body; it is, however, very much 'in character', for Hippolytus' almost pathological distaste for women (revealed in his speech to the Nurse) has now been concentrated on Phaedra who has falsely accused him of attempted rape.

Euripides' characters present their cases in the organized framework of rhetoric but they are driven by irrational forces working below the surface. His drama cherishes no illusion that mankind is capable of choosing the good; Phaedra sums up the human dilemma in a short but chilling sentence: 'We know what is right, we recognize it clearly, but we don't achieve it' (τὰ χρήστ᾽ ἐπιστάμεσθα καὶ γιγνώσκομεν | οὐκ ἐκπονοῦμεν δ᾽..., 380–1). The mind is not strong enough to combat the weakness and violence of our nature. Phaedra is talking about her love for Hippolytus, and this, the most irrational of human passions, is a theme predominant in Euripidean drama – a point pressed home by Aristophanes' Aeschylus, who claims that he never brought 'whores like Phaedra' on stage nor for that matter 'any woman in love' (*Frogs* 1043–4). 'Eros', sings the chorus of *Hippolytus*, 'you that make desire flow from the eyes ... may you never ... come to me beyond due measure ... Eros, tyrant over men, who comes upon mortals with destruction and every shape of disaster' (525–42). It was this aspect of Eros, the destructive, which fascinated Euripides: the delirium of Phaedra and, later, her love turned to hate, the jealous rage of the barren wife Hermione, the unforeseen violence of Medea's revenge, the love of brother and sister in the lost *Aeolus*, the Potiphar's wife plot of the lost *Stheneboea*. Euripides in fact is the creator of that three-walled room in which the imprisoned men and women destroy each other by the intensity of their loves and hates, of that cage which is the theatre of Shakespeare's *Othello*, Racine's *Phèdre*, of Ibsen and Strindberg.

It was this preoccupation with women's loves and hates which won Euripides his reputation, widespread in antiquity, as a misogynist; a whole play of Aristophanes is devoted to the hilarious results of the decision taken by the women of Athens to punish him for his sins against them. This is of course comic exaggeration, but it may well reflect the feelings (at least the public feelings) of Athenian wives, for Euripides' characters shattered the polite fictions about female docility which both men and women paid lip service to. 'A wife's honour' Pericles is supposed to have said 'is – to be least talked about by men, for good or bad' (Thuc. 2.45.2); but Phaedra, to protect her honour, contrives the death of Hippolytus, and Medea, invoking the male code of honour, revenges herself by the murder of her sons. Yet, though it is not likely Athenian wives would have defended such extreme measures, the Euripidean plays are sympathetic rather than critical. Phaedra is the victim of Aphrodite and her account of her struggle to overcome her passion puts her in a noble light. And in the case of *Medea*, Euripides chose to emphasize the issue of women's social subordination; it is the argument Medea uses in her famous speech. 'Of all creatures that have life and intelligence, we women are the most afflicted stock' (πάντων δ' ὅσ' ἔστ' ἔμψυχα καὶ γνώμην ἔχει | γυναῖκές ἐσμεν ἀθλιώτατον φυτόν, 230–1). She touches on one sore point after another in what must have been the grievances of many an Athenian wife: the dowry with which women 'buy an owner of their body'; the risk involved (for if the husband turns out badly 'divorce does a woman's reputation harm'); their lack of preparation for marriage and a new household; the man's freedom to leave the house for distraction, the wife's obligation 'to keep her eyes fixed on a single human being'. The routine male justification of their privileges – that they fight the wars – is rejected: 'I'd rather stand in the battle lines spear in hand three times than give birth once' (230–51).

Medea is of course an extraordinary figure, an eastern princess, grand-daughter of Helios, but this speech cannot be discounted on the grounds that she is a barbarian and witch – it comes too close to home. The chorus of Corinthian women are won over; they welcome Medea's announcement that she plans revenge with an ode which rejects the male literary tradition on the subject of women. It was not to women that Apollo gave the gift of song, for if he had 'I would have sung a hymn to counter the male sex' (426–7). It is significant that this remarkable critique of the tradition occurs in a play which presents the revenge of a wronged wife in the heroic terms usually reserved for men and, in what must have been a very disturbing ending for the audience, shows her victorious over her enemies and, aided by Helios, escaping unpunished to Athens.[1] 'In my plays' says the comic Euripides in the *Frogs* 'the woman spoke ... and the young girl and the old woman ...' (949–50). It is in fact remarkable how important female roles are in Euripidean drama compared with that of his fellow dramatists. In play after play it is a woman who plays the principal part or, in a secondary role, makes an indelible impression.

It is typical of Euripides that he could take a figure as exotic as the princess from Colchis, the awesome priestess, prophet and magician of Pindar's fourth Pythian Ode, and present her in a context of domestic strife which is painfully realistic. 'One word will floor you' says Medea, countering Jason's claim that he is marrying the princess only to advance the family interest. 'If you were an honest man, you would have tried to persuade me and then married the girl, instead of concealing it ...' (585–7). The retort is quick and to the point. 'And you, of course, would be giving me a helping hand in the project – all I had to do was mention the word "marriage". Why, even now you can't

---

[1] Cf. Knox (1976).

bring yourself to renounce the huge rage in your heart' (588–90). It is all too human, it verges in fact on the sordid. And it is not a solitary example; Euripides' treatment of the mythical figures is often realistic in the extreme. Once again Aristophanes knew his man; his Euripides boasts that he introduced into tragedy 'domestic affairs, the kind we deal and live with' (οἰκεῖα πράγματ' εἰσάγων, οἷς χρώμεθ' οἷς ξύνεσμεν . . ., 959).

Euripides' treatment of some of the most prestigious myths suggests that he must have asked himself the question: 'How would these people act and speak if they were our contemporaries?' The results are often disconcerting, nowhere more so than in his handling of the figures of Electra and Orestes. His *Electra* is from start to finish a clear challenge to the canonical Aeschylean version; in fact it contains, among its many surprises, what can only be regarded as a parodic critique of Aeschylus' recognition scene (509ff.). The setting of the play is the house of a farmer in the countryside; he delivers the prologue and gives us the unexpected news that he is Electra's husband. The heroine herself carries a pot balanced on her head as she goes to draw water. Orestes acts like a fifth-century exile returning home in secret to conspire; instead of going to the palace, he comes just over the border to this remote farm, ready to run for safety if there is no local support for his plans. When the farmer invites Orestes and Pylades (their identity still cautiously concealed) into the house for a meal, Electra scolds him shrewishly for not realizing that his poor house is no place to entertain what are obviously high-class visitors. The effect of this domestic tone is to strip Electra and Orestes of the heroic stature conferred on them by the legends, so that we see the treacherous murder of Aegisthus and the cold-blooded killing of their mother not as the working of destiny or a curse, not even the fulfilment of a divine command, but rather as crimes committed by 'men as they are' – Sophocles' description of Euripidean characters.[1] In *Orestes* the realistic presentation is even more extreme. The hero, after the murder of Clytemnestra, is afflicted not by the Erinyes (in his delirium he takes Electra for one of them) but by sickness – and we are spared no detail. 'Take hold of me' he says to his sister 'and wipe the caked foam from my miserable lips and eyes' (219–20). Helen has put on mourning for her sister but 'she cut her hair just at the ends' Electra tells us 'so as not to spoil her beauty. She's the same old Helen still' (127–8). Menelaus is a cautious trimmer who according to Aristotle (*Poetics* 1454a) is 'an example of unnecessary baseness of character'. Tyndareus is a vindictive and violent old man, while Orestes, Electra and Pylades, as they enthusiastically discuss their plans to murder Helen and hold Hermione hostage, emerge as juvenile delinquents of a start-lingly modern depravity. The great moral and legal dilemma posed by the myth, Orestes' conflict of duties, is dismissed in cavalier fashion by Clytem-

---

[1] Aristotle, *Poetics* 1460b33.

nestra's father, Tyndareus, who condemns Orestes' killing of his mother in surprising terms. 'He took no account of justice, had no recourse to the universal Hellenic law ... Orestes should have charged his mother with murder ...' (494–500). To this reversal of the canonical order of events (in Aeschylus the law court was convened for the first time in history precisely to deal with Orestes' killing of his mother) no one in the play takes objection; Orestes answers Tyndareus on other grounds. Its effect, for the moral context of Orestes' action, is devastating; he is stripped of all justification except the command of Apollo, the god whom he accuses of deserting him.

These two plays are widely criticized as artistic failures in their unconvincing endings; in each case the god from the machine announces, in what seems to be a deliberately banal fashion, a bundle of future marriages, apotheoses, etc. which seem incongruous with the desperation portrayed in the body of the play. But it is hard to see what else Euripides could have done. His realistic treatment has destroyed the heroic and moral values underlying the myth and no ending which could re-identify the Orestes and Electra of these plays with their heroic prototypes is conceivable; perhaps he thought it best to underline, by the deliberate artificiality of the form of his ending, the irrelevance of its content.

In contrast to this realistic remodelling of central myths stands Euripides' exploitation of the romantic and exotic material offered by others which deal with the adventures and ordeals of heroes in far-off lands. The *Andromeda* was such a play; it opened (as we know from the hilarious parody in Aristophanes' *Thesmophoriazusae*) with the heroine bound to the rock awaiting the sea-monster and the arrival of Perseus, her rescuer. Two extant plays of this type suggest that Euripides is the inventor of a genre of romantic melodrama which turns on the rescue of the heroine from the clutches of backward foreigners by adventurers who take advantage of the natives' superstitions. Both *Iphigenia in Tauris* and *Helen* are built on this formula: Iphigenia, spirited away from the sacrificer's knife at Aulis by Artemis, now serves the goddess as a priestess presiding over the human sacrifices offered by the barbarians, while the real Helen (as opposed to the image of her which went to Troy) is in Egypt, resisting the demands for her hand made by the local king Theoclymenus. In both plays the recognition scenes are models of skilful dramaturgy; the Iphigenia scene, in the technical brilliance of its prolongation of suspense (it was singled out as exemplary by Aristotle, *Poetics* 1455a) and the Helen scene in its sophisticated wit. Both plays end with the appearance of gods from the machine: Athena in *Iphigenia* prevents the recapture of the fugitives, whose ship has been thrown back on the shore, and the Dioscuri in *Helen* prevent Theoclymenus from killing his sister Theonoe, who helped Helen and Menelaus escape. But these interventions are not a mere dramatic convenience. In

Iphigenia the failure of the attempt to escape is not necessary; it seems to have been deliberately contrived to motivate the divine intervention, which has the important mythical-religious function of linking the action with the foundation of the Artemis-cult at Brauron in Attica. In *Helen*, the assurance brought by the Dioscuri that Helen and Menelaus will be immortal is less urgent a motive, but their intervention does make possible the dramatic final scene of the action proper: Theoclymenus' attempt to vent his frustrated rage on Theonoe; in any case she is a fully developed and sympathetic character who cannot be left to suffer for the help she has given the heroine.

These 'romantic' plays come comparatively late in Euripides' career; the plays (*Heraclidae, Supplices*) which have been described as 'patriotic' (more recently and accurately as 'political')[1] date from the years of the Archidamian War. They deal with topics which recur in Athenian patriotic orations: the rescue of Heracles' children from their persecutor Eurystheus by Theseus' son Demophon, the intervention of Theseus himself to force the Thebans to allow burial of the seven fallen champions. In the *Heraclidae* a daughter volunteers herself for sacrifice to save her family; *Supplices* has no such sacrifice scene (though the widow of one of the Theban champions throws herself on to his funeral pyre) but its main theme is the same: the celebration of Athenian martial valour not in self-defence but to protect the rights of the helpless and oppressed elsewhere. Such plays were standard fare; Aeschylus had already in his *Eleusinii* dramatized Theseus' intervention on behalf of the Theban widows and had also produced a *Heraclidae*. But the two extant Euripidean examples of this genre are not simple-minded patriotic propaganda. In both cases the principal character representing the persecuted victims rescued by Athens is an ambivalent figure. Adrastus in *Supplices*, who asks for aid to get the bodies of his champions buried, is reproached by Theseus in harsh terms which must have made some in the audience think of their own involvement in the Archidamian War.

> 'You ruined your city, your wits disturbed by young men, who in their desire for glory promote the cause of war unjustly and bring ruin on their fellow citizens – one because he wants command, another to get his hands on power and use it harshly, another for profit – and not one of them considers what harm war brings to the masses of the people.' (231–7)

In fact Theseus refuses to risk a war on behalf of a man who acted so unwisely and consents to help the Argives only when his mother Aethra reminds him that Athens is the traditional champion of the weak and oppressed. And in *Heraclidae* Alcmena, the children's grandmother, ends the play by ordering the execution of a captured Eurystheus who had been promised his life by the

---

[1] Zuntz (1955).

Athenian victors: worse still, she orders his dead body to be thrown to the dogs (1045ff.).

This emphasis on the ugliness and waste of war becomes a major theme in other plays which however lack the patriotic appeal; in *Hecuba* and especially in *Troades* the sack of Troy serves as a general symbol of war's destructiveness. In both plays the chorus consists of enslaved Trojan women, and in *Hecuba*, as they contemplate the sorrows of their queen, they recreate for us the terror of Troy's fall.

> 'My end came at midnight...The dances and sacrifices over, my husband lay
> at rest, his spear hung on the wall...I was arranging my hair...gazing into the
> fathomless light of the golden mirror...preparing to fall into bed, when a shout
> rang out in the city, a war-cry...I left my familiar bed, dressed in one robe
> like a Dorian girl...I saw my husband killed, was taken away over the sea,
> looking back at Troy...' (914–38)

But it is in *Troades* that the most vivid tableau of war's terror and cruelty is staged. Greek literature from the *Iliad* on had been much concerned with war, but war had been seen always from the point of view of the men who fought it – the Achaean heroes, the soldier of fortune Archilochus, the aristocratic partisan Alcaeus, the Spartan regular Tyrtaeus. This play presents it from the standpoint of the captured women; the characters are a royal grandmother Hecuba, who in the play learns of the death of a daughter and a grandson; an unmarried princess, Cassandra, who is taken as his mistress by the Greek commander; a mother, Andromache, who is assigned as concubine to the son of the man who killed her husband and whose infant son is thrown to his death from the walls. The chorus who brood desperately on what their individual fates will be, represent a whole female population sold into slavery after the slaughter of their men (a punishment which Athens had inflicted on the city of Scione six years earlier and on the island of Melos in the preceding winter).

That the play stems from concern over the plight of war-torn Greece there can be little doubt, but the position that it is specifically an attack on Athenian imperialism can be maintained only with difficulty. For one thing, the chorus, speculating on their eventual destination in Greece, pray that they may come to the 'blessed land of Theseus' (209) and not 'to the eddies of the Eurotas' (210), the river of Sparta. And, for another, the fundamental question raised by the debate between Hecuba and Helen, that of responsibility for the war, is left unanswered. Helen's case is that Troy was responsible since Hecuba bore Paris; Priam, though the gods warned that Paris would be a firebrand to burn Troy, failed to kill him. This case looks weak in the context of the suffering we see in the *Troades*; but the audience had seen, as the first of the sequence of plays in which this play came last, the *Alexander*, which was

EURIPIDES

concerned with precisely this question and seems to have suggested that Helen
was not entirely wrong. Like the 'patriotic' plays, the 'anti-war' plays of
Euripides are complex and ambiguous.

No less ambiguous is the treatment of war in *Iphigenia in Aulide*. The action
gives a picture of the moral cowardice and personal ambition of Agamemnon
so vivid that many have taken Iphigenia's speech accepting self-sacrifice for
the Panhellenic cause as Euripides' ironic symbol of the insanity of war – an
innocent girl who gives her life for tawdry slogans in which no one but she
can believe. Yet this theme, Panhellenic unity against the barbarians, is not
only a leitmotiv of the play but was also a policy urged by many voices in the
last years of the war which saw Athens and Sparta competing for Persian help.

The play is a sombre tragedy of war, but it contains one scene which shows
an entirely different side of Euripides' genius, a scene which in its lightness
of touch and its exploitation of the nuances of a social situation foreshadows
the atmosphere of Menandrian comedy. It is the meeting of Clytemnestra and
Achilles. The queen has brought her daughter to Aulis believing that Achilles
is going to marry her. But Achilles has never heard of this proposed marriage;
Agamemnon lied to Clytemnestra to get her to bring her daughter to be
sacrificed. Clytemnestra and Achilles have never met, but, inside the royal tent,
she hears him announce his name as he calls for Agamemnon; she comes out
to make the acquaintance of her future son-in-law. He professes embarrassment
in the presence of a beautiful woman (he does manage to pay her that compliment) and with the manners of a *grande dame* she puts him at his ease:

CLYT. No wonder you don't know who I am; we have never met. And my
compliments on your modesty.
ACH. Who are you? Why have you come to the camp, a woman among men
at arms?
CLYT. I am Leda's daughter, my name is Clytemnestra, my husband lord
Agamemnon.
ACH. Thank you for telling me the facts in such compact form. But I am
ashamed to be exchanging words with a lady... [*He moves off.*]
CLYT. [*Detains him*] Wait! Don't run away! Put your right hand in mine – a
happy first step to a wedding.
ACH. My hand in yours? How could I face Agamemnon if I took hold of what
I should not?
CLYT. But you *should* – since you are going to marry my daughter...
ACH. Marry? Marry whom? I am speechless, lady. But – perhaps this strange
statement comes from a disturbed mind...
CLYT. It's a natural reaction in everyone to be embarrassed when they set eyes
on new family connexions and discuss marriage. (823–40)

They finally realize that they are both under a misapprehension and the play
resumes its prevailing mood of grim foreboding. But this scene alone would be

enough to suggest that Euripides was a forerunner of Menander, a claim which is in fact made in a headless sentence from an Alexandrian *Life of Euripides*: '. . . towards wife, and father towards son and servant towards master, or the business of reversals – virgins raped, babies substituted, recognitions by means of rings and necklaces. For these are the sinews of New Comedy, and Euripides brought these dramatic means to perfection.'[1]

The forceful wooing of a maid by a god, the complications involved in bringing up (usually in secret) the resultant offspring, and the ultimate recognition of the child's high lineage – these were all commonplaces of heroic genealogy; Euripides seems to have used them as an intrigue formula for a series of plays (now lost) which exploited the possibilities with virtuoso skill. But there is one surviving play which is based on this formula and does in fact suggest, in clear outline, the shape of the New Comedy to come. The *Ion* presents us with a virgin princess overcome by a god (Creusa, in fear of her father, exposes Apollo's child), and on a lower level, a girl seduced by a human suitor (Xuthus remembers his affair with a local girl at Dionysiac revels in Delphi). The whole plot turns on substitution of children (Apollo foists his son by Creusa on Xuthus, persuading him, from his oracular shrine, that Ion is his own illegitimate child) and one of the signs by which Creusa recognizes Ion's identity is a golden snake collar. And though much of *Ion* is played on a serious note, there is one scene at least which is undeniably high comedy: the false recognition scene in which Xuthus, misled by the oracle, takes Ion for his son and Ion, appalled, takes Xuthus for a would-be seducer or perhaps insane. Like the Clytemnestra–Achilles scene, this depends on *agnoia*, ignorance of identity, the mainspring of New Comedy; in fact in Menander's *Girl who has her hair cut off* the goddess Agnoia delivers the Prologue. The poets of the New Comedy recognized their indebtedness; a character in Menander's *Arbitrants* proposes to recite a speech from the *Auge*, a Euripidean play which, like that in which the speaker is appearing, turned on identifications through tokens left with a child.[2] And a character in a play of Philemon is given the line: 'If I were sure of life beyond the grave, I'd hang myself – to see Euripides.'[3]

But it is not only in the ingenuity of his intrigue-plots and the sophistication of his tone that Euripides foreshadows the drama of Menander and Philemon; he also developed a conversational style for his characters which was closer to normal speech than anything so far heard on the Attic stage. The dialogue of the Euripidean characters, though still subject to the demands of metre and the decorum of the tragic genre, creates an illusion of everyday speech, perfectly suited to the unheroic figures and situations of his drama. In fact in its avoidance of sustained metaphor, its striving for clarity, precision and point, the style sometimes verges on the prosaic. Yet this plain surface is cleverly contrived,

---

[1] von Arnim (1913) 5 (col. VII).   [2] Menander, *Epitrepontes* 1125.   [3] 130 K.

as Aristotle pointed out: 'the best concealment of art is to compose selecting words from everyday speech, as Euripides does, who was the first to show the way' (*Rhetoric* 1404b5).

One effective instrument for Euripides' purposes was his gradual loosening of the iambic trimeter which (as we saw above, p. 64) provides a rough guide for dating the plays. In the strict metre of the Aeschylean trimeter the appearance of two short syllables in succession (and *a fortiori* of three) was avoided as much as possible; in Euripides it is admitted more frequently as his style develops. Not only did this give his dialogue a much more natural sound (for in Greek conversation, as is clear from early Platonic dialogues where natural speech is the effect aimed at, runs of short syllables are frequent), it also allowed him to employ new syntactical combinations and to make extensive additions to the vocabulary of spoken dialogue. The list of such additions is long; two types predominate. The first consists of compound verbs made with prepositions, most of which, in Greek, consist of two short syllables – *apo, dia, meta* etc. The prepositional prefixes of these words limit and direct the action expressed by the main verb to a particular attitude or context; their precision allows Euripides to make logical distinctions, and also subtle psychological differentations. The second type consists of nouns and adjectives which bring into tragic dialogue the new intellectual dialogue of sophistic debate on the one hand and on the other everyday words for household objects and situations of domestic life.[1] In the *Frogs*, 'Euripides' jeers at the heroic, metaphorical style of Aeschylus and claims that the poet should 'express himself in human terms' (*anthropeios* 1058); this is exactly what Euripides did.

It is characteristic of this paradoxical figure that he is also a great lyric poet. Plutarch tells us that some of the survivors of the Athenian disaster at Syracuse, wandering about the countryside after the battle, were given food and drink in exchange for singing some of his lyrics (*Life of Nicias* 29). And his *Life of Lysander* contains the story (immortalized by Milton) that in 404, when the fate of defeated Athens hung in the balance, the Peloponnesian generals were diverted from their projects of enslavement and destruction by the performance, at a banquet, of the Parodos of the *Electra* (167ff.): 'They felt' says Plutarch 'that it would be a barbarous act to annihilate a city which produced such men.' These stories may not be true but they are eloquent testimony to the strength of Euripides' reputation as a lyric poet.

In this area, too, he was an innovator. We can no longer assess the new-fangled musical style which he adopted from the dithyrambic poet Timotheus

---

[1] A few examples: *hypotithemi* (suggest), *anakalypto* (reveal), *epigameo* (marry a second wife), *metagrapho* (rewrite), *isotes* (equality), *anomia* (lawlessness), *philotimia* (ambition), *paradoche* (tradition), *sphagida* (meat-cleaver), *ochetos* (irrigation-ditch), *sanida* (plank), *diabrochos* (soaking wet), *mysaros* (disgusting), *kerkida* (shuttle).

(cf. *CHCL* I, Part I, 202); all we can say is that in a few passages of late Euripidean lyric, repetitions and syntactical vagueness suggest that the music has become more important than the words (the same impression emerges from the merciless parody in the *Frogs* 1309ff.). But two other innovations are perfectly clear: the transference of much of the musical performance of the chorus (*stasimon*) to individual actors (*monody*) and the comparative detachment of the choral odes proper from dramatic context.

Lyrical exchange between actor and chorus (*kommos*) had been a feature of tragic style from the beginning (cf. the great *kommos* of the *Choephori*, p. 35) and appears regularly in Euripides (often in the Parodos, e.g. *Troades* 121ff., *Orestes* 140ff., *Ion* 219ff.). But just as frequent are lyric arias of a single actor and lyric dialogues between two – both rarities in Sophocles and existent only in rudimentary form in Aeschylus. The lyric dialogue is frequently used for highly emotional moments such as recognition scenes (Iphigenia–Orestes in *I.T.* 827ff., Ion–Creusa in *Ion* 1445ff., Helen–Menelaus in *Helen* 625ff. – this last the target of a devastating parody in Aristophanes' *Thesmophoriazusae* 911ff.). The monodies display a rich variety of passions and dramatic reactions: Cassandra's mock marriage-hymn with its undertone of baleful prophecy (*Troades* 308ff.); the blinded Polymestor's curses and revengeful threats (*Hecuba* 1056ff.); Ion's 'work-song' as he performs his duties as a Delphian acolyte (*Ion* 112ff.) and, in the same play, Creusa's confession and her accusation of Apollo (859ff.); most innovative of all, the Phrygian slave's elaborate, ornate account of the attempt on Helen's life in *Orestes* (1369ff.).

The choral stasima are less firmly bound to their dramatic context than those of Sophocles and Aeschylus (though there is always an exception to any statement about Euripides – in this case it is the *Bacchae*). Sometimes, in fact, especially in the 'romantic' plays, the connexion seems tenuous and becomes a matter of scholarly debate; but the view that late Euripidean odes are musical interludes entirely unrelated to context goes too far. The connexion is usually one of mood rather than thought; in the *Troades* the choral odes are not linked directly with preceding or succeeding stage action but they are variations on a fundamental theme – the tragedy of Troy's fall. Similarly, the stasimon in *Electra* which celebrates the glories of Achilles' shield (432ff.) throws into sharp relief the unheroic nature of Orestes' return to Argos. Often the choral poems recreate a religious atmosphere and background which, missing in the action, is needed to give the final divine appearance authority (this is perhaps the function of the ode to the Great Mother in *Helen* 1301ff. and the celebration of the birth of Apollo in *I.T.* 1234ff.). The content of many of the choral poems is, like so much else in Euripides, a hint of the future. They are insistently pictorial: the evocation of the temple at Delphi (*Ion* 184ff.) as of the landscape traversed by the mourning Demeter (*Helen* 1801ff.), the account of the golden-fleeced lamb of Atreus in *Electra* (699ff.). All these passages, with their fullness of sensuous detail and colour, point the way to the genre pictures so dear to the hearts of the Alexandrian poets, especially Theocritus.

But it is as a tragedian that Euripides made his real mark on Greece and the world. In spite of his faults in other respects, Aristotle says, he is 'the most tragic of the poets'; the context suggests that this judgement refers specifically to a preference for unhappy endings, but it is valid in a wider sense. For in his representation of human suffering Euripides pushes to the limits of what an audience can stand; some of his scenes are almost unbearable. The macabre details of the death of Pentheus in *Bacchae*, of the princess in *Medea*, of Aegisthus in *Electra*, are typical of the Euripidean assault on the audience's feelings. And Hecuba's funeral lament over the shattered corpse of Astyanax is the work of a poet determined to spare us nothing. 'Poor child, how dreadfully your head was sheared by the walls your fathers built . . . the locks your mother tended and kissed; from them now comes the bright gleam of smashed bone and blood . . .' (*Troades* 1173ff.). In Euripidean drama man's situation is more helpless than in the tragic vision of the other poets; his plays give no hint of a divine purpose in human suffering and his characters are not so much heroes who in their defiance of time and change rival the gods, as victims of passion and circumstance, of a world they cannot hope to understand. The only useful virtue in such a world is silent endurance, and this is what Talthybius recommends to Andromache as he takes her child away. 'Let it happen this way . . . take your pain and sorrow with nobility (*eugenos*) . . . be silent, adjust yourself to your fate . . .' (*Troades* 726–7, 737).

This despairing tragic vision was prophetic; the world became Euripidean as the chaos of fourth-century Greece paved the way for Macedonian conquest and the great Hellenistic kingdoms. In that new world, where the disappearance of the free city-state reduced the stature of the individual, where the huge Hellenistic kingdoms waged their dynastic wars, locked, like Euripidean gods, in seemingly endless conflict, in that age of uncertainty, doubt and anxiety, Euripides won at last the applause and veneration which had eluded him during his life. And thanks to his adaptation by the Roman dramatist Seneca, who carried over into Latin in exaggerated form his psychological insight, his rhetorical manner, his exploitation of the shocking and the macabre and above all, his brooding sense of man as victim, it was Euripides, not Aeschylus or Sophocles, whose tragic muse presided over the rebirth of tragedy in Renaissance Europe.

6. MINOR TRAGEDIANS

For us, Greek tragedy begins with the *Persae* of Aeschylus (472 B.C.) and ends with the posthumous performances of Sophocles' *Oedipus at Colonus* and

Euripides' *Bacchae*, both just before the turn of the century; we have inherited from late antiquity and Byzantium a selection from the work of three tragic poets which represents, all too inadequately, the splendid flowering of this native Athenian art in the great period of imperial democracy. But of course there were other tragic poets, who competed with the canonical three in their lifetime. Most of them are known to us mainly or solely as targets of Aristophanic abuse; Morychus, whose passion was for the good life (βίον γενναῖον, *Wasps* 506) and especially eels (*Ach.* 887); Theognis, whose frigid verses are compared with the snows and frozen rivers of Thrace (*Ach.* 138ff.); and Morsimus, whose set pieces earned those unwise enough to have them copied out exemplary punishment in the next world – to lie in excrement together with the perjurers and father-beaters (*Frogs* 151ff.). But three fifth-century tragic poets, Ion, Critias and Agathon, achieved a certain eminence in their day and, though only fragments of their work survive, they stand out as distinct literary personalities.

Ion of Chios first competed at the Dionysia in the 82nd Olympiad (451–448 B.C.); he won third prize the year Euripides came first with the *Hippolytus* (428). On one occasion, when he was awarded first prize, he is said to have supplied the entire Athenian population with wine from his native island. He wrote prose memoirs, the *Epidemiae* (*Visits*); one fragment (*FGrH* 392 F 6) tells a delightful story of Sophocles at a banquet he attended on Chios while on his way, as one of the ten generals, to the Athenian fleet blockading Lesbos (441). The fragments of Ion's tragedies (which include an *Agamemnon*) are unfortunately all short; no extended passage gives us an idea of his style. But we do have an estimate of his poetic achievement by a much later critic – the author of the treatise *On the sublime* ('Longinus').

> Take lyric poetry: would you rather be Bacchylides or Pindar? Take tragedy: would you rather be Ion of Chios or Sophocles? Ion and Bacchylides are impeccable, uniformly beautiful writers in the polished manner, but it is Pindar and Sophocles who sometimes set the world on fire with their vehemence, for all that their flame often goes out without reason and they collapse dismally. Indeed, no one in his senses would reckon all Ion's works put together as the equivalent of the one play, *Oedipus*.[1]

An uncle of Plato, Critias, who, as the leading figure among the Thirty Tyrants, clamped a reign of terror on Athens after the surrender to Sparta in 404 and died fighting the resurgent democracy in 403, is credited in our sources with three plays which were also thought by some to be Euripidean. One other play, *Sisyphus*, is specifically cited as his; an important speech from it survives. His skill as a poet is clear from the impressive fragments of his elegiac poetry (*IEG* II 52–6) and since Plato, once in an early dialogue (*Charmides*

[1] 'Longinus' 33.5 tr. D. A. Russell in Russell and Winterbottom (1972) 493.

162d) and once in a late (*Critias* 108b), seems to hint at a career as a tragic poet, he may well be the author of the disputed plays: *Tennes, Rhadamanthys* and *Pirithous*. Some thirty fragments of the *Pirithous* remain. It dealt with Heracles' rescue of Pirithous and Theseus from Hades; Pirithous was punished with imprisonment in a stone chair for his attempt to kidnap Persephone, and Theseus loyally stayed with him. We have what seem to be the first sixteen lines of the play, a vigorous dramatic opening in which Aeacus, guardian of the gate of Hades, challenges Heracles, who proudly identifies himself and reveals that he has been sent on another impossible mission, the capture of Cerberus. From the *Sisyphus* comes the famous speech which caused Critias to be ranked by the later doxographical tradition among the atheists. Sisyphus himself, the trickster who cheated even death, describes the origin of religion. Man's life was at first anarchic (ἄτακτος) until laws and punishments were prescribed. But when wrongdoers began to break the law not violently but stealthily, then some wise man 'invented for mortals the fear of the gods ... introduced divinity ... a spirit everlasting ... that would hear every word spoken and see every deed done ... the most pleasant of doctrines ... concealing the truth with a false story ...' (fr. 19 Snell).

Agathon, whose victory-celebration in 416 B.C. was used, many years later, as the setting for Plato's *Symposium*, seems to have been a much more innovative poet than would appear from the surviving fragments of his works, which are, for the most part, rhetorical *jeux d'esprit* or cleverly turned moral clichés. According to Aristotle (*Poet.* 1451b19) he was the first poet to abandon mythical (and historical) subjects for wholly invented plots and characters and he was also (ibid. 1456a) the first to introduce choral lyrics which had nothing to do with the plot and could in fact fit into any tragedy – *embolima*, Aristotle calls them – 'interpolations'. Like Euripides, he left Athens for Macedonia in the last years of the long war, as the city, torn by internal faction and facing the prospect of defeat, resorted to ever more desperate measures. And in Aristophanes' *Frogs*, produced in 406, the god Dionysus delivers, with a pun on the poet's name, the city's regretful farewell: 'He has gone off and left me – an excellent (*agathos*) poet, and one much missed by his friends' (*Frogs* 84).

These lines come from a scene which, in spite of the comic situation – the effeminate Dionysus, dressed in the garb of Heracles, confronting his all-too-masculine model – sounds a serious note, it is a sort of comic requiem for fifth-century tragedy. Dionysus is going to Hades to bring Euripides back to life; he needs, he says, a 'clever poet'. Heracles asks him what is wrong with the living – with Iophon, Sophocles' son, for example? Dionysus admits some merit there, but suspects Iophon is still using his father's work – a reason for waiting a while and also for not bringing Sophocles, rather than Euripides, back to life. Agathon has gone, Xenocles (who won first prize in

415 against Euripides' *Troades*) is dismissed with a curse, Pythangelus is ignored and the host of 'young effeminates' who turn out talkative Euripidean-style tragedies by the ten thousand, are rejected in a characteristically salty Aristophanic metaphor: 'barbarous chatterbags, who, once they are awarded a chorus, just take a leak on tragedy and disappear – search as you may, you won't find a seminal (γόνιμον) poet any more . . .' (*Frogs* 93ff.).

This lugubrious estimate by the god of the tragic festival seems to have been prophetic. For the whole of the fourth century, new tragic poets competed at the Dionysia and Lenaea but, though they were extraordinarily productive (Astydamas, we are told, wrote 240 plays, the younger Carcinus 160), they did not make enough of an impression on later ages to ensure the survival of their work. Many of them are cited and some of them praised by Aristotle and in their own time they were generally admired; in fact, Astydamas (whose first victory was in 372) was honoured with a bronze statue in the theatre ten years before the Athenian statesman Lycurgus paid similar honours to Aeschylus, Sophocles and Euripides. Invited to compose the inscription for the statue, Astydamas produced something so boastful that his name became a proverb: 'you praise yourself, as Astydamas once did'. The meagre fragments do little to explain his great popularity. Plutarch singles out his *Hector* for mention but the one certain quotation from this play is far from reassuring. It clearly comes from a dramatic version of one of Homer's greatest scenes, the meeting of Hector and Andromache; Hector tells a servant 'Take my helmet so that the boy won't be frightened' (fr. 2 Snell) and this choice of subject, though it speaks volumes for Astydamas' self-confidence, raises doubts about his judgement.

Such a direct challenge to Homer on his own ground is something the great tragic poets of the fifth century seem to have been wary of; though they drew heavily on the epic poems of the cycle, tragic adaptations of material from the *Iliad* and *Odyssey* are rare.[1] But one play which has come down to us in the Euripidean corpus, the *Rhesus*, presents a dramatic version of the events of Book 10 of the *Iliad*: the capture of the Trojan spy Dolon by Odysseus and Diomedes and their successful raid on the Trojan camp to kill Rhesus, the newly-arrived Thracian ally of Troy. The ascription of this play to Euripides was questioned in antiquity and the debate continues into modern times. If it is Euripidean, the infrequency of resolution in the trimeter demands an early date (before the *Alcestis*). On the other hand many features of the style and stage action suggest that if it is indeed by Euripides it belongs to much later in his career. But it is more likely to be a product of the fourth century. The large number of speaking roles (eleven, cf. *Phoenissae*) in what is the shortest tragedy extant (996 lines), the rapid succession of short scenes, the complete

---

[1] The lost *Ransom of Hector* (Aeschylus) and *Nausicaa* (Sophocles) are among the exceptions.

absence of gnomic pronouncements, the complicated entrances and exits of ll. 565–681, the goddess Athena's assumption of the role of Aphrodite in order to deceive Paris, the fact that the whole of the action is supposed to take place at night – all this, and more besides, seems to bear witness to a post-classical phase of tragedy, one which has abandoned fifth-century ideals of artistic economy for a lavish, varied display of individually exciting scenes. The *Rhesus* seems to be striving for that ideal of 'variety' (ποικιλία) held up as the standard for the tragic poet in a fragment from a satyr play of Astydamas: 'the clever poet must offer the complicated bounty, as it were, of a luxurious dinner . . .'.[1]

Aristotle's pupil and friend Theodectas was an orator as well as a tragic poet, the author of fifty plays: it is perhaps significant that three of the passages where Aristotle quotes him are in the *Rhetoric* and one in the *Politics*. About 65 lines have survived; since, unfortunately, most of them come from Stobaeus' collection of moral maxims, the overall impression is one of glib sentiment and skilful versification. Athenaeus, however, preserves a reworking of a Euripidean *tour de force*, which had already been imitated by Agathon – the description by an illiterate peasant of the letters spelling the name of Theseus (fr. 6 Snell); and Strabo quotes a passage in which Theodectas attributes the black skin and woolly hair of the Ethiopians to the action of the sun (fr. 17 Snell).

Carcinus, too, is cited in the *Poetics* (1455a26), but for writing at least one of his plays without visualizing the action; he seems to have written a scene which would have passed scrutiny if heard or read, but, seen on stage, contained a glaring contradiction. Aristotle also refers to his use of recognition tokens in his *Thyestes* (1454b23) and from the *Rhetoric* (1400b9) we learn that his Medea was tried for the murder of her children and put up a sophistic defence. Not much more than a score of his verses remain, but a recent papyrus discovery bears witness to his almost classical stature in the eyes of his contemporaries. In the *Aspis* of Menander, the slave Daos acts the part of a man overcome by despair at news of his master's mortal sickness; he rattles off a series of tragic clichés, in which a citation from Aeschylus is followed by 'Carcinus says: "For in one day a god makes the happy man unhappy"' (417ff.).

Daos quotes a line from another contemporary tragic poet, who is mentioned by Aristotle – Chaeremon (411). Aristotle cites him as one of the ἀναγνωστικοί, which has been taken to mean that his plays were written for reading or recitation rather than performance. The context, however (*Rhet.* 1413b8ff.), suggests that Aristotle means merely that Chaeremon, unlike some of his more rhetorical competitors, is as effective when read (ἐν ταῖς χερσίν)

---

[1] Fr. 4 Snell. The Eupolidean metre however seems to indicate a comic provenance.

as on the stage.[1] His style is characterized as ἀκριβής 'accurate, precise', and the fragments (some 75 lines) exhibit a richness of descriptive detail and a special emphasis on colour which seem almost Alexandrian. A celebrated description (fr. 14 from the *Oeneus*) of girls resting after Dionysiac dance (inspired by Euripides' *Bacchae* 678ff.) gives some idea of his pictorial, sensual quality:

> One lay down, her shoulder-strap undone, revealing a white breast to the moonlight. Another had exposed her left flank in the dancing – naked to the gazes of the air she made a living painting... Another bared the beauty of her forearm as she embraced a companion's tender neck. Still another, her robes ripped open, showed her thigh beneath the folds...

A note of comic relief is sounded by the tragic offerings of Dionysius, tyrant of Syracuse (not mentioned by Aristotle), who, we are told, won a victory at Athens in 367. Judging by the universal contempt expressed for his poetry by later writers, this award must have been a conciliatory political gesture on the part of the Athenians. Even though he purchased what purported to be the writing tablets of Aeschylus, he could get no better inspiration from them than whatever it was that inspired the pathetic line: 'Alas, alas, I've lost a useful wife' (οἴμοι γυναῖκα χρησίμην ἀπώλεσα, fr. 10 Snell). And one wonders what the audience thought when one of his characters announced: 'For tyranny is the mother of injustice' (fr. 4 Snell).

Also not mentioned by Aristotle (his debut may in fact have occurred after the philosopher's death) is a tragic poet called Moschion, about whom we would like to know more. He revived an old fashion – historical drama (see pp. 5f.): we have a three-line fragment of his *Themistocles* and one of his plays, the *Pheraioi*, dealt with the death of Jason, the cruel tyrant of Pherae in Thessaly. The most interesting fragment (6) is a speech, 33 lines long, which is the latest variation on a theme often exploited by Attic playwrights – the history of human progress; the speech of Prometheus (*P.V.* 436ff.), the famous first stasimon of the *Antigone*, Theseus' speech in the *Supplices* of Euripides (201ff.), even Critias' speech about the invention of religion, belong to this tradition. Moschion's *Kulturgeschichte* follows the usual patterns at first: men lived like beasts, in caves, without benefit of grain, wine or metals; but a new, sensational detail is added to his description of the primitive state – cannibalism. 'The weak was the food of the strong.' Finally, time brought the age of discoveries which transformed human life, whether this was due to the thought of Prometheus, to necessity or to 'long experience, with nature as instructor'. Among the marks of civilization is the custom of burying the dead; this is presumably the point of the speech in the dramatic situation exploited by this play (for which we have no title). The trimeters are regular, extremely so, for

---

[1] *IG²* v 2118 records a third-century performance of Chaeremon's *Achilles Thersitoktonos* by an athlete-actor.

the Euripidean innovations have been abandoned; in the 33 lines there are no resolutions.

Though tragedy lived on in Athens and elsewhere through the third century B.C. and even beyond (our latest inscription recording a victory with a 'new tragedy' belongs to the twenties of the first century B.C.),[1] we know nothing of it but names. From the whole of this period, from Athens and the theatres built all over the Greek world in the fourth and succeeding centuries, from the widespread activities of the guilds of 'the artists of Dionysus' in the Hellenistic world, even from Alexandria where the so-called Pleiad produced tragedies on a lavish scale (Lycophron is credited with 46 or 64, Philieus with 42) we have less than fifty lines that were thought worth preserving. 'Nothing in the history of the transmission of Greek drama', to quote Sir Denys Page, 'is much more remarkable than the earliness, totality and permanence of the eclipse of Hellenistic Tragedy.'[2]

[1] *Fouilles de Delphes* III 2, 67. 'Thrasycles the Athenian . . . competed in his own country with a new tragedy and was victorious . . .' (177 Snell).
[2] Page (1951c) 37.

2

THE SATYR PLAY

In classical dramatic traditions there seems to be a recurrent tendency to present serious drama and broad farce in immediate juxtaposition. Much as, for instance, Roman tragedy was followed by *exodia* (usually consisting of Atellan farce), Japanese No plays by *Kyogen*, and Elizabethan tragedy by jigs, so for most at least of the fifth century B.C. the three tragedies of a trilogy were followed by a satyr play, composed by the same author, the only known exception being Euripides' *Alcestis* of 438 B.C., presented instead of a satyr play and therefore termed a 'prosatyric' play. Most satyr plays were lost in antiquity; only Euripides' *Cyclops* survives in the manuscript tradition. Modern papyrus discoveries, however, have greatly increased our knowledge of the genre.

The principal features of the satyr play were:

(1) Invariable use of a chorus of satyrs; these are small rustic creatures, half-goat, half-human, elemental and often comically grotesque. They are regularly accompanied by their father Silenus, who is a dramatic character in his own right but also functions as a choral spokesman.

(2) Use of mythological plots, with mythological travesty a principal source of humour.

(3) Absence of satire of contemporary people and events, overt or covert.

(4) Use of the same language, metres, and dramaturgic resources as tragedy, modified by special generic requirements: occasional colloquial and bawdy language, boisterous dances, etc. There is somewhat greater metrical freedom than in tragedy: Porson's Law is sometimes disregarded and cyclic anapaests outside the first place in the iambic line are admitted.

(5) Use of a relatively few stereotypes of situation, theme and characterization.

(6) A typically spirited tone, with occasional touches of slapstick and scurrility.

(7) Comparative shortness in length, as in Euripides' *Cyclops* (slightly more than 700 lines).

(8) The evidence seems to indicate that satyr plays occasionally parodied elements in the preceding tragedies.

Demetrius, *De elocutione* 169, describes the satyr play as 'tragedy at play', a fine aphorism for the specific nature of satyric humour, which largely derives from humorous re-employment of the language and dramaturgy of tragedy, from travesty of the same mythological world peopled by the same gods and heroes, and from the absurdity created by the intrusion of Silenus and the satyrs into this world. To a large extent, therefore, the humour of satyr plays consists of poking fun at tragedy, in order of course to provide comic relief.

This comically subversive assault on tragedy takes many forms. The satyr play features, above all, a comedy of incongruity. The satyrs are elemental creatures, at once fey and subhuman, perpetually interested in immediate gratification of their appetites, lazy, arrogant when sure of themselves, craven when they are not. In a satyric *Oeneus*, or perhaps *Schoeneus*, possibly by Sophocles, they present themselves for an athletic competition (the prize is the hand of the king's daughter) with the following self-description:

> We are children of the nymphs, devotees of Bacchus, and neighbours of the gods. Every worthwhile art is embodied in us: fighting with spears, wrestling, horseman-ship, running, boxing, biting, crotch-grabbing; in us you will find musical song, knowledgeable prophecy with no fakery, discriminating knowledge of medicine, measuring of the heavens, dancing, lore of the Underworld. Hey, is this fund of learning fruitless? All of this is at your disposal – just give us your daughter.

Almost invariably these satyrs are introduced into a mythological situation in which they have no legitimate place, creating an incongruity that is initially absurd and funny, and that can be further exploited. An incident which in the *Odyssey* is characterized by a certain grimness and horror and by the suffering of sympathetic characters, and which serves as a parable of barbarism and civiliza-tion, is dramatized by Euripides in *Cyclops*. These values are preserved in the play, but the presence of Silenus and the satyrs provides a continuous comic counterpoint. Thus, for instance, when Odysseus is seeking to make Polyphemus drunk, Silenus keeps trying to steal the wine and the satyrs lend their comically feckless assistance to Odysseus when he is attempting to blind the ogre. The presence of the satyr chorus performs another function in this and similar plays. They give an aura of unreality to an otherwise distressing situation, thereby signalling to the audience that Odysseus' predicament need not be taken over-seriously. Thus when he first lands on the Cyclopes' island he sees the satyrs and rightly exclaims that he has stumbled upon a sort of Dionysiac Never-Never Land: 'we seem to have invaded the polis of Dionysus!' (99).

The satyr play's comic assault on tragedy takes other forms. One technique is to create a momentary mood reminiscent of tragedy, and then deliberately destroy it. In *Cyclops* Odysseus makes a dignified and altogether serious appeal to Polyphemus for mercy, and then Silenus chimes in with one of his typically idiotic remarks (313–15). Similarly, in Aeschylus' *Dictyulci* Silenus is seeking to bully Danae into a marriage (perhaps intended to parody a serious situation in the tragedy *Polydectes*), and she delivers herself of a miniature replica of a tragic heroine's lament (773–85). But then she ends with a distinctly off-key 'that's all I have to say'.

The heroes of tragedy are often treated comically. A hero or villain who appears as larger than life in tragedy reappears in satyr plays either as a serious figure surrounded by incongruous absurdity, whereby his own seriousness appears humorously inappropriate, or as himself a comical figure. The former technique is employed in *Cyclops*. Odysseus himself is treated with complete respect, but humour is generated by the fact that, despite his initial exclamation that he has stumbled upon the kingdom of Bacchus, he reacts in deadly earnest to a situation which we perceive to be less than wholly serious: the Cyclops is essentially no more than a mock-blustering bogeyman from a fairy tale. In other satyr plays the traditional Greek heroes might themselves be presented as ludicrous and grotesque. Thus in Sophocles' *Syndeipnon*[1] the Achaean warlords engaged in a comically degrading squabble at a banquet, and one of them, perhaps Odysseus, received the contents of a chamber-pot over his head. Heracles was a common character in satyr plays, and often was featured as a gargantuan eater, drinker, and wencher.

If the satyr play takes a humorous look at the heroes prominent in tragedy, and perhaps at tragedy's ideals of heroism in some more general sense, so too it displays a nose-thumbing attitude towards some of the characteristic attitudes of tragedy. In tragedy, for instance, cleverness and deception are presented with toleration, most notably in Euripides' rescue plays, *Iphigenia in Tauris* and *Helen*, which have other significant points of contact with the satyr play and may even themselves, like *Alcestis*, have been prosatyric (cf. p. 100). Otherwise, when a clever man appears in a tragedy, he is usually represented as unprincipled and dangerous. One thinks of the anonymous demagogue in Euripides' *Orestes*, and above all of Odysseus in such plays as Sophocles' *Philoctetes*, and Euripides' *Hecuba* and *Iphigenia in Aulide*. But in many satyr plays, such as Sophocles' *Ichneutae* and *Inachus*, and Euripides' *Autolycus*, *Cyclops*, and *Sisyphus*, the plot hinges on sly misrepresentation, and a clever man or trickster is often the hero. Many satyr plays deal with subtle plots for overcoming ogres, monsters, and other villains, and wily schemes for theft and deception, and there is every reason to think that these were presented as tolerable, or even admirable. The Greeks always liked a tale of a good piece of deception, and the satyr play seems frequently to have catered to this taste. Also, the hero of many satyr plays was some such trickster as Odysseus (who is a hero in satyr plays just as frequently as he is a villain in tragedies), Autolycus, Sisyphus, and the patron deity of trickery and theft, Hermes. Other mythological figures noted for their cleverness may have also been characterized as tricksters in satyr plays, such as

---

[1] Ancient evidence wavers between *Syndeipnon* and *Syndeipnoi*. If the play is satyric, *Syndeipnon* is the more likely title, since *Syndeipnoi* would imply a chorus not of satyrs but of Achaeans.

Oedipus in Aeschylus' *Sphinx* and Prometheus in his *Prometheus pyrkaeus*. (We know that Prometheus was presented as a trickster in some comedies: cf. Aristophanes, fr. 645 and Eupolis, fr. 456 K.) Similarly, the many moral shortcomings of Silenus and the satyrs seem to have at least been regarded with toleration rather than condemnation, a sharp contrast with the morality of tragedy.

This tendency to use the satyr play as a mock-tragedy, as a means of disarming the tension and anxiety tragedy creates, was carried to its logical conclusion in instances in which a satyr play was contrived to parody elements in the tragedies of the preceding trilogy. This is most evident in the satyr plays of Aeschylus, in which the principal character of the trilogy reappears in a comic situation in the accompanying satyr play. Thus Lycurgus appeared in both the *Lycurgeia* trilogy and the following *Lycurgus satyricus*, and Oedipus in the *Oedipodeia* and *Sphinx satyricus*. In a variant of this parodizing technique, the satyr play presents a humorous counterpart not of a tragic character but of a dramatic situation which in the tragedy or trilogy is treated seriously, as in *Amymone*, the satyr play produced with the Danaid trilogy which included the extant *Supplices*. Amymone, pursued by the satyrs wanting to reduce her to sexual bondage, appeals for aid and finds a protector in Poseidon (cf. Hyginus, *Fab.* 169, 169A Rose). This presents a parallel to the situation of the Danaids in *Supplices*. Similarly, *Dictyulci* may have been presented with a *Perseus* trilogy containing the tragedy *Polydectes*, and it has been suggested that Silenus' attempt to marry Danae parodies that of Polydectes in the tragedy.

It is possible that the writing of satyr plays parodying accompanying tragedies persisted after the time of Aeschylus. Sophocles' *Ajax* and *Ichneutae* are commonly assigned to the middle or late 440s, and several resemblances between these plays suggest they were written together and that *Ichneutae* parodies elements in *Ajax*. The description in *Ichneutae* of Apollo searching for his missing cattle and their thief distinctly recalls that of Odysseus searching for the killer of the Achaean herd; the divided chorus of searching satyrs (*Ichn.* 85ff.) seems to parody the divided chorus of searching sailors (*Aj.* 866ff.), and both plays conclude with a scene of reconciliation.

There are stronger grounds for thinking that Euripides wrote his *Cyclops* as a parody of *Hecuba*.[1] The blinding of Polyphemus parodies that of Polymestor even in detail of diction (cf. *Hec.* 1035ff., *Cyc.* 663ff.). Both plays are concerned with the problem of civilized behaviour, expressed in terms of *nomos*. Both contain a plea for mercy based on idealism turned aside with a cold lecture about expediency. If the two plays were performed together there is an ironic contrast between Odysseus' rejection of Hecuba's plea in the tragedy and his

---

[1] The dating of *Cyclops* is disputed, cf. Sutton (1974a). The arguments for a date substantially later than 424 (the probable date of *Hecuba*) are not compelling.

own plea to Cyclops in the satyr play. Polymestor appears to be an invention of Euripides, and his characterization seems modelled on that of the Cyclops. These correspondences suggest that *Cyclops* is a comic foil for *Hecuba*, and although no external evidence exists, it is an attractive idea that the correspondences are intentional, that is, that both plays were produced in the same year.

A notable feature of the satyr play is marked dependence on a limited repertoire of stereotyped themes, situations, narrative elements, and characterizations; *Cyclops* incorporates a number of these generic stereotypes. One of these, the frequent importance of trickery and trickster-figures, has already been noted. A second, perhaps the commonest of all, is the overthrow of ogres, monsters, and giants. As in *Cyclops*, and such other plays as Aeschylus' *Cercyon*, Sophocles' *Amycus*, Euripides' *Busiris*, and Sositheus' *Daphnis* or *Lityerses*, the villain is an ogre who molests wayfarers until he makes the mistake of practising his art on a passing hero who destroys him.

In many such plays the villain challenges passers-by to an athletic match or similar contest. Athletics and competition also figure frequently in satyr plays with other types of subject such as Aeschylus' *Theoroi* or *Isthmiastae*, in which the satyrs run away from Dionysus and decide to become competitors in the Isthmian Games, and the (possibly Sophoclean) *Oeneus* or *Schoeneus*, about an athletic contest for the hand of the protagonist's daughter.

Another theme frequently associated with this typical situation – the ogre who molests passers-by – is that of abused hospitality. This is explicit in *Cyclops* (cf. especially 299ff.), and probably in similar plays. But this theme of hospitality and its abuse also figured in satyr plays with other types of subject. In Sophocles' *Inachus*, for instance, Hermes apparently first comes to Inachus' kingdom disguised as a foreign stranger (he is described as a *karbanos aithos*, 'swarthy barbarian', *P.Oxy.* 2369 ii 26) and is received hospitably by Inachus.[1] Then he transforms Inachus' daughter Io into a cow, and Inachus and the satyrs, unaware of his benevolent motive, are naturally enraged: their indignation was probably all the greater because they thought he had abused hospitality. There may have been a similar disruption in Sophocles' *Iambe*, a dramatization of the *Homeric Hymn to Demeter*, if the play contained the incident where the king and queen of Eleusis find Demeter baptizing their son on the fire and misconstrue her motive.

Again, many plays, such as *Cyclops*, about the defeat of wayfarer-molesters featured the theme of escape or rescue. Like Odysseus, the hero would fall into the clutches of the villain and destroy him in order to regain his freedom. In such plays the satyrs could always be introduced plausibly as slaves of the

---

[1] Some think the stranger is Zeus himself, but this is unlikely if the stranger appeared on-stage in the early scenes: the tragic poets were reluctant to represent Zeus as an on-stage character. On the other hand, if Inachus and the stranger did not meet on stage it is hard to imagine what could have filled the first 280 lines of the play.

villain, to be released as part of the play's happy ending. This was presumably the case, for instance, in Euripides' *Sciron*. The evidence of vase paintings suggests that in Aeschylus' *Circe* they shared with Odysseus' crew a transformation into bestial shape and eventual release from it. Escape and rescue appeared in many forms: in the plays of Aeschylus, for example, one may mention escape from bestiality in *Circe*, from foreign lands in *Proteus*, from sexual bondage to Silenus and the satyrs in *Amymone* and *Dictyulci* and the Suitors in *Ostologoi*,[1] and from the Underworld in *Sisyphus drapetes*.

Usually, as in *Cyclops*, the satyrs have been forcibly separated from their natural master Dionysus 'whose service is perfect freedom', and are allowed to return to him at the end of the play. Aeschylus, however, sometimes reverses the normal process: in *Isthmiastae* the satyrs (temporarily – we do not know how the play ends) seek escape from Dionysus, and in *Amymone* and *Dictyulci* they are themselves the villains who threaten the heroine.

Another frequent narrative element is magic and the miraculous. Taking, for example, the satyr plays of Sophocles, one may note the appearance of the Cretan 'robot' Talus in *Daedalus*; the possible baptism by fire in *Iambe*; a magical flute, and headgear that confers invisibility, as well, of course, as Io's transformation into a cow in *Inachus*; Hermes' magical growth in *Ichneutae*; the cure of Orion's blindness in *Cedalion*; a magic philtre conferring immortality in *Kophoi*, etc. Similarly, witches such as Circe and Medea, wizards such as Proteus, and numerous monsters and similar fabulous beings appeared as characters in satyr plays.

All these satyric stereotypes may also be seen as aspects of a more general tendency to employ elements reminiscent of *Märchen* and fairy tales. For many of the narrative elements found in satyr plays can be related to familiar folklore motifs. Thus, to name a few, Aeschylus' *Sphinx* features a riddle contest, and his *Proteus* a 'shape-shifter'; Sophocles' *Iambe* and *Kophoi* present variants of the theme of loss of immortality through folly. Euripides' *Cyclops*, like other satyr plays about the destruction of wayfarer-molesting villains, dramatizes a variant of the 'Jack the Giant-Killer' situation: the defeat of an ogre by a plucky and clever hero.

Also, in *Cyclops*, which seems representative of plays of its type, the original viewpoint of a fairy tale is preserved intact. Odysseus is a simple hero, and Polyphemus a simple villain. The quality of Odysseus' revenge is scarcely called into question, either in respect of its brutality or its fraudulent nature. Even the gruesomeness of Polyphemus' cannibalism and of his blinding is presented with the comic exaggeration of a fairy tale, intended to evoke the same pleasurable *frisson* of horror as children derive from such stories. This, like the unreality conferred by the presence of the satyrs, keeps the play from

---

[1] There is no real reason for doubting that *Ostologoi* was satyric, cf. Sutton (1974*b*) 128.

having a distressing effect out of keeping with its function of providing comic relief.

Two other common characteristics of satyr plays may be noticed. The first is that many satyr plays are set either in the countryside or in exotically alien locales: Asia Minor, Egypt, Libya, etc. Second, almost by definition a satyr play must have a happy ending. In the few instances where the poet seems to have selected a plot that did not end happily, he must have adapted his material so as to minimize the unhappy aspects.

If tragedy affirms the existence of some kind of general world-order, so does the satyr play. Many satyr plays end with the defeat of villains of one kind or another, so that even if the satyr play is tolerant of the chorus' shortcomings and of cleverness, it is scarcely an amoral genre. It holds a comic mirror up to tragedy, but at the deepest level it affirms its values. For all its humour, for instance, one should not forget that *Cyclops* is no less cautionary in intention than is its Homeric prototype.

Euripides' *Alcestis* was presented in 438 B.C. instead of the usual satyr play, and a number of satyric stereotypes recur in this play: hospitality, rescue from bondage, use of folklore themes,[1] drunken carousal and gluttony (for comical banqueting scenes were not uncommon in satyr plays, e.g. Sophocles' *Syndeipnon* and Euripides' *Syleus*), and the appearance of Heracles, a frequent satyric character. Also, familiar satyric elements are found in Euripides' *Iphigenia in Tauris* and *Helen*: defeat of a villain, violation of hospitality, trickery (which is condoned rather than criticized), and exotic settings, and these are combined much as in *Cyclops*. The Euripidean romance was created by the introduction of satyric themes into the tragic performance. Indeed, since these plays resemble *Alcestis* in this respect, it is tempting to consider them prosatyric. This is especially true of *Helen*, since it seems to have parodied a tragedy in the same set, *Andromeda*, and since its treatment of Menelaus' heroism has a distinctly comic flavour. The length of these plays, particularly of *Helen*, might be deemed an objection to this theory. But *Alcestis* is already substantially longer than any known satyr play, and in view of the length of Euripides' later plays generally, this is probably not a fatal objection.

It is a striking fact that the typical subject matter and scenes of satyr plays are also those of the *Odyssey*: incidents involving the defeat of villains and ogres presented with the same simple, readily-identifiable polarization into good and evil; the theme of hospitality and its abuse, functioning, as in plays like *Cyclops*, as a litmus test for the identification of sympathetic and unsympathetic characters; use of cleverness and of a clever man as hero; situations of escape or rescue from actual or impending bondage; use of folktale narrative elements, magic and the miraculous, wonderful and terrible beings, and exotic settings to

---

[1] Schmid–Stählin 1 3, 537 n. 5.

create a highly romantic universe. The *Iliad* is essentially grimly realistic, and by contrast the *Odyssey* is romantic. Though it is not itself escapist in intent, it may be regarded, since it contains these elements, as the ultimate ancestor of all western literature of escape, romance, and fantasy. It is precisely these elements which are carried over into the satyr play.

The satyr play provides comic relief by allowing us to escape from the universe of tragedy, which is realistic in the same sense as that of the *Iliad*, into a colourful and fabulous world of boundless possibility. At the same time, since this is a palpable fantasy world, and since a happy ending is obligatory by the rules of the game, we may be excited by the predicaments of satyric characters without being moved or distressed. So besides being a romantic universe, this is an optimistic one. The satyr play thus presents a roseate vision of life counterbalancing that of tragedy.

Tragedy is also realistic in that it reproduces the moral ambiguities of life. The unending debate over the rights and wrongs of Antigone and Creon is witness to the fact that the universe of tragedy is not peopled by simple heroes and villains. In imitating the *Odyssey* by adopting a simple and readily comprehensible polarization of heroes and villains, often in starkly agonic terms, the satyr play offers relief from the necessity of confronting a complex universe. This contrast is posed dramatically in the instance of *Hecuba* and *Cyclops*. Polymestor and Polyphemus are similar ogres destroyed by their victims, who wreak their vengeance with particular savagery. In *Hecuba*, by such devices as the final prophecy and the creation of a measure of sympathy for Polymestor when he genuinely grieves over the murder of his children, Euripides adds a moral complication by casting doubt on the quality of Hecuba's revenge, which in retrospect is made to seem barbaric and otiose. But in *Cyclops* a similar incident is recounted in the simple, unquestioning terms of a fairy tale. It is almost as if we view the same incident twice, through the eyes of an adult and a child. This release from the need to respond to complex moral issues must also have been experienced as a form of relief.

We have seen that clever men and tricksters are frequently cast as sympathetic central characters in satyr plays. Indeed, these are so common that the clever man, if anybody, may be characterized as the satyric hero. Again, this recalls the contrast between the *Iliad* and the *Odyssey*, for the tragic hero is notoriously a linear descendant of Achilles, and this satyric hero is equally descended from Odysseus. Like Achilles, the tragic hero who attains greatness because of his heroic self-assertion is guided by exalted and rather forbidding standards. Odysseus in the *Odyssey*, however, is great for entirely different reasons: persistence, shrewdness, self-reliance, industry, adaptability, and similar 'middle-class virtues'. After tragedy's presentation of exceedingly uncommon, often great, individuals, the satyr play's presentation of more ordinary virtues may have been experienced by the audience as another form of relief. Moreover, the great problems posed by tragedy are genuine and genuinely terrifying, while the satyric hero is regularly confronted by nurseryroom monsters like Polyphemus who are mock-terrifying straw men to be sent down to routine and predictable defeat.

By 340 B.C. (cf. *IG* II² 22.2320) the dramatic festival of the Dionysia was re-organized, and satyr plays were thenceforth performed independently of tragedy. Thus they no longer served to provide comic relief after tragedy, and it is probably no coincidence that shortly after this date evidence appears for a new kind of satyr play, which retained the satyr chorus but gravitated into the orbit of contemporary comedy, abandoning mythological plots in favour of contemporary satire, and adopting the dramatic techniques and metres of comedy.

The two best known such plays are Python's *Agen* and Lycophron's *Menedemus*. *Agen* was written and produced at the behest of Alexander, to satirize and discredit his fallen minister Harpalus. It was probably produced in 324, when Harpalus was still alive and a potent threat to the internal security of Alexander's empire; if so, this is an interesting example of the use of literature as political propaganda. *Menedemus* seems to have been a good-natured lampoon on the notorious frugality of this philosopher.

There is evidence for other such plays. Although Sositheus is best known as a reviver of the classical mythological satyr play, perhaps in response to the rise of bucolic poetry (cf. Dioscorides' epigram *Anth. Pal.* 7.707), a satyr play ridiculing the philosopher Cleanthes is probably attested by Diogenes Laertius 7.173, and the Eupolidean metre of a fragment of Astydamas Minor's *Heracles satyricus* quoted by Athenaeus suggests that it may have been a similar play.

Wilamowitz's suggestion that Timocles' *Ikarioi satyroi* was a satyr play rather than a Middle Comedy is nowadays unpopular,[1] but Athenaeus 9.407d seems to say that Timocles the comic poet and Timocles the contemporary tragedian were one and the same, and there is nothing in this play's fragments uncharacteristic of other late satyr plays. More conclusively, titles consisting of plural nouns and *Satyroi* are otherwise reserved for satyr plays; comedies with satyr choruses, such as Cratinus' *Dionysalexandros*, received different types of title. Thus, if this was a satyr play, the common suggestion that Python invented this new kind of satyric drama must be wrong, for while *Agen* ridicules Harpalus for establishing a cult for his newly deceased mistress Pythionike, *Ikarioi* speaks of her as still living. Timocles, who was, in fact, virtually unique in writing both tragedies and comedies, and was quite possibly working at the time of the re-organization of the festival (his name appears on the inscription cited above), would be admirably situated to make this innovation.

---

[1] Wilamowitz-Moellendorff (1962) IV 688f.; the most recent argument to the contrary is that of Constantinides (1969) 49–61.

3

COMEDY

I. INTRODUCTION

'It was produced in the archonship of Euthynus at the Lenaea by Callistratus. Result, first; second, Cratinus with *Kheimazomenoi* (not preserved); third, Eupolis with *Noumeniai*.' So runs the record for our earliest surviving comedy, the *Acharnians* of Aristophanes, and it refers to an occasion in the year we call 425 B.C.[1] At that time Aristophanes and Eupolis were near the beginning of their careers, young men in their twenties; Cratinus had won his first victory at the festivals some thirty years before, and Aristophanes, on the way up, could portray his distinguished rival as a figure from literary history, now a neglected old has-been with a drink problem.[2] It happens that the first date in that literary history is some thirty years earlier still, in a year reckoned to be 486 B.C., when a competition for comedies was instituted at Athens as an official event at the Dionysia, and the winner was one Chionides, a man remembered by posterity for little else.

If Chionides and Magnes are the names to mention from the first generation of writers of Athenian Old Comedy, as they are for Aristotle in the *Poetics* (1448a34), then Cratinus and Crates represent the second generation; Eupolis and Aristophanes are of the third and last. What we know about Old Comedy still depends, in overwhelmingly large measure, on the selection of eleven plays by Aristophanes which survive in medieval copies together with an inheritance of interpretative commentary, a corpus of marginal scholia which has offered a perennial invitation to scholarly interest and may have been of decisive importance in keeping the text alive through times when so much other literature was lost.[3] As to the rest: papyrus fragments of plays or commentaries recovered by modern excavation, inscriptional records of productions, remains of theatres, works of art representing masks, actors, and choruses, quotations from lost plays and numerous statements of widely varying date and value about plays

---

[1] Ar. *Ach.* hyp. 1 Coulon: nothing else is known about either of the competing plays mentioned, and it has been suggested that 'not preserved' originally applied to both.
[2] Ar. *Knights* 526–36.
[3] See *CHCL* I, Part 4, 191–2.

and their authors – all this catalogue of material contributes to the construction of a fuller and more balanced account than can be given from Aristophanes alone, but it is still an account with a strong Aristophanic bias. We cannot help seeing the rest in terms of similarities to Aristophanes and (more cautiously) differences from him; and it is good to have that in mind from the first. Menander is another part of the story. His first plays were produced more than sixty years after Aristophanes' last, when the mode of comedy, like so much else in the Athenian world, had been transformed. Yet a reference to Menander and the New Comedy is in place here because the very substantial accessions of text from papyri published in the twentieth century must be admitted to have some effect on our views of comedy's earlier age. The new discoveries suggest new comparisons and contrasts, but they also remind us, if we care to look back to the time before their making, how great can be the differences between whole, partial and fragmentary knowledge.

For all their variety of theme and incident, Aristophanes' plays have a common basic pattern: a revolutionary idea, a way to change a situation which the hero will not tolerate, is carried against opposition and pursued through some of its consequences, which are good for some and bad for others. In *Acharnians*, for instance, a man who has had enough of wartime life in Athens makes a personal treaty with Sparta and sticks to it through all accusations of traitorous behaviour to enjoy his monopoly of the benefits of peace – an open market for imports, feasting, celebration and the chance to go back home again to his farm. Or in *Plutus*: the hero takes charge of the blind god Wealth, and, despite opposition from Poverty, has Wealth's sight restored by a miraculous cure so that poor but honest men (like himself of course) can be prosperous. It is characteristic of this kind of comedy that the issues involved are those of the public world – peace against war, right and wrong distribution of wealth – and that those issues are simplified and made concrete by being transposed into the private world of individual people and their families. Among other things, the public world includes education, modern versus traditional, as in *Clouds*; and it includes the performing arts, especially tragedy, as in *Thesmophoriazusae*, *Frogs* and elsewhere.

As the themes of the plays are varied, so are their characters. Some, like Heracles and Dionysus, are familiar figures from myth, and probably appealed to many in the audience as old stage favourites: 'Heracles cheated of his dinner' is mentioned as a stock routine of comedy in the *Wasps* (60). Others represent real people of present or past (the latter can be seen in, or summoned from, the Underworld); and it is a good question how true to life the 'real people' are or were ever supposed to be. The art of Aristophanic portraiture is well compared to that of a modern newspaper cartoonist; it exploits, and indeed helps to create, the popular image of public figures, and (again like the modern cartoonist) it will sometimes present a satirical hybrid between the real person and a second imaginary identity, as when Cleon in the *Knights* becomes a Paphlagonian slave in the household of Demos of Pnyx Hill, the sovereign people. Demos, like John Bull or Uncle Sam, is an imaginative summation of the qualities of a senior member of the electorate. Here he serves to remind us that the very common tendency of the ancient Greeks to personify concepts, whether verbally or visually, can in comedy take the form of bringing the personified entity on stage: thus Reconciliation (Diallage) is thought of by the chorus of Acharnians as a fine young girl, just the one to set up house with in the country (*Ach.* 989); while in *Lysistrata* she actually appears in a walk-on part to bring Athenians and Spartans together (1114ff.). From the viewpoint of later comedy, and hence that of much modern drama, the specially interesting group of Aristophanic characters is the large one of fictional ordinary (and not so ordinary) people in their everyday social or professional relationships, ranging from leading characters like Strepsiades in the *Clouds* down to such as the lodging-house keeper and her friend in the *Frogs* (549ff.). Strepsiades interests us here not as the comic hero who has adventures with Socrates, but rather in the role he is given at the start of the play, a man with a teenage son whose life-style he cannot support. If such people often seemed like familiar contemporaries to their audiences, there were still ways in which their special identity as stage characters and their remote origins as part of a ritual were recalled. Comic actors, like all others, wore masks; but there was also a traditional comic costume, with padded paunch and posterior and (for males) a leather phallus worn outside their tights which showed under short clothes and, according to Aristophanes, could be used to raise a laugh from the small boys.[1] This costume, which is documented from representations contemporary with Aristophanes, can be traced back in art to a time long before we have any texts, as can the tradition of choruses made up of creatures of the wild (animals, birds, insects, fish), an inheritance which Aristophanes himself associated with early comedy in the person of Magnes, and was to exploit inventively in his own plays.[2]

The variety of visual effect is something that the reader of Aristophanes learns to recapture in imagination; the appeal of the music and dancing is irreparably lost, though the pattern and language of the lyrics can still evoke a response; and in his portrait of Cratinus in the *Knights* Aristophanes recalls two songs from the old master which were popular hits and became all the rage at parties (529ff.). From lyric writing to dialogue at a casual and unaffected level of everyday speech, the fifth-century comic poet has a whole vocabulary of

---

[1] *Clouds* 539: the phallus, like the padding (*Frogs* 200), could be referred to and used for comic by-play or taken for granted and ignored; on jokes for the boys, cf. Eupolis, *Prospaltioi* 244 K.

[2] Magnes: *Knights* 520ff. (see below, p. 112 with n. 2).

different modes of expression at his command, and within them, like a modern comic entertainer, he can be both mimic and creator; he can produce laughter and suggest criticism. One main line of development in comedy, which can be seen in Aristophanes in the contrast between his latest plays, *Ecclesiazusae* and *Plutus*, and the earlier ones, is the trend away from this highly colourful and 'poetic' writing to a much more uniform and naturalistic manner, to be perfected in the end by Menander. But for earlier comedy, the alternation between song and speech, between chorus and actors, is something vital and organic; and its nature cannot be properly appreciated without at least some consideration of the forms which that alternation takes.

2. STRUCTURAL PATTERNS IN OLD COMEDY

The simplest kind of pattern in Aristophanic comedy, and the one that is basic to its structure, is an alternation in the form A B A′ B′, where A and A′ are lyrics in responsion to each other, and B and B′ are blocks of lines either for the speaking voice or to be recited to some form of accompaniment in the manner loosely called 'recitative': the technical term is *iambic syzygy* when lyrics interlace with the iambic trimeter of regular soliloquy and dialogue; it is *epirrhematic syzygy* where the longer tetrameter lines, anapaestic, trochaic and iambic, are concerned.[1] Not all of Aristophanes is written in syzygies: for instance, in prologues, before the chorus arrives, there are sequences of scenes without intervening lyrics; episodic composition, in scenes marked off by non-linking lyrics or none, is specially favoured late in the plays; and these sequences do sometimes have balancing elements, if only because some comic effects are enhanced by repetition. But the four-part syzygy pattern is basic; it can be varied in order, prolonged, and variously embellished; a great volume of critical work centres on attempts to define and explain its different manifestations in relation to the content and dramatic design of the plays, and in particular to project backwards from those features which seem most genuinely traditional towards a proto-form of comedy or comic revel. This whole line of enquiry stems largely from research into the origins and development of Attic comedy by Zieliński (1885); some important successors are Mazon (1904), Pickard-Cambridge (*DTC*: 1927, rev. 1962), Gelzer (1960), Händel (1963) and Sifakis (1971). Discussion can usefully begin from the choral parabasis, a characteristic feature of the fifth-century plays of Aristophanes which is absent from the two surviving fourth century plays, *Ecclesiazusae* and *Plutus*.

In full form, the choral parabasis has seven parts. It consists of an epirrhematic

[1] 'Recitative' means, in layman's language, something between speech and song; but, given that there was such a mode of delivery, it still is unclear how far this was varied, e.g. for different kinds of tetrameters or different styles within one kind: see for a brief discussion *DFA* 156ff., esp. 164.

syzygy prefaced by a block of lines in a long metre, commonly anapaestic tetrameter, with their own matching introduction and conclusion. The whole pattern can thus be written A B C D E D' E'; but there are various ways in which it can be reduced, and it always is reduced when it is used for a second parabasis within one play. In the main parabasis of *Knights* (498–610) the correspondence between form and content is particularly close. In the syzygy, the two lyrics, D D', are miniature hymns, in which the chorus of knights invokes first Poseidon, then Athena; the two epirrhemes, E E', are each 16 lines of trochaic tetrameters (both the metre and the length, sixteen lines or twenty, both multiples of four, are canonical); the first subject is praise of the traditional valour and virtues of the knights, the second a euphoric account of their horses' novel and recent success in a landing of cavalry on an enemy shore. In this wartime play (424 B.C.) part of the appeal is the topical one to popular sentiment, but the chorus can be a comic chorus as well as representing the cavalry and the upper-class Athenians who served in it, and the victory they specially hope for is victory in the festival (591–4). In any case the dramatic action of the play is in suspense. The break with what has gone before is marked, here as elsewhere, in the short opening section we have called A, which sees the departing hero off the stage with a wish of good luck, and invites the audience to 'pay attention to our anapaests' (B C). The dramatic identity of the knights is not quite forgotten, for (507ff.): 'if any of the comic dramatists of old had tried to make us come forward (*parabainein*) to face the theatre and speak lines, he wouldn't have got his way easily' – but now, they continue, the poet deserves support as a brave outspoken man with whom they have enemies in common. Essentially, however, the lines are an advertisement for Aristophanes and an appeal for a favourable reception (end of B into C) which is hung on the peg of a defence: this is the first play, after a dramatic début three years ago, that Aristophanes has produced in his own name.[1] The *apologia* includes, among other things, Aristophanes' celebrated description of Cratinus and other comic poets which has been mentioned above already.

The reference to 'our anapaests' and the use of the term *parabainein* which we have just noted would of themselves suggest what is abundantly confirmed by the extant plays and recognizable fragments: namely that for the third generation of writers of Old Comedy and their audiences a parabasis such as we have described was an established component of a play, with certain familiar conventions. But the balance between convention and innovation was not always evenly poised, and there are some ways in which we can see it shift. The first five plays, *Acharnians, Knights, Clouds, Wasps, Peace,* were successively

---

[1] Aristophanes was not alone in having some of his plays produced by others, and he went on doing so (e.g. *Frogs*). We do not know why this was done, but can accept that rivals and critics might carp: see *DFA* 84–6, with Plato Com. 99–100 K and *P.Oxy.* 2737 fr. 1 ii 10ff. (= *CGFP** 56, 44ff.).

produced in the years 425–421, *Clouds* and *Peace* at the Dionysia and the others at the Lenaea. Of these, *Acharnians*, *Knights* and *Wasps* have a full parabasis, but in *Peace* there is one without epirrhemes (i.e. A B C D D'); in *Clouds*, where the other plays have their anapaests, the surviving revised version offers a single block of lines in another variety of parabasis metre, the Eupolidean (i.e. B for B C). Each time, with interesting consistency, the anapaests or their equivalent present a kind of literary discourse, an *apologia* for the poet, which can be spoken in the first person as if by him as well as in the way exemplified above from *Knights*; though in *Acharnians* (628f.) Aristophanes has the chorus claim that he has not previously seen fit to advertise himself. We can note here with the complete plays the evidence of a commentary on a lost play (?*Anagyros*) first published in 1968, which gives some quotations in sequence from anapaests and from the lyrics and trochaic tetrameters of a syzygy.[1] The four complete plays from the later fifth century are *Birds* (414 Dion.), *Lysistrata* (411, (?) Len.), *Thesmophoriazusae* (411, (?) Dion.) and *Frogs* (405 Len.). Of these, only *Birds* has the full form of parabasis; in *Thesmophoriazusae* the syzygy is reduced to a single epirrheme (E for D E D' E'); in *Frogs* there is simply a syzygy; in *Lysistrata* (614–705) there is a carefully balanced structure including two pairs of ten-line epirrhemes which looks like a special variant for a play with a chorus representing twelve men plus twelve women in two opposed halves.[2] The *apologia*, which was so prominent earlier, has now gone, even where, as in *Birds* and *Thesmophoriazusae*, there are the anapaests to accommodate it. Also absent from *Lysistrata*, *Thesmophoriazusae* and *Frogs* is the second parabasis, which, though shorter and more variable in form, is a regular feature of the earlier plays, granted that *Acharnians* is a special case.[3] We noted at the outset that *Ecclesiazusae* (produced in 393 or 392) and *Plutus* (388) have no parabasis at all.

The parabasis is sometimes thought of as a kind of fossil, a survival from remote origins in a ritual, which has preserved and somehow transmitted to other parts of the play as they evolved the patterning which its own precise balance marks so clearly. What we see in Aristophanes is then the end of a long story: this component of the play, which is exclusively choral and does nothing to further the dramatic action, is in decline as the interest in organized dramatic action grows and the role of the chorus diminishes. It is easier to subscribe to the second part of this view than to the first, though one should still beware of supposing that the process of decline was necessarily as tidy as the limited set of data we have makes it look. In fact there is another well established claimant,

---

[1] *P.Oxy.* 2737 (see p. 107 n. 1 above).

[2] We know of other plays in which the chorus was similarly divided, as between rich and poor in Eupolis, *Marikas* (421 B.C.), but not enough survives to show the shape of their parabases: see Webster in *DTC* 160; and for *Marikas* (*P.Oxy.* 2741) *CGFP* no. 95, 29n.

[3] The choral performance at *Ach.* 971–99 can perhaps be seen as a hybrid between a second parabasis and the sort of ode which would be regular at such a place: Sifakis (1971) 35.

some say a still stronger one, to be an archetypal element of comedy. This is the formal debate, for which the name *agon*, like much other technical terminology, is a legacy of the nineteenth century. In its canonical form, the agon has balancing epirrhemes in tetrameters in which the two principals present their arguments (E); each of these runs into a conclusion, like the anapaests of the parabasis, for which the traditional name is *pnigos* 'choker' (P); each again is prefixed by a matching exhortation (*katakeleusmos*) from the chorus (K); each half of the debate, so constituted, has one of a pair of lyric odes (O), and the whole sequence is rounded off by a concluding section, like that of the anapaests of the parabasis, namely the *sphragis* or 'seal' (S). Thus the basic alternation of ode and epirrheme is elaborated to the form O K E P O' K' E' P' S. If we now recall the simplified statement of the basic pattern of a play which served us for a moment above, 'a revolutionary idea . . . is carried against opposition', then we can say that an *agon* in the first half of the play tends to accommodate the main dramatic issue. But from the first Aristophanes is master of the pattern, not its slave.

In *Acharnians*, the revolutionary idea of a personal peace treaty with Sparta arouses powerful opposition, and might have been expected to offer a suitable theme for an epirrhematic agon in full form, but it does not: Dicaeopolis' main defence of his actions, when we reach it, is a speech in iambic trimeters based on the famous long speech by Telephus in Euripides' lost play *Telephus* of 438 B.C., and the whole unit (490–625), which is sometimes called a quasi-agon, is in form a simple four-part syzygy, with two matching choral parts in dochmiac metre and a further iambic scene roughly in balance with that of the speech. Then *Knights* has two epirrhematic agons, one before the main parabasis and one after; *Clouds* has two, both in the latter part of the play; in *Peace* 'there is not, strictly speaking, an agon as regards either matter or form', and so on.[1] But however the definitions are drawn, the pattern verifiably persists, and is still recognizable in the fourth-century plays when reduced to half of itself or less: *Ecclesiazusae* 571–709 shows the form O K E P; and *Plutus* 487–618, the role of the chorus still further reduced, has simply K E P for the debate between Chremylus, in favour of restoring sight to Wealth, and the figure of Poverty. In spite of all the variations, such a structure in a regular simple form could be imagined as the core of a primitive drama for chorus and actors, and as the growth point for the symmetries and balances which are seen elsewhere in the plays. The problem with this exercise in imagination, even though the patterns found in Aristophanes can be traced to some extent in fragments, is given by the two generations of plays which are lost; and Dover, writing in 1954, put the point crisply when he said 'we cannot extrapolate from Aristophanes'.[2] But if the search for patterns of proto-drama must at present remain a speculative one, the study of relationships between form and content in the surviving plays can

---

[1] *DTC* 200.   [2] In *FYAT* 139.

be more rewarding, for the patterns are under pressure not only from the demands of subject matter within particular parts of plays, but from the trend towards an organized plot composed in the units we call 'acts' and away from a participating chorus. That trend we can to some extent follow by way of Aristophanes' later work to the *Dyskolos* of Menander and other plays of New Comedy. But there are still the missing generations in between.

3. THE EARLIEST COMIC DRAMA

If ever we recovered a series of comedies dating back to 486 B.C., it would still be an interesting question how much further the history of comedy could or should be pursued. What was the essential change which made the revel-songs of *komodoi* into comedy, and when did it occur? Aristotle confronted the problem, and much modern discussion takes off from the few remarks of his on early comedy which appear in the surviving part of the *Poetics*.

According to Aristotle, stages in the evolution of tragedy were marked by innovations associated with particular people (for example, Sophocles and the use of a third actor); but for comedy the innovators were generally unknown 'since in the beginning it was not taken seriously'.[1] The official recognition of comedy at Athens came 'quite late' (this is our date of 486 B.C.) and by then, when the names of the first comic poets are recorded, it had already 'certain formal characteristics'; before then, performances were by volunteers. Comedy, like tragedy, originated in improvisation.[2] The pattern of 'improvisation' Aristotle had in mind seems to be the one common to the Hellenic and many other cultures, with leader and responding chorus or group: the leader initiates the occasion and may 'improvise' or compose orally; the response of the group is previously composed or otherwise predictable; and there may, of course, be more than one leader and more than one group. Such a pattern can be illustrated from the lament for Hector in the *Iliad* (24.719ff.) where there are singers (*aoidoi*) to lead the lament; the women and then finally the whole people responding, while in turn Andromache, Hecuba and Helen intervene with speeches expressing their personal grief. Whether rightly or not, Aristotle saw the genesis of tragedy in 'the leaders of the dithyramb'; for comedy he thought of the leaders of the phallic songs (*phallika*) 'which still survive as institutions in many Greek cities'. But the claim to have originated comic drama came from more than one quarter. The mainland Megarians, notes Aristotle, claimed that comedy arose with them in the time of their democracy (i.e. in the period following the expulsion of the tyranny in the early sixth century); the Megarians of

---

[1] This paragraph quotes from chapters 3, 4 and 5 of the *Poetics*: here 1449a37ff., with 18f. on Sophocles, and continuing from 1449b1.
[2] 1449a9ff.

Megara Hyblaea in Sicily also put in a claim, on the ground that Epicharmus, who was 'much earlier than Chionides and Magnes' came from there; and there were some dubious etymological arguments about 'drama' and 'comedy' in support.[1] Not surprisingly, when he looked back from the comedy of his own time, Aristotle found the element of invective and personal abuse a striking feature of early comedy, which he seems to have thought of as the natural successor in this respect to the development represented by Archilochus and other writers of abusive personal poetry.[2] The start of a movement away from that concept of comic writing is the one development on which he is precise: 'plot-composition came first from Sicily; of the Athenians, Crates was the first to move away from the iambic convention and write plots with subjects of general [and not particular] reference'.[3]

When he derives comedy from *phallika* such as were known in his own day, Aristotle is in some way using surviving primitives to confirm an evolutionary hypothesis. Descriptions of performances by *phallophoroi*, *ithyphalloi* and others compiled by scholars of the Hellenistic age can be taken to indicate what he had in mind.[4] These traditional ceremonies, which have their parallels in other cultures, offer a number of points of contact with fully developed comedy: for instance, the performers are sometimes masked, and there can be a prominent element of invective and abuse which, as we have just noted, was something which struck Aristotle as characteristic of early comedy. What Aristotle found wanting, and what we lack also, is any record of the stages of development that may have intervened; and this is still true even if we make the most of the links between comedy and the hypothetical proto-comedy at the expense of their differences, and discount as far as possible the point that, by the time Aristotle and his successors made their observations, there was ample opportunity for the ostensibly primitive performances to have absorbed elements from formal comedy at a developed stage.[5] In short, Aristotle's derivation of comedy is a hypothesis which is interesting and possibly correct, but he does not offer, and we cannot adequately supply, the means by which it might be verified.

We do not know how far Aristotle, if pressed, would have extended a definition of *phallika*; but the picture we can form of *komoi* that are possibly related to comedy is of increasing interest and diversity as the evidence of vase

---

[1] 1448a29–b2.

[2] 1449a9ff.: in other words, comedy became the natural medium for those who would earlier have been writers of iambics. See also 1451b10ff. and *Eth.Nic.* 1128a16–31.

[3] 1449b5ff.: in mentioning Sicily, Aristotle no doubt had Epicharmus and Phormis in mind, whether or not their names were originally intended to be cited in some way.

[4] The principal texts are from Sosibius (*c.* 300 B.C.: *FGrH* 595 F 7) and Semus of Delos (2nd cent. B.C.: *FGrH* 396 F 24); these are quoted by Athenaeus 14, 621d–f, 622a–d, and translated and discussed with others in *DTC* 132–47.

[5] See *DTC* 132–47 with special reference to Webster's contributions to the revised version.

paintings and other works of art is exploited by intensive study and enhanced by new discoveries. Among the earliest to be quoted and the best known are the Attic vases which offer a line of ancestry for the theriomorphic choruses of Aristophanes and others: Sifakis (1971) includes an admirable discussion of previous interpretations. Examples are an amphora in Berlin (F 1830) and an oenochoe in the British Museum (B 509), both dated 500/480 B.C., which show a piper with two chorusmen dressed as cocks: the first one has them wrapped in mantles, and perhaps marching on, while on the second they are in a running dance-step. Another amphora in Berlin (F 1697) is dated as early as the mid-sixth century, and has a piper with three young beardless men in armour on the backs of three bearded men with horse masks and horse tails: Athenian knights, a century and a quarter before Aristophanes used them as a comic chorus.[1] Unfortunately (and this is generally true of the monuments which concern us here) there is nothing to show what occasion the representations recall, or with what cult it was connected. The vase with the knights was painted long before our date (486 B.C.) for the official recognition of comedy at the Dionysia, but could perhaps represent a performance there by the 'volunteers' mentioned by Aristotle. The two pictures of bird-dancers may be earlier than or just later than 486, but whether they are regular comic chorusmen, 'volunteers', or something else, they were painted in the lifetime of the first generation of Attic comic poets, and may therefore give a fair idea of the appearance of the chorus in the *Ornithes* of Magnes, whose flappings are mentioned by Aristophanes, the future author of plays called *Birds* and *Storks*.[2] Music, movement and colour were obvious elements to exploit in choruses of this kind, and the *Birds* is an outstanding example of what could be done. Such choruses could, like any others, have generated a patterned structure of composition by alternation with a leader; being very markedly special beings (even aristocratic young men on horseback) they might be expected to have something special to say to introduce themselves and dilate on their relationship – past, present or future – to the spectators; but something more is needed before a pattern of dramatic action appears.

Another important group of monuments consists of vases with padded or exaggeratedly fat (and sometimes phallic) dancers whose costume seems to relate them on the one hand to the human characters of classical Attic comedy in their conventional stage dress and on the other hand to satyrs and other semi-feral companions of Dionysus. Prominent among these are the Corinthian *komos-*

---

[1] These three vases are nos. 27, 26 and 23 in the List of Monuments in *DTC* 300ff.; they are illustrated in that book and often elsewhere, as in Sifakis (1971) plates i, vi, vii–viii; Bieber (1961) figs. 124, 123, 126; cf. Trendall and Webster (1971) under 1, 12 and 1, 9.

[2] Ar. *Knights* 520ff.: the other choruses referred to are *Barbitistai* 'Lyre-players', *Lydians*, *Psenes* 'Gall-flies' and *Batrachoi* 'Frogs'; the 'lyre-players' could be musical satyrs, the *Ornithes* (*pace* Aristophanes) could as well mean 'Cocks' as 'Birds', and in this instance chronology does not rule out the idea that the two vases actually commemorate the play. Cf. Muscarella (1974) no. 49, a terracotta statuette possibly recalling Aristophanes' *Birds*.

vases which are the subject of a special study by Seeberg (1971); they are the source of some scenes that have often been discussed, since a very influential article by Körte (1893), for the sake of the evidence they may give for early Dorian dramatic dances and hence for the claims by some Dorians to have originated comedy itself. Of special interest here are the elements of story or plot that have been recognized. An amphoriskos in Athens (NM 664), dated 600/575 B.C., shares with other vases a representation of the Return of Hephaestus: Hephaestus had imprisoned Hera by his magic, and now Dionysus and companions bring him home, fuddled with wine on a mule, to release her; two 'padded dancer' figures are present.[1] A fine (but notoriously puzzling) column-krater of the same period in the Louvre (E 632) has two scenes which are possibly to be read in sequence: in one, alongside a dancing padded figure with a companion who pipes for him, two figures named Eunos ('Kindly') and Ophelandros ('Helpmate') are carrying off a krater, watched by a third figure with two sticks, whose name is Omrikos ('Rainer' or 'Umbrian' or what?); while in the other scene two male figures are imprisoned next to a stack of kraters, and a female seems to be bringing them food.[2] The story of the Return of Hephaestus, a popular myth, can be seen as an ancestor, perhaps even as a prototype, of adventures like Dionysus' quest in Hades in Aristophanes' *Frogs*; it is known from Epicharmus, one of the first generation of comedy writers.[3] Eunos and Ophelandros are persuasively interpreted as satyr-like followers of Dionysus in an escapade of stealing wine and then suffering for it (Ombrikos is recorded as a title of Dionysus at Halicarnassus); or they have been taken as thieving slaves; or as part of the preparations for a party; and the story of crime and punishment (if that is what it is) is compared with that of the 'men stealing produce' which (we are told) was a theme of a traditional form of folk-drama in Sparta acted by players called *deikeliktai*.[4] But the party that leads from simple celebration to boisterousness, violence and then redress is a recurrent topic of comedy from Epicharmus onwards;[5] and the transforming effects of wine may be the link between the two scenes of an Attic black-figured cup of 530/510 B.C. in Thebes (BE 64.342), which was first published in 1971. This skyphos has on both sides a frieze of old men with large heads, well taken as representing masks, and long white hair and beard; both times they are accompanied by a piper, but

---

[1] Seeberg (1971) no. 227a (with 227b–c and 228); *DTC* no. 38 and fig. 5 (with nos. 39 and 47; and Attic versions, nos. 8 and 11); Bieber (1961) fig. 130; Trendall and Webster (1971) 1, 9

[2] Seeberg (1971) no. 226; *DTC* no. 41; Bieber (1961) fig. 132; Trendall and Webster (1971) 1, 6.

[3] *Komastai or Hephaestos*: an entry in Photius confirms the subject that the title suggests, but the fragments (84–6 Kai, 47–9 Ol) add little: see further Webster (1959) 62–4 and in *DTC* 171–3, 265; *CGFP* under no. 85.

[4] The source is Sosibius, as cited above, p. 111 n. 4.

[5] Epicharmus 148 Kai, 175 Ol; Ar. *Wasps* 1253–5; and later Eubulus, *Semele or Dionysus* 94 K; Alexis, *Odysseus hyphainon* 156 K.

the first set stride or dance along in a decorous way, wearing large *himatia* and leaning on big sticks with white or woollen caps to them; the second set are standing on their heads waving their legs to the music, like Hippoclides half a century before, who did this in front of his prospective father-in-law, and 'danced away his marriage';[1] one recalls also Philocleon in Aristophanes' *Wasps*, and his progress from respectable (if obsessive) juryman to uninhibited reveller (1253–5; 1299ff.).

If the useful result of investigating the structure of fifth-century comedy proves to be the recognition of basic and potentially productive patterns rather than the extraction of a single archetypal proto-form, the study of pre-literary *komoi* may likewise be better directed towards those elements of myth and motif which we can see were productive rather than to a search for origins and development in an Aristotelian sense. Yet one of the most interesting circumstances (it may be) is revealed by Aristotle's remark that comedy 'was not taken seriously' from the first, and gained official recognition at Athens relatively late. There may have been many centuries of pre-history in which cult-ceremonies made no recognizable move in the direction of drama. Judged by the test of results, the most significant moves in that direction were made in sixth-century Attica, though one sees that cross-influences between different cities' institutions could easily occur, and rival claims easily arise over matters that often can have admitted no very precise definition. In time, tragedy and satyr play gained the measure of identity that organized festival competition presupposes; comedy could take, in response to them, a no-holds-barred attitude to conventions, and perhaps carried already, in the variety of forms its early constitution accommodated, the capacity to adapt and transform in the ways it so strikingly did. The mainstream became Attic, and possibly always had been.

As to the Megarians (returning to Aristotle for a moment) not much dependable information survives, but we can at least confirm that there was a local comic tradition from occasional – and of course condescending – references in Attic writers.[2] The claim from the Megarian side that comedy developed there in the time of their democracy seems to be asserting that comedy in the 'iambic' tradition was a Megarian invention. That claim is matched by, and possibly responsible for, the setting up of a founder of Attic comedy called Susarion, from Icaria (like Thespis, the founder of tragedy), and of a date, duly recorded in the third-century Parian chronicle, for the first comic performance (the date fell somewhere between 581 and 560 B.C.: the part of the inscription which gave it is now lost); nor are we astounded to find a tradition that Susarion was a

---

[1] Trendall and Webster (1971) 1, 13, referring *inter alia* to Hdt. 6.129 for Hippoclides and to Pollux 4.104 for a Laconian dance of *hypogypones*, old men with sticks.

[2] 'Laughter stolen from Megara', of stock routines, Ar. *Wasps* 57 (422 B.C.); other allusions by contemporaries in Eupolis 244 K (referred to above, p. 105 n. 1) and Myrtilus, *Titanopanes* 1 K; earlier, Ecphantides 2 K.

Megarian anyway.[1] What core of truth there is in all this will probably never be known. If there had been any substantial amount of information about sixth-century comic artists in the Athens of Aristotle's day, it is hard to credit that what we gather from him about the dispute over priorities would take the form it does; but the pointers to the earlier sixth century are interesting in view of the independent evidence from the *komoi* of the vases, which must have been organized by someone, 'volunteer' or whoever. Epicharmus, though we know much less of him than we should like, is of a different order of reality; and if Plato and Theocritus can rank him as the supreme writer of comedy and as its inventor, then the citizens of the Sicilian Megara, which claimed him as a favourite son, were not simply men labouring under delusions of local loyalty.[2] It is to Epicharmus and the west that we should now briefly turn our attention, before further exploration of the Attic mainstream.

4. EPICHARMUS AND OTHERS

Syracuse was a Corinthian colony; Corinthian influence has been seen in sixth-century representations of dancers produced in Sicily;[3] and there are reports from Hellenistic sources of *komoi* in the west similar to those of the Greek homelands and like them of indeterminable antiquity.[4] The early colonists could have been expected to transport and foster institutions from their mother-cities; but growth is often different under another sky. Epicharmus, by repute, lived to be 90 or more; he was perhaps born, as some think, as early as the mid-sixth century; in later ages, and possibly from his own lifetime onwards, he acquired a remarkable reputation as guide, philosopher and friend to everyman from the miscellaneous didactic poetry that circulated under his name. If we believe that he really was 'much earlier' than the Athenians Chionides and Magnes, we may wish to think of him as active at a date before 500 B.C.;[5] but for our purposes, he comes most clearly into focus as a comic writer in the Syracuse of Hieron I in the 470s, in a circle whose distinguished visitors included the lyric poets Simonides, Bacchylides and Pindar, and the tragedian Aeschylus, who wrote his *Aetnaeae* in honour of the foundation of a new city of Aetna and also gave the *Persae* its Sicilian première. In writings of this time Epicharmus

---

[1] Parian chronicle: *IG* XII.5, 444 ep. 39 = *FGrH* 239 A 39, quoted with other relevant texts in *IEG* II 147–8; cf. West (1974) 183f.

[2] Plato, *Tht.* 152e; Theocritus, *Ep.* 18, an inscription for a statue set up in Syracuse.

[3] *DTC* nos. 67–8; cf. Payne (1931) 124.

[4] For *phlyakes* as the south Italian equivalent of the Spartan *deikeliktai* etc., see Semus of Delos (quoted above, p. 111 n. 4); and cf. *schol. in Theocr. vetera*, p. 2 Wendel, on a *komos* to Artemis Lyaea at Syracuse: *DTC* 135ff., with text p. 296.

[5] The three ways of escape from Aristotle's 'much earlier' (*Poetics* 1448a33: see above) are that it is corrupt, interpolated, or an exaggeration, and each has found advocates: perhaps most of the data are satisfied if E. was born about 530 and became known in the decade before the first (as opposed to the second) Persian War.

and Pindar both allude to one of Hieron's incursions into mainland Italo-Greek affairs, when he set himself up in 477 B.C. as the protector of the western Locrians;[1] Aeschylus met with the comic poet's mockery over a favourite word of his; but it is (unfortunately) no more than a possible conjecture from the title that Epicharmus' *Persians* is connected with its Aeschylean namesake.[2] References elsewhere to the iambic writings of Aristoxenus of Selinus and to the choliambic poet Ananius suggest that Epicharmus and at least some of those for whom he wrote were well enough acquainted with poetry in the 'iambic tradition'; but the abusive political topicalities of a Cratinus were not for him, and, one supposes, hardly could have been in the ambience of Hieron's court.[3]

Individual play-titles, when we have virtually no text, may only serve to remind us of what we should like to know and do not; but when studied collectively they can show something of the trend of a dramatist's interests. In lists and from quotations, we have some 40 titles of plays by Epicharmus (biographical sources give figures of 35, 40 and 52; but there is no saying in any case what proportion survived of those he wrote); of these, about half indicate subjects from myth, like the *Komastai or Hephaistos* which has been mentioned already in connexion with the Return of Hephaestus as a subject of sixth-century vase-painting. *Komastai or Hephaistos* and at least two other titles (*Bakchai, Dionysoi*) suggest themes from adventures of Dionysus; others who provided subjects for several plays each are Heracles and Odysseus, the hero of strength and the hero of resource. The context often seems to have been given by the story of a confrontation with a special trial, giant or monster, as for instance in *Heracles and the girdle* (of the Amazon Queen, or another?), *Odysseus the deserter* (in the army before Troy), *Bousiris* (Heracles and the king of Egypt who proposed to sacrifice him), *Cyclops*, *Sirens*; and similarly with other heroes, as in *Amykos* (Castor, Pollux and the pugilist king of the Bebrycians); *Pyrrha or Prometheus* (the Flood); *Skiron* (starring Theseus, presumably) and *Sphinx*. The take-off point can be a particular treatment in more serious poetry (and no doubt was, more often than we are sure): the Sirens sing to Odysseus' crew in a parody of a Homeric hexameter; but then, from a scrap of dialogue which survives, the temptation they offer is the typically comic one of feasts with a variety of delicious seafood.[4] The contrast between heroic occasion and unheroic behaviour is seen again in *Odysseus the deserter*, which has been thought

[1] Pindar, *Pyth.* ...Off., with Schol. *ad Pyth.* 1.98 (= Epich. 98 Kai, 121 Ol); it is anyone's guess if the play in question, *Nasoi* 'The Islands' also alluded to the Syracusans' attempt to colonize Pithecusae/Ischia after their famous naval victory over the Etruscans in 474 (Strabo 5.4.9; Livy 8.22.6).

[2] Schol. *ad Aesch. Eum.* 626 (= Epich. 214 Kai, 194 Ol); for Aeschylus' *Persae* in its Sicilian context, cf. Pindar, *Pyth.* 1.71–80, an ode written for Hieron's chariot victory of 470.

[3] Aristoxenus: *Logos kai Logina* 88 Kai, 112 Ol. Ananius: *Hebas gamos* 58 Kai, 22 Ol; note Pindar, *Pyth.* 2.54ff. on Archilochus; and for the abuse in *Megaris* (90 Kai, 114 Ol) cf. *Wasps* 1308ff.

[4] *Seirenes* 123–4 Kai, 70–1 Ol; *Odyssey* 12.184ff.

to take off from the story of Diomedes and Odysseus in *Iliad* 10; it has two characters, probably these two, in a scene where Odysseus seems to be preparing some kind of cover story for an operation that had gone by no means according to plan; in another snatch of text, a Trojan apparently says he has been accused of traffic with the Greeks because he accidentally lost a neighbour's piglet, and one can look ahead to Aristophanes' debunking of the emotions which cause war in the *Acharnians*, with his fiction of the contraband puppy that launches three hundred ships.[1] One of Heracles' gifts to the comedian was his legendary appetite for food and drink. There is a vivid description of him at the table in *Bousiris*, guzzling, champing, snorting and wagging his ears (21 Kai, 8 Ol); his wedding feast in *Hebas gamos* (revised as *Mousai*) called forth a virtuoso narrative, which, to judge from the surviving excerpts, must have catalogued a good number of the edible creatures of the Mediterranean as well as other delicacies.[2] But the flavour of the writing is not easy to catch, whether from short excerpts or gappy papyrus fragments; there is no evidence for the shape and structure of the plays, and no sign of the metrical variety of fifth-century Attic comedy; if the source which reports that two plays were written wholly in one metre really had whole plays and not abridgements, we have to think of a very different use of actors and chorus.[3] That said, there are in the non-mythological as well as in the mythological plays a number of motifs which had interesting developments elsewhere, and it could be among plays of this group above all that Aristotle found a trend towards the kind of comedy whose beginnings in Athens he associated with Crates. Perhaps the most often quoted is a figure with many descendants in fourth-century comedy and its derivatives, the professional sponger or parasite, from *Hope or Wealth* (35 Kai, 103 Ol) – a man who will dine anywhere given an invitation (or not), who flatters and sides with his host at every opportunity, eats and drinks well, and then goes home alone through dark and mud, facing a mugging, to a bed with no bedclothes.

Some other titles are of special interest because they point in two directions, both to Attic drama and to the much less well-documented tradition of the literary mime, which extends from Sophron (whose early years in Syracuse probably overlapped with Epicharmus' old age) to those Hellenistic writers whose work may have been specially influenced by Sophron, among them Theocritus and Herodas. Epicharmus' *Thearoi* 'Visitors to Delphi' (79 Kai, 109 Ol) has a description of dedications to Apollo which recalls Euripides'

[1] *Odysseus automolos* 99–100 Kai, 50–1 Ol, augmented in 1959 by text from *P.Oxy.* 2429, *CGFP* no. 84; Ar. *Ach.* 541ff.

[2] *Hebas gamos/Mousai* 41–75 Kai, 11–40 Ol; among unidentified fragments of Doric comedy is one which may be *Bousiris*: *P.Heid.* 181, *CGFP* no. 223.

[3] Hephaestion, *De metris* 26.10, on *Epinikios* and *Choreuontes*, wholly in anapaestic tetrameters. Some deny that Epicharmus had a chorus at all, probably unrealistically, given some of his plural play-titles; if he had, neither its size nor the distinction between actors and chorus need have been the same as in Attic comedy.

chorus in the *Ion* (184ff.) and Herodas' ladies in a temple of Asclepius in the fourth Mimiamb; to the same family belong Theocritus 15, the ladies at the Adonia, as well as lost works by Aeschylus (*Theoroi or Isthmiastae*), Sophron (*Tai thamenai ta Isthmia*) and a late comic poet Euphron (*Theoroi*, 7 K). Another literary family with representatives in Epicharmus is the dialogue or debate, as of *Land and sea* (23–32 Kai, 93–102 Ol) and *Logos kai Logina* 'His argument and hers' which immediately recalls the two *Logoi* in Aristophanes' *Clouds*, Right Argument and Wrong, as the other recalls a mime-title of Sophron's 'The Fisherman and the rustic'.[1]

There were other writers of comic plays in the Doric dialect besides Epicharmus: we have slight records and remains of Phormis, mentioned as a contemporary, and Deinolochus, of a younger generation. It is fairly easy, and sometimes of significant interest, to mark out common ground between these writers and Attic drama, much harder to be sure how far common developments speak for influence in one direction or the other. The plain story is that in the course of the fifth century, Attic drama became overwhelmingly dominant, and the Athenian festivals set the standard; where local and dialect drama survived, it was not to compete with established tragedy and comedy, but essentially to fill the gap in popular entertainment that full-dress plays left open. Some few names survive of people whose developments or recreations of these local traditions were thought worth remembering; among them is that of Rhinthon of Syracuse (or of Tarentum?) writing about 300 B.C. and blending, apparently, the literary tradition of tragic burlesque with that of the local festival performers whom the Italian Greeks called *phlyakes*.[2] Once Athenian comedy turned away from its involvement with the life of contemporary Athens and became universal (a movement which, as we have seen, Aristotle traced to Sicily), western Greeks could join others from all quarters in writing in the Attic mode, whether in Athens or elsewhere; but that is basically the story of the age after Aristophanes.

5. MYTHS AND MYTH-MAKING

Near the end of their journey through the Underworld in Aristophanes' *Frogs*, Dionysus and Xanthias hear a mysterious noise, and then see a most remarkable creature, large, frightening, and all shapes at once: now a cow, now a mule, now a beautiful woman; but then suddenly dog-like with a face lit by fire;

---

[1] On this kind of dialogue see Coffey (1976) 29f. Drama and non-dramatic discourse can be very much alike in it, as in a papyrus fragment which has been thought of both as a speech by a comic doctor in a play by Epicharmus and as part of a (?pseudo-)Epicharmean treatise, perhaps *Chiron*, spoken by the centaur Chiron himself: *P.Sak.* inv. 71/2 GP 6 5673, first published by Turner (1976) 48ff.

[2] See above, p. 115 n. 4. Rhinthon is later than the last of the so-called 'phlyax vases' which document performances of Attic and of local comedy in southern Italy from the late fifth century through the first three quarters of the fourth: see Trendall (1967) 9ff.

'it must be Empusa', says Dionysus (293); and it has, finally, one leg of bronze and the other of cow-dung. 'The cow-dung', notes Radermacher in his commentary, 'is probably comic invention.'

Comedy can be very interesting for the fragments it preserves of old myths and popular beliefs; and here indeed is a primitive-looking apparition, a sinister compound of animal and human, like a thing from a child's nightmare or a folk-tale. The opposite point, that comedy refashions and recreates its mythical material, is one that is rightly stressed in a valuable study by Hofmann (1976) of myth in comedy with special reference to Aristophanes' *Birds*; and this applies to a story of the creation like the one told in the *Birds* or to the gods and heroes and their adventures at large in just the way that it does to such a detail as the leg of an Underworld bogy.[1] If it is hard to define precisely what we mean by myth, it is not easy either to form a view of the various ways in which myth (in one sense or another) inspired the comic imagination. The possible importance of that source of inspiration has been indicated already by our rough reckoning that about half of Epicharmus' plays had themes from myth. When we come to stress, as we now must, the variety of use that comedy makes of mythological subject matter, Empusa and some kindred figures can open up the topic in a way that may be instructive.

With mythical material, as with anything else in comedy, the control to interpretation given by context is a vital complement to what can be learnt by static analysis and comparison. Empusa in her context in *Frogs* is part of a sequence designed to give the impression of a magical mystery tour through Hades. The leg of cow-dung (let us agree) is probably comic invention; it adds momentarily to the laughter. But whatever else, Empusa has two elements, sexual attractiveness and terror, which are present and emphasized precisely because Dionysus is to react to them: these emotions here and elsewhere in the play are part of the comic portrait (for the god of the *Frogs*, in matters of sex and courage, is a good step nearer those followers of his, the satyrs, than is the god of Euripides' *Bacchae*); and the traditional Empusa figure, with the emphases given by context and comic refashioning, plays its minor part in bringing this out. Later on in the *Frogs*, there is another interesting apparition, namely the dream from Hades which comes to the Girl in Distress in Aeschylus' parody of a Euripidean solo lyric (1331ff.). This is that well-remembered child of black Night, with a shiversome dreadful face, black corpse clad, looking bloody murder, and equipped with a soul that is no soul and big nails. From Rau, Barlow and others one can follow in detail the working of the parody and assess its validity as a reflection of Euripides' lyric style;[2] our point here is simply that this time Aristophanes has put a monster together which is something more than

---

[1] Hofmann (1976) 161ff.; and 177–96 on the creation story in Ar. *Birds* 685ff.
[2] Rau (1967) 132f.; Barlow (1971) 44f.

a denizen of the Underworld: it is part of a demonstration piece in musical and dramatic criticism. Similar components are found in the imagery of political attack. At *Knights* 75ff. Cleon is a relatively plain kind of monster, a giant, all-seeing, with one leg in Pylos and the other in the Assembly, as well as other parts in places chosen to suggest theft, venality and moral turpitude; but at *Peace* 751ff. Aristophanes looks back in anger, and imagines himself having attacked, in the spirit of a Heracles, a creature with a whole gallery of un-amiable characteristics, some of them borrowed from Hesiod's Typhoeus (*Theogony* 820ff.): there is a horrible smell; instead of snake-locks, the tongues of a hundred flatterers surround its head; it has snapping dog-teeth, a voice like a toxic torrent, and so on. In this final example, an element of story or action is just perceptible if we reflect that Aristophanes casts himself in the role of Heracles performing a labour. The unlovely portrait is perhaps something that gave Aristophanes special satisfaction: it is repeated in *Peace* almost word-for-word from *Wasps* (1029ff.).

Of course, more elevated figures still from the mythological pantheon can be pressed into service. For instance, Plutarch's *Life of Pericles* recalls from comedy not only Pericles and Aspasia being satirized as Heracles and Omphale, or Heracles and Deianira, but quotes from Cratinus' *Cheirones* a bogus Theogony in lyric, in which Stasis and Cronos unite to produce the supreme tyrant, Pericles Lord of the Dome (his head, not the sky), and Katapygosyne (Lady Lewdity) bears Aspasia to be his Hera.[1] More elaborately still, in the *Dionysalex-andros*, Cratinus involves Dionysus in a comedy of mistaken identity over the Judgement of Paris and the Trojan War and (we are told) 'Pericles is satirized very cleverly by indirect means as having brought the war on the Athenians'.[2] Perhaps these are enough instances to carry the point that the fifth-century Athenian's inheritance of myth and folk-tale could be exploited in comedy for anything from a passing allusion to a whole sequence of action or plot, and that sometimes complicated sets of overtones could be conveyed. Cratinus' lyric Theogony is being satirical about mythical genealogies and at the same time about certain personal qualities of Pericles and Aspasia, but he also chooses to present it in a manner which debunks the elevation of the high mode of choral lyric. The adventure story of the *Dionysalexandros* is amusing at one level because it makes a romp (and sometimes a decidedly down-to-earth romp) of a story of gods and heroes; but it also gives a kind of framework for reflecting on and criticizing contemporary politics which we can legitimately set alongside the framework from everyday life which Aristophanes provides for his fantasy of Demos and the politicians in the *Knights*.

[1] Plut. *Per.* 3 and 24 (Crat. *Cheirones* 240–1 K): Cratinus called Pericles *kephalegeretas* after *nephelegereta*, the Homeric epithet for Zeus Cloudgatherer.
[2] *P.Oxy.* 663, col. ii fin. = *CGFP* no. 70: see below, pp. 126, 131.

What kinship (if any clearly traceable one) may exist between the comic poet's mode of creating figures like Demos or Right Argument and the process which created figures of myth is a question which needs to be opened here rather than discussed. The special case of mythological comedy which does need our attention is that of myth as reflected in tragedy, and conveyed to the comic stage by derivative and allusive treatments for which there are many varieties and names (travesty, parody, burlesque, quotation, imitation and so on). The full influence of early tragedy on early comedy is not likely to be well assessed without more texts of both than we have; but parody and tragic allusion in Aristophanes have been very carefully studied;[1] we have noted already in discussing structure that Aristophanes' interest in the *Telephus* of Euripides has certain possible implications for the composition of the *Acharnians*, and (little though we still know of the *Telephus*) there is something more to add if one also relates the sequence of incidents in that play to the *Thesmophoriazusae*.[2] Wholesale burlesque of tragedy, especially the thrilling kind of Euripides, is something that begins in the fifth century and is extremely popular in the first half of the fourth; unfortunately, our only complete specimen of this genre is the putative original of Plautus, *Amphitruo*, perhaps to be dated about 330 B.C. What we can sometimes trace is the way in which, in time, comedy absorbs from tragedy some of what might be called the grammar of dramatic composition: a motif or a piece of technique is taken over by way of parody or burlesque, and comes to stay as part of the comic dramatists' stock-in-trade. An example might be the recognition scene in Aristophanes' *Knights*, full of pointed parody, in contrast with that of Menander's *Perikeiromene*, where the fainter hints of a poetic tone are hardly more than a reminder to the audience that life is sometimes like literature.[3]

The words 'myth-making' in the heading to this section were put there to call attention to the point that, though comedy borrows so much of its mythical material, it often transmutes what it takes. There is, of course, quite another sense in which comedy can be said to make myths, and that will escape no one who has considered what the effect of Aristophanes' portraiture has been on the impression posterity has of Socrates, Cleon and Euripides. Further thought on the nature of these portraits must enter into our discussion of some other kinds of comedy; the entry of mythical elements into all of them will make it plain that any tight classification is out of the question.

---

[1] Rau (1967) with bibliography 220–3.

[2] Handley and Rea (1957), Rau (1967) 19–50, Webster (1967) 43–8.

[3] Ar. *Knights* 1232–52, with Rau (1967) 170–3; Menander, *Pk.* 349ff. (779ff. Sandbach), with *Entretiens Hardt* (1970) 126–8 and 41–2; and see below, pp. 133, 143, 168f.

6. POLITICAL COMEDY

The *Acharnians* opens with a scene in which Aristophanes faces the audience for a few moments with a man who, like themselves, is waiting for something to happen. He is thinking over, as perhaps they are, some past experiences of music and drama at the festivals. He specially liked 'the five talents that Cleon disgorged' (6). It is a guess (but a good one) that this is a reference to a recent comedy, probably Aristophanes' own play *Babylonians*, produced the year before. He will return to the topic of that play. What the man is waiting for, it soon appears, is an assembly of the people; but 'the Pnyx here is empty' (20) and he is the only one on time.[1] What he wants is a formal motion on peace with Sparta; all he gets is Reception of Delegates and Reports – or that would have been all, but for the fact that he is an Aristophanic hero, and there is one Amphitheus there, whose pedigree from Demeter (no less) plus a contribution of eight drachmas travelling expenses, makes possible a miraculous journey to Sparta and the personal peace-treaty, the hero's revolutionary idea, from which the rest of the action springs. The mixture of fantasy and realism is about to become more diverting still. There is violent opposition from the men of Acharnae, who form the chorus; their hatred of the enemy is sharpened by what they have lost themselves in the invasions of Attica, and our hero must defend himself. To do this, he borrows, in the way we have already noted, from the role of Euripides' hero Telephus, the king of Mysia who came to Agamemnon's palace in disguise, and found himself defending the Trojans against Greek demands for invasion and revenge.[2] But twice, briefly, yet another identity appears, that of the playwright, speaking with the actor's voice: 'And I know what happened to me with Cleon because of last year's play, when he dragged me into the Council and slandered me practically to death...' (377); 'Cleon will not slander me now for abusing the city in front of foreigners: this is the Lenaea, and we are on our own' (502ff.). This sequence of incidents illustrates as well as any single example can the diversity of elements which make up ancient political comedy. It was, as we gather, an exciting game for a good young player.[3] It is one where the play, at our distance of time, is not at all easy to follow.

We are far from knowing the full story of Cleon's action against Aristophanes. But it shows well enough that in fifth-century Athens, as in other societies which have taken pride in being free, there was still tension, sometimes aggravated into conflict, between those who pushed their freedom to its utter limits

---

[1] Line 20, as quoted here, gives the scene; the man's name, Dicaeopolis, becomes known much later (406).

[2] See above, pp. 109 and 121; and below, pp. 132f.

[3] This view assumes that Aristophanes personally was the object of Cleon's attack; the actor is then speaking for the writer (but need not have been Aristophanes himself); the matter is disputed because the play was officially in the name of Callistratus (above, p. 103; p. 107 with n. 1).

and those who, for various reasons, sought to draw those limits tighter. In or about 442 B.C., when Aristophanes was no more than a child, comic productions at the Lenaea gained the official status they had already had at the Dionysia for some forty-five years.[1] This must reflect some measure of growing public enthusiasm for comedy, even if we allow for the consideration that productions of tragedy were similarly recognized at the same time or soon after. The other side is given by the record of a decree of the year of the archonship of Morychides (440/439 B.C.: schol. *ad* Ar. *Ach.* 67) 'against attacking people by name in comedy'. One would like to know much more about the terms and effects of this measure, and not least who was supposed to be protected by it; it was repealed in the third year after its passing. 'They do not allow comic attacks and abuse directed against the People', says a critic of the Athenian democracy writing not far from this time, 'or they might suffer abuse themselves; but against individuals they encourage this.'[2] In the affair of the *Babylonians*, Cleon must have been able to argue that the production of Aristophanes' play had been contrary to public interest; and Aristophanes, for his part, can hardly have found the proceedings before the Council a pleasant experience. Yet within the year he was at work on the *Knights*, with Cleon cast as a rascally slave, with Demos, the Sovereign People, as a gullible old master (even if he is transformed at the end) and with an unflattering description of a debate in the Council thrown in for good measure.[3] The *Knights* won first prize. Within weeks, the villain of the piece was voted into office as one of the ten generals.

Plainly, in favourable circumstances, both comic poet and politician had a capacity to bounce back from blows which might have been expected to floor them. What happened when popular support was less sustaining is harder to say. What (for instance) did attacks in comedy contribute to the discredit and suspension from office of Pericles in 430?[4] How influential was opposition to the comedy of personal attack (in particular laws against it) in the movement away from that kind of comedy in the later fifth century and the early fourth?[5] The problem with such questions is not only the limited amount of contemporary evidence that bears on them; it is that the nature of comedy's image-making is in itself so infinitely varied. Plato, at all events, was someone who understood and did not underrate the comic poet's capacity to make his images live on in the mind, whether for evil effect or not. In the *Apology* (18b–d, 19c) Socrates

---

[1] *IG* II² 2325, *DFA* 113 with 40f.

[2] Pseudo-Xenophon, *Ath.Pol.* 2.18.

[3] *Knights* in progress, cf. *Ach.* 301; debate in the Council, *Knights* 624ff.; see also *Wasps* 1284ff. with MacDowell (1971) *ad loc.*

[4] See Schwarze (1971) with Gomme (1956) on Thucydides 2.65.4 and de Ste Croix (1972) 231ff.

[5] Horace (*A.P.* 282ff.) and others treat the transformation of comedy by legislation as a fact of literary history; yet the only legislation we know of for sure is the decreee of 440–439 B.C. already mentioned; and its effect was transitory.

COMEDY

presents the *Clouds* as a prime example of the man-in-the-street's idea of him
as an unscrupulous intellectual quack; and it could well be that the play fostered
the prejudice which was to prove so powerful a weapon in his accusers' hands.
Then in the *Symposium* (221b) Alcibiades is praising Socrates' behaviour as a
member of a defeated and retreating army, and Plato (this time with a more
benevolent recollection of Aristophanes) has him allude to a description, again
in the *Clouds*, of Socrates stalking through the streets of Athens with an air of
superiority to his surroundings, his eyes scanning the scene.

As to political policies, in the *Frogs*, written twenty years after the clash with
Cleon, the chorus is still claiming the right to offer the state good advice
(686ff.). Through his chorus, Aristophanes there advocates the restoration of
full citizen rights to the disenfranchised and the dismissal of low-class politicians
in favour of leaders with some of the traditional values and virtues. This does
not perhaps at first sight seem like particularly stirring stuff; but one ancient
scholar is quoted for the statement that the play was so much admired for its
parabasis that it was actually given a repeat performance.[1] Whether or not that
was so, the parabasis in which the advice was given begins with a spiteful
allusion to a contemporary politician who could be taken, and was no doubt
intended to be taken, as a type-specimen of the species that Aristophanes holds
up for disapproval. The politician is Cleophon, with his voice like a Thracian
barbarian's (675ff.); and it was the same man who gave his name to the play
which came third to the *Frogs* in the festival competition, the *Cleophon* of Plato,
the comic poet who was Aristophanes' slightly older contemporary. The years
of war and revolution which have intervened since Aristophanes' youth still
leave it possible, in 405 B.C., for politics to enter into comedy and even to be a
foreground subject of it.

Wars with Sparta and her allies in fact went on almost continuously through
Aristophanes' early life, from his 'teens to his forties; and in modern times, when
war and fear of war have affected people universally, his expression of some of
man's basic longings for peace is something which has had a special appeal.
Yet if we slip into thinking of plays such as *Acharnians*, *Peace* and *Lysistrata*
as if they were part of a political campaign, there is a danger of overlooking
something more basic about the way in which Aristophanic comedy operates.
The pains and problems of the complex, intractable world of political reality
are transformed by Aristophanes into a simpler and more colourful world where
they will yield to a man's wishes if he has pluck and luck enough. That is not to
say that the portrait of a contemporary situation can simply take leave of reality.
There would be no fun in a new fantastic solution to the real world's problems
if the real world itself seemed to be being left behind. The comic poet can be an
acute observer, and may be motivated by strong (and not necessarily system-

---

[1] Dicaearchus in Ar. *Frogs* hyp. 1 (= fr. 84 Wehrli).

atized) views of his own. But his selection of detail and his presentation of issues and arguments need only answer to the demands he sets himself within the medium of a comic play designed to amuse a large audience and capture the public imagination; he need not respond to the different demands which would be made of a documentary reporter or a propagandist.[1]

Wars bring death, mutilation and misery; but comedy does not dwell on these things. Its portrait of the effects of war, much like that in some wartime plays of later ages, is more of the ordinary man's frustrations, discomforts and longing for a better life. The painful depths remain unplumbed, just as the heights of courage or patriotic devotion are not scaled. But ordinary everyday things, on which most people focus for most of their lives, have more evocative power than is commonly admitted; and it would be wrong, if we return again for an example to the opening of the *Acharnians*, to see no more than an amusing allusive monologue in the words of the man who, as he says, hates the city and longs for the place where he belongs, his home in the country where he could produce basic necessities and not have to buy them from traders in the streets (33–5). The theme of peace and plenty and rustic bliss is a recurrent one in this play and the *Peace*, as well as in the fragments of *Georgoi* (so one would expect from a play with a chorus of farmers); and after several years of war, the audience can hardly have needed much prompting to respond to it.[2] But Aristophanes is often much more direct. 'How can you say you love the People?' Cleon is asked in the *Knights*, '– when for seven years now you've seen them living in barrels and turrets and places for vultures to nest in, and you don't care: you've got them shut up and you're taking all the honey'; and still (the accusation continues) you scorn and reject proposals for peace when we get them.[3] The 'No Peace, no Sex' campaign, the brilliant idea by which the women in the *Lysistrata* end the war, is a theme which allows Aristophanes to give something of a woman's-eye viewpoint. There is the wife who wants news (510ff.): 'Often enough, at home, we'd hear how you men had gone wrong over something big; and we'd smile and ask with a sinking feeling inside "What was it you decided to add to the treaty in the Assembly today?" "What's that to you?" he'd say, "Shut up!" And I did.' Then later (591ff.) Lysistrata points out that though she and the other wives miss their men in wartime, it is worse for the girls growing old without a husband. 'But don't men grow old too?' she is asked. 'Not the same thing at all. A man can come back from the war with grey hair, and he's married to a young girl in no time; but women are so soon past their best...' Naturally there were other sides to the picture of war: the young cavalrymen

---

[1] The point is well put by Gomme (1938) 102f.; on A.'s political outlook in general, see de Ste Croix (1972) 355–71.

[2] See for instance *Ach.* 247–79, 665ff., 989ff. (p. 105 above); *Georgoi* frs. 107, 109, 110 K; *Peace* 556ff., 571ff., 1140ff.

[3] Ar. *Knights* 792–6; for background see Thuc. 2.16–17, 52.2; 4.15–23, 41.4.

who form the chorus of *Knights* present themselves with plenty of panache; Dionysus recruited to the fleet can be drilled by Phormio like the rawest of raw recruits; early in the war, Pericles can be accused by a comic poet of downright cowardice for not living up to his brave oratory.[1] But basically, war and comedy did not agree with each other; and if the Aristophanes of *Peace* and *Lysistrata* sometimes seems over-sentimental in his vision of the warring states working together for peace and rejoicing together when they get it, there is still no reason to deny him a core of sincere pacifist feeling beneath all that.

One thing which the comic poet shares with the common man is a realistic, not to say earthy, attitude to the motives on which people act, especially eminent people. Thus in the passage of *Knights* referred to above, it is not enough simply to charge Cleon with not caring about overcrowding in Athens; it is insinuated by the metaphor of taking honey from the bees that he is somehow using the situation to line his pockets as well. Bribery and corruption, with whatever truth or degree of truth, are constantly said to have been at work whenever a person or a policy earns strong dislike; personal idiosyncrasies, especially social and sexual behaviour, are freely admitted to a kind of relevance by association. Pericles 'the Olympian' and his Aspasia, as we have noted, lent themselves readily to translation into a number of mythological roles.[2] The insinuation in Cratinus' *Dionysalexandros* that Pericles somehow, like Paris, plunged the world into war from self-interest, for the sake of a woman, is akin to, and may in part have inspired, the notion in Aristophanes' *Acharnians* that the root cause of the whole embroilment was three brothel-girls, one kidnapped Megarian and two from Aspasia's house taken in retaliation: that was why the Olympian stirred up a certain local commercial friction with his Megarian decree worded like a drinking song (*Ach.* 515ff.). Looking back in the *Peace*, in a passage which has been called a 'malicious and quite unnecessary sideswipe at Pericles', Aristophanes has Hermes say that the trouble began with the trial of Phidias (he was accused of fraud over gold supplied for the making of the statue of Athena for the Parthenon); and then Pericles stirred up the flames of war to make a smoke screen for himself and avoid any similar attacks.[3] Fortunes change: inside ten years, in the *Demoi*, Eupolis is resurrecting Pericles as one of the great statesmen of the past who will scrutinize Athens' present condition and advise her.

The scope of ancient political comedy is wide. It ranges from passing

[1] Ar. *Knights* 498–610 (above, p. 107); Dionysus joins Phormio's fleet in Eupolis, *Taxiarchoi* (250ff. K, with *P.Oxy.* 2740 = *CGFP* 98; and cf. pp. 131ff. below; Pericles as 'King of the Satyrs', Hermippus, *Moirai* 46 K, cf. Schwarze (1971) 101–9.

[2] See above, p. 120 with n. 1.

[3] *Peace* 605ff.; the quotation is from de Ste Croix (1972) 371; for attacks on Pericles' friends, see Gomme (1956) on Thuc. 2.65.4.

allusions to contemporary people and events as far as the embodiment of a whole political situation in a play; and that situation can be transformed just as well into a setting from myth as it can into one of everyday life. But further, since the field of Athenian public affairs that might be called political is so extensive, a discussion of political comedy could take illustrations from many more passages and deal with many more topics than have been selected here – not least passages concerning the management of state finances and the administration of justice. In those areas, political comedy, especially as seen in the *Wasps*, shades over into what is more conveniently called social comedy. As to their political attitudes, comic poets, as critics of the present, are very easily labelled by turns as conservatives and as idealists; for they most naturally contrast what is bad now with what was good then or what would be good if... For Aristophanes, in so far as we can recognize the man beneath the work, there seems no reason to deny either label; yet for someone of Cratinus' generation, he was a smart young man, tarred with the same brush of intellectualism as Euripides.[1] One feature of the representation of public affairs in comedy, whatever selection we make, is so prominent in its importance both for a historical and for a literary approach that it deserves a final word of stress. That feature is the element of creative imagination or fantasy which dominates the design of a play, however true to the real world details and individual incidents or characters may be; for one good part of the effect of the well-conceived play is to offer an escape from that world into a fictional one where dreams (or at least some of them) come true.[2] It is that aspect of comic invention which must be our next main concern.

7. ADVENTURE AND FANTASY

The *Birds* of Aristophanes begins with the entry of two men who are on a journey. Popular fiction is fond of far away places; and fifth-century Greek comedy is no exception. The very idea that people are travelling, be it far or near, is one that can be relied upon to make reader or audience take notice. Three other plays of the eleven, *Thesmophoriazusae*, *Frogs* and *Plutus*, all begin with two people going somewhere. In *Birds* (as indeed in *Peace*) the journey is to the world above the earth; in *Frogs*, as in the *Demoi* of Eupolis and in other plays known only from fragments, a part of the action takes place in Hades. The dramatist enacts an escape from the world about us by physical transposition of the action into another.

The *Birds* missed the first prize in 414 B.C., but won second. One wonders if anyone asked Aristophanes, in the course of the celebrations, how he arrived at

---

[1] Cratinus 307 K kills two birds with one stone by coining the verb *Euripidaristophanizein*.
[2] This point is well taken by Connor (1971) 180f.

the idea that two people should leave Athens in search of peace and quiet and end up founding a new city in the sky, Nephelokokkygia – that Cloudcuckooland whose name has entered the English language as that of a specially insubstantial kind of Utopia. Perhaps he could have told his questioner, perhaps not: creating is one thing, reconstructing the process another. For readers of a remote age, there are still more hazards in the way; yet there is still some point in reflecting on certain of the elements in the creation and how they relate to each other, even if we do not presume to be drawing an Aristophanic mental map.

Why birds for a chorus? *Ornithes* was not a novel title; and Aristophanes had known as much for ten years and more (*Knights* 522: above, p. 112 with n. 2). But the non-human chorus, which we have taken (and Aristophanes himself may have taken) as a survival from a very primitive type of comedy, is something that still held its place in the later fifth century precisely because it continued to offer possibilities to the imagination. Not least, such a chorus, by challenging or inviting the audience to identify with it, offers a kind of transposition, not necessarily in physical space (though moving to the bird-world in the sky does this) but at any rate into a new non-conventional and perhaps purely escapist system of values. 'If you will follow our way' the argument tends to run 'you will have all these good things which you do not now have.' Accordingly, Aristophanes' chorus of birds, after more elaborate claims on the attention of mankind, which include asserting their role in the Creation,[1] at last come on to some very concrete benefits of being winged: with wings, a man could go home from the theatre for lunch and return; he could fly off and ease himself in comfort; or he could fit in a visit to another man's wife while her husband was safe in his front seat (785–96). Two variants of the same motif can be noted in passing. At *Clouds* 1115–30, the chorus of Clouds addresses the judges, promising them good weather if they favour the play, and bad if not (in the event they did not);[2] and in a fragment of the *Theria* of Crates the animals which gave the play its name are to be found arguing the benefits of men eating radishes and fish: this was in fact one of a series of plays with fantasies on the 'Land of Cockaigne' theme – free and effortless food, whether in an idealized past or somewhere else over the rainbow.[3]

One can of course have a fantastic plot without running to a non-human chorus, just as one can have a strikingly decorative chorus without imitating the creations of nature. But the choice of birds as a chorus gave Aristophanes some very special opportunities, visual and musical, and one can see from the text how eagerly he grasped both. It is a main function of the first two hundred lines of the play to build up to an elaborate sequence of song and choral

[1] See Hofmann (1976) quoted above, p. 119 with n. 1.

[2] The play came third, and Aristophanes did not conceal his disappointment (hyp. VI Coulon with 524f.); for the form of this appeal, cf. *Birds* 1101ff.

[3] On this theme see Baldry (1953).

parade.[1] The bird motif is present from the first, and in a form typical of the way in which Aristophanes creates stage spectacle from language. *Ornis* means both 'bird' and, by extension, 'omen'. Ordinary men might be expected to have an omen for their journey, but Aristophanes' two heroes have the literal thing, a bird each from the market. Their errand is to a bird-man, Tereus, the legendary king who became the hoopoe. Before they meet him, there is a preliminary routine with a bird-servant;[2] then dialogue with the Hoopoe leads to the idea of founding a new bird city, and the birds are to be called together to be persuaded. Music and song are natural to the occasion. The Hoopoe first calls to his mate, Procne, the nightingale, in an attractive little lyric (209ff.), to which the response is nightingale song in the form of a solo by the piper; and then he summons at large birds of field and garden, of mountain, marsh and sea (227ff.). The words ingeniously slip from bird-call to human speech and back again; the metrical structure hints, but hints clearly, at a virtuoso song and dance with changing mode and movements as each group of birds is summoned.[3] At last, when the birds do arrive, there are individual decorative costumes to excite comments and wonder. There were other plays in which members of the chorus had individual identities (Eupolis' play *Poleis*, for example, appears to have had a chorus of individually named cities, frs. 231–3 K), but it is hard to see that there can have been a better opportunity for show. Certainly for later ages the *Birds* represents the musical side of ancient comedy at its spectacular peak.

Less tangible, perhaps, but still significant as a constituent of the play, is the set of ideas which relate to air and the elevated setting in the sky. 'Elevated', *meteoros*, is a word which prompted one of Aristophanes' best-known visual jokes of all, when in the *Clouds* he presents Socrates elevating himself literally in a basket so that he can raise his mind (figuratively) to higher things and mix his thought with the air which (he asserts) is its like (227ff.); similarly, words for 'fly' and 'take wing' (as at *Clouds* 319) can refer to intellectual excitement as well as literal elevation. The relationship between *Clouds* and *Birds* in the use of this complex of imagery has been perceptively recognized;[4] and it is well represented in the long sequence with the men who want wings from the new bird city. Cinesias, the dithyrambic poet, wants wings to fly and collect material for preludes from the clouds, preludes full of air, snowflakes and heavenly chinroacuro (1383ff.). An informer, who is the next applicant, is given a discourse on the power of words to make men's minds 'take wing' (1437ff.). There is a way in which the whole play can be seen as an imaginative take-off from reality into a world of air in which a man with nerve and a good gift of

---

[1] Gelzer (1976) gives a well-balanced discussion of the early part of *Birds*.
[2] Like master, like man: so with Euripides' servant at *Ach.* 395ff. and Agathon's at *Thes.* 39ff.
[3] Fraenkel (1950); Dale (1959).   [4] Gelzer (1956) esp. 79ff.

arguing can have things all his own way and end by bringing even the Olympian gods to make terms. Gilbert Murray (1933), for whom *Birds* is a type-example of a 'play of escape', gives a good sketch of the trials and tensions of Athenian home and foreign affairs at the time of the play, from which an escape would no doubt have been welcome. There were many things of pressing concern to contemporary Athenians which do not strike the surface in *Birds*. On the other hand, as Murray rightly emphasizes, there are still stinging references to some of Aristophanes' pet political hates – Cleonymus, Peisandros, Dieitrephes, Cleisthenes. Typically of the technique of political comedy, these men are mercilessly attacked for their real or exaggerated personal foibles, a godsend to the modern political cartoonist just as to the ancient comic poet: a fat figure, lack of a beard when most men wore one, the classic cowardice of throwing away one's shield in a retreat that has become a rout.

There is, for all that, in *Birds* as in other fifth-century comedy, another kind of engagement with reality which has a special role in relation to plays with fantastic situations. Somehow, it seems, the dream is only delectable if the real world keeps rearing its head. So if (as happens at 1035ff.) a professional drafter of decrees visits Cloudcuckooland, his offerings – which, be it noted, are in prose[1] – are not only amusing as a reflection of the ways of political legislators: we recognize the invasion of the real world into the clouds as having a function akin to those vividly realistic elements we sometimes meet in pleasant dreams. The mission of Poseidon, Heracles and a foreign god to negotiate a deal with the birds has both elements of fantasy and elements of satire against established (in so far as it can be called established) Olympian religion. But what is also interesting, not least with the perspective given by our knowledge of later developments in comedy, is the degree of character contrast between three individuals engaged in the same action: Poseidon, consciously senior; Heracles, tough and simple, ruled by appetite and mood; foreign god, the racially under-privileged element, with (among his other problems) broken Greek. At the beginning of the scene (1565ff.) an extra dimension is given by the fact that Our Hero, whom the gods have come to visit, is far too preoccupied with cookery (grilling birds, condemned rebels against the ornithocracy) to notice his visitors; as negotiations develop, points of Attic law (including a quotation from Solon, 1661ff.) come into the argument: these realistic details point up the fantasy, the satire and the component (in so far as we recognize it) of social commentary.

Of the play that was placed first over *Birds*, the *Komastai* 'Revellers' of Ameipsias, we know no more than that one fact. Third came a play of which just enough is known to make us wish, as so often, that we had more: namely, the *Monotropos* 'Solitary' of Phrynichus. 'I am called solitary –' (so runs a quotation, fr. 18 K) 'I live the life of Timon: no wife, no slaves, sharp temper,

---

[1] So is the law quoted at 1661ff., and the prayer at *Thes.* 295ff.

unapproachable, mirthless, speechless, my own man entirely.' Here was another way of escape – misanthropy, the conscious rejection of one's fellow men and their ways. A few years earlier, at the Lenaean festival of 420 B.C., Pherecrates had put on a play *Agrioi* 'Savages' whose chorus apparently gave a collective portrait of a similar sort, of life without its conventional values and encumbrances. Timon appears again as a type-example of misanthropy at *Birds* 1549, and once more when Aristophanes takes up the theme in 411 B.C. in a lyric of *Lysistrata* (805ff.). Two points concern us here. Timon of Athens, thanks above all to Lucian and Shakespeare, is better known as a fictional personality than as a real one; but real he apparently was, and he is worth remembering as an example of the way in which real people do lend parts of their identities to imaginative creations. What begins as satirical portraiture of an individual sometimes persists and contributes to the establishment of a dramatic type. It does not of course follow that Pherecrates or Phrynichus was interested in the ethical motivation of their respective misanthropes in the way that Menander was interested in the hero of his *Dyskolos* or *Misanthrope* a century later (indeed it is most improbable that either was). But if Timon is first of all useful as a reminder of one more way in which reality becomes fantasy, a kind of comedy which turns on one or more of its characters' social behaviour is well worth observing as one of the fifth-century developments which was to have a long future.

If 'fantasy' in this discussion has seemed to be a somewhat elastic term, there are ways in which 'adventure' could be stretched even further. Merely to encounter a body of (let us say) Ant-men, a chorus of Goats or Fish, makes for an adventure as typical of Old Comedy as it is untypical of life or literature in general. Yet there is one kind of adventure story which deserves special mention here, however brief. That is the kind which involves adventures of the god of drama himself, Dionysus, of which the type-example is *Frogs*; other plays with Dionysus by Aristophanes' principal rivals have already been referred to above, namely *Dionysalexandros* by Cratinus and *Taxiarchoi* by Eupolis.[1]

Adventures of Dionysus are a theme common to tragedy, satyr play and comedy. From the point of view of comedy they have a particular interest, like that of the animal choruses, in representing what is very likely to be a primitive element with a very long history which still held its place in fifth-century competitions. A motif which is recurrent in Dionysus plays and which has a future in plots of adventure and mistaken identity, is that which can be conveniently called disguise (the precise application of this term to a god in one or more human roles is not something that need detain us here). In *Dionysalexandros*,

---

[1] *Dionysalexandros*, *P.Oxy.* 663, as cited above, p 120 with n. 2, with quoted fragments 37ff. K; it is arguable that *P.Oxy.* 2806 (*CGFP* *76) is from the play's parabasis: Handley (1982a). *Taxiarchoi*, see p. 126 n. 1.

Dionysus, for what reason we do not know, appears in the role of a shepherd on Mount Ida, no doubt a bungling novice, and finds himself standing in for Paris, judging the goddesses' beauty-contest, collecting Helen from Troy, vainly disguising himself as a ram and her as something else (perhaps a goose) in order to escape detection and revenge; then finally he is handed over to an imprisonment which – we are sure – he will escape. The chorus was of satyrs (though there may have been a subsidiary chorus of shepherds or herdsmen); the occasion of the play, for the sake of which we have referred to it already, was an elaborately contrived attack on Pericles. In *Taxiarchoi* (the chorus was presumably made up of officers of that rank), Dionysus is not a *soi-disant* shepherd, but a recruit to the fleet of Admiral Phormio, in which (among other things) he learns some drill and has a rowing lesson which Aristophanes very likely remembered when it came to the rowing scene of *Frogs*.[1]

Frogs, like *Birds*, is a play with a very full measure of music and poetry; and that is by no means solely because it has a contest between tragedians as a major theme. Like *Birds* with its re-embodiment of the creation myth, it refashions for its Dionysiac adventure plot a set of popular images of the Under-world. As with *Ornithes*, Aristophanes knew *Batrachoi* as a very old title.[2] The *Frogs*' chorus, which is a splendid extra, gives place to the chorus of Initiates in the Mysteries for the elaborate sequence of processional hymns which is the choral parodos. Dionysus, first playing Heracles, then as literary critic, has an air of the happy amateur such as we seem to recognize in him when he plays shepherd or sailor. Looking back from later comedy, we can see how this early comic tradition of adventure with mythical background is very heavily overlaid by the type of myth-burlesque which derives primarily from tragedy, especially the later and more adventurous kind of Euripidean tragedy. That, together with the part of *Frogs* which means most to most people, the literary debate, will be among the topics which concern us next.

8. THE LIFE OF THE MIND

In 438 B.C., when Euripides produced the tetralogy of plays which includes *Telephus*, Aristophanes was still a boy. He may have seen the production on his first or an early visit to the theatre; but whether or not, thirteen years later in *Acharnians*, we find him using one of the high spots of the play, its hero's major speech, as a model for a speech by the hero of his comedy, and taking over much of the context as well. Another fourteen years pass: in 411, in *Thesmophoriazusae*, the whole sequence is remade for a quite different dramatic context. In *Frogs*, in 405, the famous play of a generation ago is still fair game; even in *Plutus*

---

[1] Cf. Wilson (1974); Harrison (1976) 137; Handley (1982 b).
[2] See p. 112 with n. 2.

(we are by now fifty years on) there is still an allusion either to *Telephus* or to Aristophanes' own reminiscence of it in *Knights*.[1]

Many other illustrations could be chosen to show that Aristophanes' interest in forms of literature more elevated than the one he practised was not only early but lasting. But a point which the *Telephus* offers immediately is that being topical about politics and being topical about works of the creative mind can be two very different things from the viewpoint of the comic poet and his public. True, there are lasting political issues and there are matters which politicians are never allowed to forget; true also that some literary and intellectual movements are transitory. But in general the distinction suggested here seems to hold: in the life of the mind there is a certain timelessness, the creator living through his creation, and by most people strongly identified with it; this is something which it is useful to remember as a corrective to the simple idea of comedy as a mirror of the contemporary scene.

Literary allusions in Aristophanes range from Homeric epic to plays produced at the last dramatic festival. Commonest are allusions to the tragedians, and among them much the most prominent is Euripides, who is in fact a character in *Acharnians*, *Thesmophoriazusae* and *Frogs*. Here, as so often, we recognize Aristophanes as heir to a considerable comic tradition. The entertainment that comes from reinterpreting stories of the gods and heroes in new down-to-earth terms is, we find, effectively reinforced by a simultaneous downgrading into the new context of the poetic language of one or another of the previous versions of these stories. A similar verbal incongruity is created when the ordinary man in comedy rises above the everyday language which might have been appropriate to his situation and borrows elevation from a more highly-wrought poetic counterpart of the feelings he is to express. Under the terms allusion, parody and burlesque modern discussions of comedy include a whole galaxy of comic effects of this kind. Examples have been mentioned in other contexts above from early Doric comedy as written by Epicharmus as well as in Attic plays by Aristophanes' much older contemporary Cratinus.[2] Three more references to Cratinus will show that neither literary subject matter nor poets as characters were unexpected on the fifth-century stage. His *Archilochoi*, dated soon after 449 B.C., is a forerunner of the *Frogs* in the sense that it involved a contest between 'Archilochus and company' on the one hand and Homer, perhaps with Hesiod in support, on the other; the *Odysses*, a plural title of the same sort, brought on 'Odysseus and company' in a parody of the Cyclops story from the *Odyssey*; *Pytine* 'Wineflask', the play which won first prize over *Clouds* in 423, had Cratinus himself as a character, in contention between his wife Comedy and his mistress Liquor.

[1] *Plut.* 601, *Knights* 813 = Eur. fr. 713 *TGF*.
[2] Pp. 115ff., 120f.

COMEDY

It is often asked whether there was any more than sheer entertainment in the comic writers' representations of poets and poetry. In one way, perhaps, the question is a reaction against the studious pursuit and discussion of allusions by commentators: can an audience of thousands, one wonders, have shared *en masse* the educated man's reaction to a literary hit? Surely not all of them: but modern experience of satirical revue shows that it is not necessary for all of the people to see all of the jokes all of the time. Laughter is infectious; satire can have several levels; and in theatrical performance voice and gesture, sometimes allied with costume and staging, can add significantly to the effect of the words. A good example, not least because we have the whole of the text being parodied, is the take-off of Euripides' *Helen* in *Thesmophoriazusae* 846–928. The basic situation is clear and broadly comic. Euripides' kinsman (Mnesilochus, as he is often called) has been caught dressed up as a woman acting as his agent at the Thesmophoria. In hope of a rescue he takes on roles from Euripidean adventure plays, first sending a message by a device from *Palamedes*, then turning to last year's productions, *Helen* and *Andromeda*, for Euripides to play the hero to his heroine in distress. When we come to detail, not only is the mock-tragic elevation of the two principals brought down to earth time and time again by the presence and interventions of a third party, an uncomprehending guard, but there are extra nuances of criticism, direct or implied. For instance, the long prologue speech of the *Helen* is transacted in 16 lines, including interruptions, with a wickedly precise selection of quotations; there are elements of visual and musical parody (855, at Proteus' tomb; 914f., lyrical moment of recognition); and there are minor quirks and distortions of language which would puzzle no one amid the general amusement, but add to the refinement of appreciation by those who knew their Euripides well.[1]

The same multiplicity of appeal is surely to be recognized in the sequence of scenes which represents the peak of ancient literary comedy, the contest between Aeschylus and Euripides in the second half of *Frogs*. It is interesting that after the Dionysiac adventure story of the first half of the play, Aristophanes takes special care to build up to the agon between the poets (738–894, prefacing 895ff.); then immediately after their debate he sets out to anticipate, by sheer flattery of the audience, any lurking objection that the scenes of competition that follow will be too highbrow (1099–118).[2] Even lacking the music, we can make something of the caricature of Aeschylean lyrics by Euripides, and of Euripidean by Aeschylus: the Aeschylean parody is full of heroes' names and recalls epic or early choral poetry with its trailing dactylic rhythms; the specimens of choral writing and solo in the manner of Euripides are presided over by a muse who appears in the role of a castanet dancer and are represented by

[1] For detailed discussion see Rau (1967) 53–65.
[2] Not only are they clever; they even read books: cf. *CHCL* I, Part 4, 162 and Turner (1952) 22.

134

Aeschylus as trivial, modern and debased below the standards of true tragic art.[1] There is a level at which all this can be appreciated as sheer ragging. There is another, potentially more serious level of appreciation if we respond not only to the portrayal of the two contrasted styles but to the technical criticisms of the metric of the lyrics, both explicit (as at 1323) and implied. But there are two other levels at which both the contrast of lyrics operates and the whole literary debate of which it is part. The individual arguments, jokes and illustrations are part of an antithesis between traditional and modern in tragedy, as it might be a clash of generations; and they are part of a further antithesis between traditional and modern morality, a clash of ideals. It is no accident that in the *Daitales* 'Banqueters' of 427 B.C., Aristophanes' first production, the Good Son has been reared on Homer and the Bad Son on rhetoric, or that Phidippides in the *Clouds* gives his father such grief by condemning Simonides and Aeschylus, and reciting a speech of Euripides about incest between brother and sister (1371).[2] The doctrine, to put it in Aeschylus' words from the *Frogs* (1054f.) is that 'little children have a schoolmaster to teach them; but the youth have the poets'. The idea that literature is to do with education is one that still causes deeply engaged argument; and it may well be that the *Frogs* was a force in its first formulation and eventual diffusion.[3]

If we ask what part the personalities of the two debating poets, Aeschylus and Euripides, have to play in this picture, it will be as well to remember that Aeschylus had been dead for more than 50 years, some years before Aristophanes was born, and neither the comic poet nor the vast majority of the audience could possibly have had any personal memory of him. Euripides could have been (though we have no reason to suppose he was) a familiar Athenian figure with personal idiosyncrasies recognizable to many; but even so, unless any feature could in some way be related to aspects of his dramatic technique, it could hardly be helpful to the overall comic effect and might even prove distracting. The scene in *Acharnians* (407ff.) of Euripides composing at home with his feet up, surrounded by the costumes of past productions, is one that at first sight might look like portraiture; but the portrait is very much more of the type of intellectual poet than of an individual; it is closely related to the purposes of the context and has close kin in the portrait of Agathon in *Thesmophoria{u}usae* (95ff.) and in a long series of works of art with portraits of poets composing.[4] If we can rely on the independence of the tradition that Agathon was a handsome man, then the scene in *Thesmophoria{u}usae* does exploit a personal characteristic in the course of a satirical portrait of the writer's poetry. The idea, interesting

---

[1] Rau (1967) 125ff.; cf. Barlow (1971) 44f.

[2] *Daitales* 198ff. K, esp. 198, 222 (= frs. 1, 28 Cassio (1977)); note also *Clouds* 964ff. on musical education old and new.

[3] Snell (1953) 113–35.   [4] Handley (1973) 106.

as part of the early history of the concept of mimesis, is that the beautiful write beautifully, that it is logical to dress up as a woman to write about women, and so on. But essentially the portrait is of the poetry, not of the person.[1]

The plain man's view of the intellectual is, as we have seen, a prominent ingredient in comedy's portraits of the literary scene. So it is, as would naturally be expected, when we come to philosophers and the comedy of ideas. The line is led by *Clouds*, with Socrates as a character; but Aristophanes was not alone in this genre: there are immediately to hand some interesting parallels with plays by contemporaries from which we may select. In *Clouds* (95ff.) the audience's first intimation of the topics which are discussed in Socrates' Reflectory is the idea that the cosmos can be understood in terms of a stove; this is noted by a commentator as having been used already by Cratinus in ridiculing the natural philosophy of Hippon of Samos.[2] Then in the *Konnos* of Ameipsias, the play that came second over *Clouds* in 423, Socrates is referred to as hungry and lacking a cloak, in a way which recalls the lines in the *Clouds* about 'the rogues, the pale shoeless men of the company of the miserable Socrates and Chairephon' (102ff.). Callias, and the sophists whose company he kept, were the target of satire in Eupolis' *Kolakes*, placed first over *Peace* in 421 (the setting of the house of Callias was used again by Plato in his *Protagoras*); finally, there is the famous quotation from an unidentified play by Eupolis, which goes: 'I hate Socrates too, the beggar, the idle talker, who has thought out everything else, but how to get food to eat is something he's neglected' (352 K: compare *Clouds* 175-9).

Forewarned as we are by now of the nature of comic portraiture and of the existence of a flourishing style of satire against the philosophers in fifth-century comedy, we need not be surprised either that the initial presentation of Socrates in the *Clouds* is of an old man talking airy nonsense while suspended in the air (218ff.), or that Plato in the *Apology* makes Socrates recall the incident and the part it played in prejudicing people against him (19c, 18b).[3] The basis of the joke is to be found in comedy's constant tendency to take metaphors literally and to translate abstract or intellectually recondite notions into concrete or familiar ones.[4] Socrates, in order to think about things above the mundane level (*meteora*), is literally *meteoros* or 'elevated' himself. But at the same time, the word *meteoros* has a range of meaning which will extend to suggest a variety of things including astronomical interests (Socrates claims to be 'thinking about the sun', 225) and supernormal brainpower (Socrates, as if god speaking to

---

[1] Cf. Bruns (1896) 156ff.; admittedly the joke is funnier because of Agathon's known effeminacy.
[2] Cratinus, *Panoptai* 155 K; DK 38 A 2.
[3] See above, pp. 123f., 129.
[4] This aspect of comic writing is well explored by Newiger (1957); cf. Handley (1959).

mortal, calls his visitor 'creature of a day'); or again, to be *meteoros* is to be in a state of excitement – no longer to have one's feet on the ground – of a kind which the plain man may find insubstantial and vaguely disreputable.[1] It is perhaps in the combination of a direct visual appeal with this periphery of verbal suggestiveness that the power of this comic image lies. But there is more to it than that. When Socrates claims to be mingling his thought with the air which is its like, and goes on to develop the point in quasi-scientific terms, he is parading a philosophical equation between mind or thought and air which was formulated by Diogenes of Apollonia.[2] The Socrates of the *Apology* (loc. cit.) explicitly denies all knowledge of such matters; yet it is possible to suppose that, as with other subjects in which he disclaimed expertise, the historical Socrates would have been willing to argue with the professed experts.

The search for a historical Socrates has been pursued with vigour from the philosophical as well as from the literary viewpoint. Though the fortunes of the Socrates of the *Clouds* have fluctuated in the debate, an approach from the side of comic portraiture makes one doubt, as with the poets of the *Frogs*, whether there is much of the personal and idiosyncratic that survives critical scrutiny, and whether in any case it could have had a primary comic function.[3] If the portraits of Aeschylus and Euripides are in essence portraits derived from a concept of their poetry, that of Socrates is in immediate contrast in having no body of writing on which it could be based. It has been claimed on the one hand that the emphasis on memory and endurance, and the technique of arguing with a pupil are Socratic features of the Socrates of the *Clouds*, but it can still be asked whether they were specifically so; and the figure who is head of a school of unwashed poverty-stricken idlers and teaches disreputable rhetoric is something which, on any reasonable account, is decidedly *un*-Socratic.[4] The verbal portrait of Socrates striding through the streets with an air of superiority to his surroundings does seem, from its recollection by Plato, to be an authentic detail (362; see above, pp. 123f.); but the supposed references to 'midwifery' (especially 137) are both of debatable allusive effect in the *Clouds* and open to question as a Platonic rather than a historical element in the Socratic tradition.[5] Aristophanes, it seems, is giving a portrait not from life, but from the popular image of an educator, which he chooses to hang on to Socrates; it is the worse as biography, but not necessarily the worse as comedy, for that.

[1] See LSJ, s.v. μετέωρος, not forgetting compounds and derivatives; on this group of ideas in *Clouds* and *Birds* especially, see Gelzer (1956) esp. 79ff.

[2] See Dover (1968) on 230–3 for references and discussion.

[3] Basic to this approach (though I do not follow it wholly) is the discussion in Bruns (1896) 181–200 and 201–424 *passim*.

[4] See Schmid (1948) and Philippson (1932), together with the more sceptical view of Dover (1968) xxxii–lvii.

[5] Burnyeat (1977).

By his own account, Aristophanes was pleased with himself when he had written the *Clouds* (521–4). *Acharnians* and *Knights*, in the two previous years, had won first prizes; but this time, notoriously, the result was a third. He made a revised version, which is the version we have. Though we are not clear about the circumstances or (in detail) the extent of the revision, he must have felt – and rightly, as events have proved – that it was a play with a statement to make, a play worth an author's second thoughts. One of the new features was the debate between the two personified Arguments, whether we call them the Worse Cause and the Better, or Wrong and Right, or whatever else (889ff.).

The conflict between generations which has been present as a theme from the first is now elaborated and developed in the form of a conflict of educational ideals; and there is a resemblance in type, as well as in structure, to the debate between the two poets in *Frogs*. Right describes the traditional way of education, painting a picture of decorously-behaved boys at music school and gymnasium learning what their fathers learnt and acquiring a certain gentlemanly athleticism. Wrong skirmishes with him in argument, then gives in his turn a prospectus for the new system, in which the technique of effective argument is supreme: once learn to talk your way out of a situation, and then you can 'indulge your nature, laugh and play, and think that nothing's shameful' (1078). Right defects: unable to beat the opposition, he joins it. From all this, Socrates is absent: 'Your son', he says, 'will learn for himself from the pair of them, and I shall not be there' (886f.). If we ask where Aristophanes' own sympathies lay, whether on these educational issues or on others, the normal (and probably basically correct) answer is that he was conservative, with a strong dash of wishful-thinking idealism about the past. But there are reservations to make. The obvious contrast with what one dislikes in the present is either a recollection of the past, however rose-tinted, or a dream of the future, however fantastic. Comic dramatists, as we have seen, naturally tend in these directions; and they know well what appeal the Good Old Days can have to an audience in a holiday mood. Thus there needs to be room to wonder how far Aristophanes, or any other writer of satirical comedy, is personally engaged in the attitudes which are recurrent in the genre. Secondly, in portraying a clash of ideals, no matter where his own sympathies lay, Aristophanes is much too good a writer to let the contest be too one-sided. In *Clouds*, Right's personality is not wholly sympathetic from the start: the aggressive old man who surrenders in the end to the educational – and sexual – ethics of his opponent's world has already shown a marked weakness for the physical attractions of the young boys whose upbringing he idealizes; Wrong is a rogue, but at times we all admire the dash and cleverness that brings a rogue his success; and so, probably, we are intended to do here. But even so, the balance of appeal need not all be put down to dramatic contrivance. A man of vivid imagination who lived through the political and intellectual revolutions of the age of Aristophanes must have felt his own opinions constantly put under test and stress. It would not be surprising if, as many have with the technological advances of the twentieth century, he admitted the excitements of the new advances of his contemporaries while deploring the accompanying decay of the inherited standards of behaviour and belief. The basic impulse to satirical writing is after all, one suspects, that of a divided mind.

9. THE SOCIAL SCENE

The latter part of Aristophanes' *Wasps* is the occasion of an interesting social gathering. Old Philocleon, the play's hero, has at last been turned, by a trick, away from the passion for jury-service which has obsessed him. He is now to be re-educated. He is given smarter clothes and new shoes, and told how to behave himself in polite company. In the event, he turns out to be a grown-up version of everyone's horror-child. Eventually, he leaves his party, which we have had described to us, and appears as a tipsy reveller on his way home with a girl-friend by torchlight (1326ff.): 'And if you're not naughty, Piglet', he says, 'I'll set you free and make you my mistress when my son's dead.' He goes on to explain that he has no money of his own yet; his son is grumpy and mean, and afraid of his coming to ruin – 'for I'm the only father he's got' (1359). There is a cluster of motifs here that interest us.

The tradition that comedy ends with a revel is likely to be a very ancient one, going back remotely beyond any of our historical documentation.[1] When the revelling of a proto-comic chorus transformed itself to represent a celebration held by men or gods, a wide variety of comic possibilities must have been opened up. Food and feasting lend themselves readily to euphoric description; then, if the behaviour of the revellers is also portrayed in words or action, the way is open to a kind of social criticism. Historically speaking, we can claim that the description of Philocleon's behaviour at the party is in a line of descent from the description of the gluttonous Heracles in Epicharmus.[2] But the reflection of the fashionable world of fifth-century Athens gives another dimension, and raises questions about the qualities of Attic comedy as a mirror of the social scene. Is Aristophanes' representation of everyday life (for example, the language people spoke in conversation) in any sense truer than what we have seen of his treatment of some of the issues and personalities from the public world of contemporary politics or literature? To look at the scene yet again, does the comic exchange of roles between father and son ('for I'm the only father he's got') imply that fathers with young sons in love, so

---

[1] See, e.g., *DTC* 132ff., 301ff.; Ghiron-Bistagne (1976) 207ff.
[2] 21 Kai, 8 Ol: see above, p. 117, and also p. 113 with n. 5 and p. 114 with n. 1.

familiar from fourth-century comedy, were already familiar enough as stage figures for Aristophanes to raise an easy laugh from his audience by standing the convention on its head?[1] If so, is there more background to the Comedy of Manners in fifth-century comedy than one would happily suppose from the general trend of the surviving plays themselves?

One lost play which has a special interest in the context of these questions is the *Korianno* of Pherecrates, Aristophanes' older contemporary, whose *Agrioi* 'Savages' of 420 B.C. has already been noted as one of the fifth-century examples of the misanthrope theme in comedy.[2] *Korianno* takes its title from a woman's name, and we know that she was a woman with lovers, for the play is included by Athenaeus (13.567c) among examples of comedies with the names or nicknames of hetaerae as titles. As in the *Wasps*, comedy is created from the generation gap between father and son, but this time, instead of undergoing a transposition of roles, they seem to be rivals: 'Oh, no: for me to be in love is natural; you're past it ... you're an old man and you're crazy' (frs. 71–2); 'Lord Zeus, do you hear what this wicked son of mine says about me?' (fr. 73). There are also some fragments from a scene with women talking together, waited on by the young daughter of one of them. Fr. 70 reads as follows: 'Undrinkable, Glyke.' 'Mixed you a watery one, did she?' 'All water, I'd say.' 'What *have* you done? How did you mix it, blast you?' 'Two water, Mummy.' 'And wine?' 'Four.' 'Get to Hell: it's the frogs you should be serving.' It is a reasonable, though unverified, guess that Korianno is both the thirsty guest and the object of the rivalry in love.

With the hindsight given by our knowledge of later comedy, we can see what a bright future there was for plays with a love-interest and an ambience of family relationships. The genre-painting (if we may so call it) of the women's drinking-session at once calls to mind the famous opening scene of Menander's *Synaristosai* 'The hen party', adapted by Plautus in his *Cistellaria*.[3] Fathers and sons as rivals in love-affairs also appear in plays of the fourth century that were to become classics, for example in Diphilus, *Kleroumenoi* 'Taking the lot', which we know from Plautus' version in *Casina*;[4] Act III of Menander's *Samia* (206–420) develops to a high emotional peak the situation in which a man thinks that his mistress and his adopted son have betrayed him together and produced a child. It is important here not to outrun our evidence. Comparable extracts from the beginning of *Clouds* (assuming we had them as fragments) could be very temptingly disposed against Terence's *Adelphoe* to suggest that *Clouds* is much more concerned with the internal relationships

[1] Wehrli (1948) 24.
[2] See above, p. 131.
[3] See on this Charitonidis–Kahil–Ginouvès (1970) 41ff.; Oeri (1948) 61, 82ff., 86; and cf. below, p. 145 n. 1.
[4] Wehrli (1948) 56ff. (though 57 n. 2 dismisses *Casina* from its natural company).

of Strepsiades' family than is the case. Moreover, to remind us that *Korianno* is a fifth-century play, and that Pherecrates, like his contemporaries, and unlike his fourth-century successors, had a strong interest in the musical side of drama, we can quote a fragment from a parabasis which is written in the metrical unit which came to be called 'Pherecratean' after him (fr. 79): 'Audience, pay attention to a novel innovation, anapaests in syncopation.'

The problem of evaluation which these quotations present is typical of the difficulties of fragmentary texts. Yet some help with it can be sought from the direction of ancient literary theory. Aristotle, we recall (and indeed others after him) made a distinction in modes of comedy between the comedy of topical satire (that is to say, writing in the mode derived from Archilochus and the iambic poets) and the comedy of fiction (that is to say, making plots with invented characters and general, not particular, reference to the contemporary scene). We met this distinction above, in discussing Aristotle's account of the earliest comic drama (p. 111), and noted his remark that 'plot-composition came first from Sicily; of the Athenians, Crates was the first to move away from the iambic convention and write plots with subjects of general reference'. Crates, for all that Aristophanes looked up to him as one of the Old Masters, has not been kindly treated by posterity; and the few fragments and play-titles which survive do not offer a way to verify Aristotle's placing of him at the head of a literary trend.[1] The matter becomes somewhat more tangible when we are told of Pherecrates by one of the better informed treatises on comedy that he was an actor, that he set himself to follow the example of Crates, that he turned against abuse and made his reputation by introducing new subjects and being inventive in plots.[2] There is much here one could question, beginning, perhaps, with the nature and validity of the distinction there was supposed to be between satirical and fictional comedy, and ending with the notion that Pherecrates came into playwriting by way of acting, which is open to suspicion as a typical device of the ancient biographer to fill the vacuum he abhors.[3] What remains, however, after due scepticism has operated, is a set of observations by someone who knew Pherecrates' work and could link him with Crates as a poet who developed a style of comedy differentiable from that of the great triad of Cratinus, Eupolis and Aristophanes, the true heirs of Archilochus. Accordingly, though we may still not feel confident enough to speak with Gilbert Norwood of 'The School of Crates',[4] there are good reasons for taking seriously what signs we have in Aristophanes and elsewhere of the emergence of that mode of fictional comedy which was to prove dominant.

---

[1] Ar. *Knights* 537–40 and *Second Thesmophoriazusae* fr. 333 K.

[2] Anon. *De com.* II 32ff. Kaibel, III 29ff. Koster.

[3] The same is said of Crates (Anon. *De com.* II 28ff. Kaibel, III 26ff. Koster) and of others, sometimes perhaps rightly; yet the main point seems to be to provide a kind of theatrical lineage.

[4] Norwood (1931) ch. 4; and see Bonanno (1972).

We are concerned not simply with the quantity of the evidence, but with its quality and the circumstances in which it comes to us.

One of the pleasures of comedy that is sometimes undervalued is the pleasure of familiarity. We feel relaxed and at home with ourselves in the presence of what is recognizable from the world around us; we can then respond all the more readily when, in one of an untold number of ways, the representation transcends the reality. Even when Aristophanic comedy is at its most fantastic, it is justifiable to look for the points of contact between the fantasy and the audience's familiar experience; even when the representation seems to be at a level of unaffected realism we need to ask, if we do not wish to be deceived, what the dramatist's fictional purpose was. Since comedy commonly represents kinds of people and activities from everyday life which do not figure in more serious literature, it offers some specially interesting data for the social and economic historian; but he must be prepared to find that the comic poet's attitude to documentation does not have much in common with his own. None the less, when all is said about the distortions of comic fiction, where the portrayal of everyday life is concerned, there is a way in which the 'familiarity principle' that we have envisaged above can work to give some reassurance. The comic poet will distort reality for amusement, or to make propaganda; he will expect his audience to meet him half-way or further in matters of stage representation; and he will stretch reality in the direction of optimism, making people eat more, travel faster, be richer (and so on) than the corresponding man in the street – but the background detail must have a degree of verisimilitude which will convince audiences and not leave them puzzled or hostile. It is the Aristophanic Euripides in the *Frogs* (959) who uses a phrase which the comic poet can hardly have formed in mind without some thought of its applicability to himself: Euripides speaks of bringing familiar things (*oikeia pragmata*) on to the stage, things people knew by personal experience or from close association and on which they could successfully criticize him.

Our knowledge of classical Greek as a spoken language is a compound. We derive it from Aristophanes and the other dramatists and from prose authors, notably Plato, on occasions when they represent people talking naturally together; with the recovery of more Menander, there are even ways in which we can distinguish fifth-century idiom from fourth-century and so sharpen our knowledge of both. The resultant picture is far from perfect, not least in that the written word can never be quite like the spoken word, the composed dialogue not the same as the conversation overheard. One of the pleasures of seeing an Aristophanic comedy must have been, for contemporary audiences, that of hearing people talk as they talked themselves. Yet in fact, as anyone knows who has tried to translate any substantial amount of Aristophanes into modern English, the range of style or tone is wide, and a mood is rarely built up with consistency or sustained for long; the comedy breaks through.

At the lower end of the colloquial (or social) scale comes the broken Greek of such characters as the Triballian in the gods' embassy in *Birds* (1565–693), or the Scythian policeman in *Thesmophoriazusae* (1001ff.); vulgarisms in the speech of the politician Hyperbolus are picked on in a fragment of the *Hyperbolus* of Plato (168 K); at least a proportion of the copious vocabulary of obscenities would be likely to have been heard in the market or the wine-bar.[1] At the upper end of the scale, we might put parody of the talk of the bright young men in the perfume shop, their heads full of the language of their rhetoric teacher; and with this might go the reference in *Wasps* to the aristocratic Alcibiades' lisp.[2] People from outside Attica can be brought on speaking in dialect (it is a hard question how authentic Aristophanes' use of non-Attic dialects was): for example, the Megarian and the Boeotian in *Acharnians* (729ff., 860ff.), Lampito and the other Spartans in *Lysistrata*. A special case of Doric speech in comedy, and one with a lasting tradition, is the doctor, talking the Doric of his Sicilian medical school; there is one line surviving from such a character in a comedy by Crates, and he runs through Middle Comedy to Menander.[3] Realism is here shading into theatrical convention, and it does so in another way when at times of high emotion the language of characters is coloured with quotation, parody, and other borrowed plumage from high poetry.[4] The social portrait given by different kinds of speech easily blends with elements of social or literary satire, as can be seen from the examples given here and many others. When, in the fourth century, comedy strove for a more naturalistic effect, it tended to lose not only the bite but the variety of the age of Aristophanes.

A passage which brings together a number of the points made so far is at *Thesmophoriazusae* 279ff. It begins: 'Here now, Thratta; follow me. Oh, Thratta, look – the torchlight, and all the people coming up, and the clouds of smoke ...' The genre is that which we have sampled in Pherecrates, the women's conversation piece: in fact a representation of someone going with her maid to the Thesmophoria. No great extent of text is needed to suggest that Aristophanes could write as much as he chose in this vein. But there is a twist to the representation, which saves it from the flatness of total familiarity. The character is in fact not a woman, but Euripides' kinsman dressed up as a

---

[1] Henderson (1975) 35ff. distinguishes 'primary obscenities' from metaphorical expressions which can be either current ('frozen wit') or literary.

[2] Bright young men: *Knights* 1375ff., cf. Radermacher (1951) XIII 1; Alcibiades, *Wasps* 44f., cf. Archippus 45 K (from Plutarch, *Alc.* 1).

[3] Crates: 41 K. Alexis, *Mandragorizomene* 142 K (from Athenaeus 14.621d, q.v.); Menander, *Aspis* 439ff. (a man pretending to be a doctor).

[4] See for instance *Knights* 1232ff. (mock-tragic recognition scene: above, p. 121 with n. 3) and *Lys.* 954–79, referred to below, p. 145.

woman, showing just how well he can carry it off; and no doubt the maid is imaginary, giving scope to the actor's talent for mime. The routine continues with an invocation of Demeter and Persephone, the offering of a cake which the maid is supposed to produce from its container; and then there is a prayer for a daughter to find a rich, stupid husband and for a son to grow up sensible – but they are referred to not as son and daughter, but in terms of their sexual organs. The kinsman is not, after all, quite the perfect middle-class housewife.

It has been said that Aristophanes sometimes cares more to have a remark made than who makes it. But the comic effect on such occasions is not simply that of the unexpected: the breaking of the image which was being built up coincides with the breaking of the normal social ban against verbal explicitness in matters of sex; and the appeal is suddenly not to our sense of realism but to our sense of fantasy, as Aristophanes lets the character say what the audience will enjoy hearing such a person say (like the stage bishop being driven to swear).

Women have major parts in both *Lysistrata* and *Thesmophoriazusae*; and there many times over, and on a much larger scale, we can examine the compounding of realistic and comic elements in the way that they and the social life around them are portrayed. They are not, of course, any more than Euripides' kinsman, the true image of the middle-class housewives they purport to be. Apart from the consideration that they are women as seen and acted by men, one of the strong features of their interest for dramatic purposes is that they are women taking on male roles. This is true whether we see them assembling at the Thesmophoria (because their ceremony is a transposition of a male one, and they make speeches like orators against Euripides) or gathering together and trying to force their husbands to political action – the making of peace – by an international 'Ban Sex' movement. But the very fact that women are so prominent in these plays, as opposed to the earlier ones, means that some kinds of relationships are explored in ways which there would have been no occasion to do with a differently oriented plot. We can take as an instance *Lysistrata* 870–979: Myrrhine has joined the Movement, and left Cinesias: 'What's wrong with you? No thought for the child, not fed or bathed for five days?' '*I* think of him, but he's got a feckless father ...' (88off.). 'You don't care that the hens have gone off with your spinning?' 'Good God, no' (896f.). 'But won't you come and – well – lie down with me just now?' 'No way – though I won't say I don't love you.' 'You do? Then why not, pet?' 'In front of the baby? – you must be joking' (904ff.). With these preliminaries Myrrhine leads Cinesias through a routine of teasing and partly undressing and breaking off to get cushions, perfume and the like; this appeals, of course, to the audience's sexual fantasies; but there is no extravagance in the style, which remains basically familiar and colloquial. Only when she finally breaks off and frustrates him is there a change, when Aristophanes moves to the level of mock-heroic, and has Cinesias complain about the agonies of his tension in dialogue with the chorus in a parody of tragic lament (954–79). We can class this episode as social comedy because, for all its other qualities, it is a depiction of a kind of personal relationship which is universal; it rests not on its comic effects alone, not on any satire of individuals, but on the author's observation of human nature in the world about him.

If it is hard to draw a clear picture of a comic poet's attitude to political events or any of the other affairs of the public world, it is perhaps harder still to pin down personal feelings in relation to the social scene. Often enough, for instance in his constant satire against homosexuals, or his propagation of the old comic theme that women are alcoholics, Aristophanes simply seems to be echoing or writing large what the man in the street holds as his own view or as an inherited prejudice.[1] Yet there are moments of subtler and keener perception. We have noticed already how, in *Lysistrata*, the war is portrayed from a woman's point of view, not least with a good verbal sketch of the wife who is anxious for news and is told to shut up (above, p. 125). A similar detail at the opening of *Acharnians* highlights the unhappiness of the country-man condemned to a wartime life within the city walls, when he has to buy everyday necessities like charcoal, oil and vinegar from street traders rather than enjoy his own produce at home (33ff.; above, p. 125). In *Peace*, when peace comes, the changes it can bring to people's circumstances are shown in two vivid instances: that of the sickle-maker and the dealer in earthenware jars, whose goods have leapt in price, and that of the arms-merchants, whose gear is a drug on the market (1197ff.). Some insight into the personal implications of a misfortune appears from the case of the old man in court, who is defeated by a smart young opponent and achieves a retort which has its elements of pathos as well as of rhetoric: 'I leave the court fined by the amount I'd saved for a shroud' (*Ach.* 691). Some of the realities of dealing with old people show through the scene in *Wasps* in which Philocleon is cosseted into agreeing to hold a trial in his own home, and, among other things, thoughtfully provided with a chamber-pot hung up on a peg (807ff.). These, and many passages like them, offer flashes of insight into people's social and economic affairs rather than studied portraiture. A passage where the portrait is somewhat more sustained is the self-description by the chorus of flatterers in Eupolis' *Kolakes*, the play which, as we have noted (p. 136), competed successfully with the *Peace* in 421 B.C.: fr. 159 reads (in part) as follows:

---

[1] Homosexuals: see, e.g., the list of 42 people attacked by name for homosexuality in comedy given by Henderson (1975) 213ff. Women and wine: e.g. *Lys.* 194ff., *Thes.* 630ff., 690ff.; more passages in Oeri (1948).

'I have these two outfits of outer clothes, very elegant, and I put on one or the other and take a spin to the market. And then, when I see some simple-minded type with money, I'm all over him. If he has something to say, I praise it strongly, and show amazement, and pretend to be delighted – and then off we go to dinner, to eat someone else's bread, and to keep joking, on the spot, or it's "out"...'

The similar character in Epicharmus' *Hope or Wealth*, as we have noted, tells the same sort of story; and both the social type and the kind of portraiture have a developing future in later comedy.[1]

In its sharpness of description, whether hostile or sympathetic, and in its strong vein of interest in the life (and to some extent the relationships) of ordinary people, fifth-century comedy had two growth points of enormous potential. With the familiarity brought by centuries of later literary history, it is easy to underrate their importance. How it was that this side of comedy, rather than any of the others, was to prove to be so fruitful, is clearly a key question to be asked in any study of the comedy of the fourth century.

10. FROM ARISTOPHANES TO MENANDER

The gap in time between Aristophanes' *Plutus* and Menander's *Dyskolos* is just over seventy years, or two rather stretched generations. Of the comedy of that period, Gilbert Norwood writes:

Between the excitingly varied landscape of Old Comedy and the city of Menander stretches a desert: therein the sedulous topographer may remark two respectable eminences, and perhaps a low ridge in the middle distance, or a few nullahs, and the wayfarer will greet with delight one or two oases with a singing bird or so; but the ever-present foreground of his journey is sand, tiresome, barren and trickling. (Norwood (1931) 38)

Yet this is the period in which Attic comedy really became international. The popularity of its plays among the Doric-speaking Greeks of the west is in evidence from south Italian vase-paintings with comic scenes dating from the first quarter of the fourth century onwards; Attic terracotta statuettes and their replicas occur in places as far apart as Ampurias near Barcelona, Olynthos, Lindos and southern Russia.[2] It was in this period that actors came increasingly into prominence as famous personalities,[3] that Aristotle delivered in Athens the lectures represented by our surviving *Poetics*, and much theatrical

---

[1] See p. 117 above, and Handley (1965a) on 57ff.

[2] South Italian vases (the so-called 'Phlyax vases') are catalogued by Trendall (1967) and listed in appropriate places by Webster–Green (1978). Terracottas: e.g. the famous set of characters from a mythological comedy in the Metropolitan Museum, New York, with numerous far-flung replicas: Webster–Green (1978) no. AT 9–23.

[3] Ghiron-Bistagne (1976) 154ff., *DFA* 279ff.; there is firm evidence for organized guilds from the early third century onwards, though they may have been known by their professional name 'Artists of Dionysus' for half a century before that (Dem. 19.192; Arist. *Rhet.* 1405a23 et al.).

rebuilding and reorganization took place, not least in Athens under the financial administration of Lycurgus.[1] It is also clear that the public had its idols, some of whom wrote very prolifically; and that success at Athens was sought for, and won, by Greeks from quite different quarters of the world, some of whom eventually gained citizenship. Anaxandrides is an example from the first generation of fourth-century comic poets. An East Greek, by report, from Rhodes or Colophon, he scored brilliantly with first prizes at the Dionysia in successive years, 376 and 375, and won a first at the Lenaea at about the same time; he ended with ten firsts in all, and we have a record of him still producing (and winning a fourth prize) in 349. Antiphanes, another great name, was a close contemporary, another non-citizen (we are told that Demosthenes was responsible for making him one), and apparently another East Greek, with three places laying claim to be his home town. Alexis is said to have come from the west, from the Athenian colony of Thurii on the gulf of Taranto; he was a copious writer who lived to a great age; some ancient critics brought him into a specially close relationship with Menander, whose life he in fact over-lapped at both ends. The fourth-century Athenian theatre freely drew in talent and freely exported plays, which were certainly written in some number: 617 were catalogued for the period called Middle Comedy – our period – according to the so-called Anonymus, *De comoedia*; and Athenaeus' figure, possibly differently based, is 'over 800'.[2] How is it that from all this activity the impression made on a modern scholar should be that of sand, 'tiresome, barren and trickling'? And can we, without prejudice to our answer, see anything of the shape of things to come in the last plays of Aristophanes?

The most tangible difference between the earlier plays and *Ecclesiazusae* and *Plutus* is the diminution of the role of the chorus. This we noted before in discussing structural patterns (pp. 106ff.). The parabasis is now gone, and the formally patterned agon reduced to half of itself or less than half; twice in the *Ecclesiazusae* and several times in the *Plutus* at places where a choral performance might have been expected the manuscripts have the heading ΧΟΡΟΥ (as one might write CHORUS in English), a notation familiar from fragmentary texts of post-classical tragedy as well as from Menander. Though there is still room for discussion about the textual history and significance of this notation (we cannot claim to be certain in either play how many times the chorus performed or what it did),[3] the main points for our purpose are sufficiently clear. The element of poetry and song is diminished: even if, at all likely points, the chorus sang and danced, the effect must still have been weaker than what

[1] Pickard-Cambridge (1946) 134ff.
[2] Anon. *De com.* 11 52ff. Kaibel, 111 45ff. Koster; Athenaeus 8.336d.
[3] See Hunter (1979).

happens in (say) *Frogs*, since their lyrics were not specially composed for the play. At the same time, with the dramatist's mind no longer so clearly focused on his alternating patterns of scene or speech and lyric, the action will almost inevitably have fallen into sections or stages demarcated by the principal choral performances. These sections will then have tended to take on a compositional status akin to what one would recognize by the term 'act'; and that process is fully realized in Menander.[1] To take an illustration: the action of *Plutus* from 802 onwards, after a XOPOY, consists of a series of illustrations of the effects of the miraculous cure by which Wealth has had his sight restored. First Carion narrates the transformation within the house – the bin full of good barley, the jars full of wine and the well of olive oil, and so on. Then there arrives the Just Man, who had been scorned by the friends he had helped, but now that Wealth is no longer blind, he brings as a thank-offering the cloak in which he had shivered for thirteen years. They are joined by an Informer, who is pushed off in the old cloak to be a bath attendant, while the Just Man is taken in to meet Wealth in person. XOPOY again (958). The parallelism is obvious and traditional, but instead of being grouped into a pattern by interlacing choral odes (like the scenes with the Farmer and the Best Man in *Acharnians* 1000ff.), the three elements come together to form a kind of unit.

We should follow the fortunes of the chorus and of lyric in comedy somewhat further. After *Plutus*, Aristophanes wrote two more plays, very likely his last, which were produced by his son Araros, namely *Kokalos* and *Aiolosikon*; *Aiolosikon*, we are told, lacked parabasis and choral lyric. In this respect, and in being a mythological comedy without personal attacks, *Aiolosikon* is presented by our source as a type-example of Middle Comedy; while in *Kokalos* (it is said) 'he introduces rape and recognition and all the other things in which Menander followed him'.[2] When Cratinus' *Odysses* 'Odysseus and Co.' is mentioned together with *Aiolosikon* it appears to be thought of by our source not simply as a mythological play, but as one lacking abuse, parabasis and lyrics as well.[3] This could be so. If so, it is a useful reminder that Old Comedy was not necessarily as regular in development as simple extrapolation from Aristophanes would make it; but there remains the possibility that our information has been garbled in the course of passing from one ancient scholar to another, or that behind it all lies a later adaptation of Cratinus' original fifth-century composition. The one substantial piece of choral performance in the *Plutus* is the parodos (253ff.), in which the chorus of old farmers enters in trochaic tetrameters (not lyrics) in dialogue with Carion. They sing a parody of a

[1] This topic, including the definition of 'act', has been much discussed: see, e.g., *Entretiens Hardt* (1970) 12ff. and Blanchard (1970).
[2] Platonius, *De com.* I 1.24f., 29ff. Kaibel, 1.22ff., 27ff. Koster; the quotation is from *Vit. Ar.* XI 69ff. Dindorf–Dübner, XXVIII 54ff. Koster.
[3] Platonius, quoted n. 2 above.

dithyramb by Philoxenus, the *Cyclops*; this is in simple iambic stanzas (290ff.). They then return to their own role with a song indicated in the text by XOPOY.[1] The Philoxenus parody, though preserved as part of the text, is in fact completely inorganic to it, and could perfectly well have been performed in similar circumstances in any other play. But the notion that a chorus might have a special identity, or do a special performance at least on its first appearance, is one that persists. Four fragments of a marble relief in Athens dated to the third quarter of the fourth century show a dancing chorus of men in soldiers' caps with staffs;[2] from the same period, Eubulus' *Stephanopolides* 'Garland sellers' had, as its title suggests, a characterized female chorus which introduced itself in a lyric of which fragments survive (104–5 K). These instances, among others, allow us to trace a little of the story until it resumes in Menander, with a chorus announced on its arrival, either in the general character of tipsy revellers (as in *Perikeiromene*, for instance) or, on occasion, with a special function or description to suit the play (as in *Dyskolos*).[3]

Menander offers no evidence for specially written choral song. There is a little evidence for actors' lyric, which could still occur in special situations (a song at a temple, recalling Euripides' *Ion*; a song and dance in honour of the Great Mother);[4] recitative, in the sense of lines delivered to a musical accompaniment, is well illustrated in the lively scene of the ragging of Knemon at the end of the *Dyskolos*, which takes on a kind of poetic colour as it rises to the description of the party which the old misanthrope has refused to attend (see below, p. 171). But the basic mode of Menandrean comedy is the speech of everyday human relationships, and his basic metre correspondingly is that which Aristotle (*Poetics* 1449a24) thought of as closest to speech, namely the iambic trimeter.

If, then, the decline of the chorus and of lyric in general is not quite so sharp and simple as a crude contrast between early and late Aristophanes would make it, it is still to be seen as a major change in comedy, part of a trend of development well marked in *Ecclesiazusae* and *Plutus* which has consequences for the shape and structure of plays as well as for the nature of their appeal to audiences. The diminishing role of the lyrical and poetic elements must to some extent account for the impression of flatness of style given by the fourth-century fragments. These contributions towards the questions we set out to answer will be augmented as other general trends in fourth-century comedy are

[1] Cf. Handley (1953) 59 with n. 4.

[2] Webster–Green (1978), no. AS3 with pl. ix; cf. also AS4.

[3] 'Paean-singers', according to the papyrus, 'Pan-worshippers' by the generally accepted correction: see Handley (1965a) on 230–2.

[4] *Leukadia*, fr. 258 Kö; schol. *ad* Eur. *Andr.* 103, cf. Handley (1969) 96 and Gomme–Sandbach (1973) 400ff.

surveyed. But there remains, before we leave the present set of topics, a scene which merits mention here both for its own sake and as an indication of what could have happened but apparently did not.

It is part of the reversal of the normal order of things in *Ecclesiazusae* that sexual relationships shall be free, but on condition that the oldest and ugliest are satisfied first (611–34). Aristophanes illustrates this situation by constructing a comic routine around a young man, a girl, and a fearsome old hag, soon to be displaced by two even more hideous competitors (877ff.). In this way he creates an opportunity to introduce pairs of songs in which his actors can take turns to answer each other ('There's something pleasant and comic about this, even if the audience don't enjoy it', 888–9). The high point, so far as we are concerned here, is the duet of boy and girl – she, in pain and longing, begs her lover to come to her, while he, again in pain and longing, stands at the door and begs her to come down and open up. Perhaps, as has been suggested, Aristophanes is drawing on the idiom of contemporary popular song; but what the incident recalls, rather than anything else in Greek comedy, is the serenade sequence in Plautus, *Curculio* (96ff., esp. 147–57). The Aristophanic scene has, among its other elements, some of the basic ingredients of romantic comedy and of musical comedy in a much more modern sense than Aristophanes would have recognized; and it is perhaps even more significant from the historical point of view as an indication of potential than as an achievement. The convergence of theme and mode of performance with Plautus is interesting chiefly to remind us of what did in fact not (so far as we know) develop in fourth-century Greece. For although music and poetry were still admitted to comedy, they never seem to have regained the status they once enjoyed in Aristophanes, still less to have taken the interesting route which led to the musical comedy of Plautus.

Myth, we have seen, is a very primitive element in comedy; mythical scenes and characters, often based on a treatment in some more elevated form of literature, continued from Epicharmus onwards to lend themselves to many different comic purposes, including those of political comedy; myth, especially myth as found in tragedy, could provide patterns of character and action which transmuted themselves into part of the comic poet's own stock-in-trade. Though much is uncertain about the chronology and content of many plays, some picture of development can be formed from the results of an investigation by Webster.[1] According to this, in the last twenty years of the fifth century just under half of the dated plays are mythological; for the years 400–350 the fraction is between a half and a third, as opposed to only one tenth of the titles assignable to 350–320. 'Mythological' can, of course, apply to several different

---

[1] Webster (1952); see also Webster (1970) 85, 259ff.

kinds of play. There is a sense in which the *Plutus* is a mythological comedy, having the mythical figures of Wealth and Poverty as characters; but the kind of play in which we are interested here is one which takes a whole fabric of plot and characters from myth, and is comic by virtue of exploiting the clash and contrast between the values and incidents of the 'parent' story and their counterparts in the world of men like ourselves or worse than ourselves. Euripides' lost *Antiope* presented, through the contrast between Antiope's sons, a conflict of ideals between the cultured intellectual and the practical man (see p. 68). In the *Antiope* of Eubulus there is a comic Boeotian speaking his own dialect (like the Boeotian of Aristophanes' *Acharnians*); and in a fragment from a messenger speech we hear that the ever-hungry Zethus is to be settled in the 'sacred plain of Thebes' (for the bread is better there), while the more etherial Amphion is sent to hungry Athens, where men drink the breezes and live on hopes. Eubulus' *Bellerophon* again recalls Euripides, it seems: in our one fragment, the hero calls for someone to steady him as his flying horse Pegasus rises; and once more we can compare Aristophanes, in his parody of Euripides' play in the *Peace*, where Trygaeus has a shaky start flying to Heaven on his dung-beetle (82ff.).[1] Examples can be multiplied;[2] but one story which is specially worth mention is that of Auge, for it involves the motifs of rape and recognition which were remarked on by ancient scholars as basic ingredients of the New Comedy of Menander and his contemporaries, and were notably present in Aristophanes, two of whose last plays, as we have seen, were taken as type-examples of what was to come in the age after him.[3] Euripides' play *Auge* is slightingly referred to in the *Frogs* (1080) for the sake of its heroine, who gave birth to her son by Heracles in the temple of which she was priestess. Comic plays entitled *Auge* are known from Philyllius and Eubulus. Philyllius' play could well have been written in the closing years of the fifth century, when *Auge* was new (it was one of Euripides' latest productions); and in that period, it seems, there originates a group of terracotta statuettes which include Heracles, a woman veiling her face in shame, an old nurse with a baby and others eminently suitable to have been souvenirs of the cast of such a comedy.[4] The continuing popularity of the terracotta types and the production of another comic *Auge* by Eubulus give some indication of the appeal this kind of story had. The fragments on food and feasting which we have in quotations by Athenaeus do something to show how the comic poets brought the story down to earth, and they remind us of Heracles' traditional comic role as a glutton; the food-and-drink motif has its visual counter-

---

[1] See also the texts quoted in *P.Oxy.* 2742, *CGFP* no. *74.
[2] See, e.g., Webster (1970) 16ff., 82ff.
[3] See above, p. 148 with n. 2.
[4] Terracottas: see above, p. 146 n. 2.

part among the statuettes in the figures of a man carrying a shopping basket and a man carrying a jar.[1]

One can see how stories like that of Auge may have admitted comic innovations and distortions in the traditional manner; single lines from the tragedians could also still be picked up and twisted to good effect. Anaxandrides, it can be said, is being Aristophanic when he takes a famous line from the *Auge* of Euripides and parodies it to make a political witticism: 'Nature willed it: she cares naught for laws' (Eur. fr. 920 *TGF*) becomes 'The city willed it: she cares naught for laws' (Anax. fr. 67 K). But such stories had other qualities too, much less tangible from our evidence. They had been (and surely still could be) so shaped as to yield a satisfactory dramatic pattern, an organic whole; they could be (as they were by Euripides) so treated as to throw into question the divine and human motivation behind the plot, even if the comic poet's means and purposes were different; and they could be so handled as to involve the audience in sympathy with the characters and their attitudes from time to time, to promote a certain feeling of identification, to evoke the smile and not the laugh. In spite of the strong Roman colour of Plautus' writing, the *Amphitruo* probably still gives a good idea of the blend of different effects in comedies of this kind. We begin with the basic and farcical confusions of mistaken identity, when Zeus/Jupiter and Hermes/Mercury masquerade as Amphitruo and his servant, so that the king of the gods can have the pleasure of adultery with Amphitruo's queen Alcmena; we move on to the elements of human sympathy in the portrait of a woman who retains her dignity in spite of the way in which she is being deceived, and in this we can see something of the side of later Greek comedy which is other than sheer light entertainment. That is a side which Menander was to develop. But for the sake of the contrast, we can note now that when Menander recalls Euripides' line about Nature and laws, as Anaxandrides did, it is not in order to make an allusive political witticism, but to give an extra dimension to the everyday affairs of the people in his play from the situation of their mythical counterparts.[2]

It was in fact the decline in political and personal satire that gave Aristotle and other ancient critics one of the clearest contrasts they could make between the comedy of the age of Aristophanes and later comedy. But how sudden and how clear cut was the change? For Aristotle, as we noted, the movement away from the iambic or satirical convention had already begun, as far as Athens was concerned, in the generation before Aristophanes, with Crates;[3] while on the other hand, the references to contemporary individuals and political events in

[1] Philyllius, *Auge* 3–6 K, Eubulus, *Auge* 15 K; Heracles, Ar. *Wasps* 60 (cf. above, p. 117).
[2] Men. *Epitr.* 765–7 (1123–5 Sandbach): see also below, pp. 168f.
[3] See above, p. 111 with nn. 2–3, p. 141 with nn. 1–2, and the texts referred to in p. 148 n. 2.

Ecclesiazusae, Plutus and later fragmentary plays of the fourth century show (to say the least) that there was no universal inhibition against such things. That is not to say that there was no tension between attackers and attacked of the kind we found when discussing political comedy in its prime. Isocrates, writing in 355 B.C., contrasts the difficulties faced by people with serious but unappealing policies to advocate (like himself) with the position of orators in the assembly, as unthinking as they are unscrupulous, and with that of comic poets in the theatre, who retain public favour while broadcasting their fellow citizens' mistakes to all Greece.[1] Isocrates was an old man at this time, turned eighty in fact, and one wonders if his mind was not on comic poets of the past, by whom he had himself been attacked, rather than on those of the immediate present.[2] Nevertheless, it is hard to divorce what he says completely from contemporary reality; and the same applies, though with different reservations, to the political theorizing of Isocrates' somewhat younger contemporary Plato, when he lays down his rigid rules in the *Laws* against personal attack in comedy or in any kind of iambic or lyric poetry (935e). From the comic poet's point of view, personal attack and political commentary were a traditional licence; and like many comic traditions, this one was preserved. For Menander, contemporary affairs are about as far in the background as the Napoleonic Wars are for Jane Austen, yet still (more than Austen) he embodies elements of social commentary in the words and actions of his characters, and still he allows himself an occasional nod in the direction of comedy's past, as in his allusions in the *Samia* and elsewhere to a notorious sponger and butt of the comic stage, Chairephon.[3]

Accordingly, with politics in comedy, as with its music and poetry, one can point to a declining trend, to a shift of interest elsewhere; and though a dramatist who ran against the trend might attract the necessary sponsorship and acceptance for an Athenian production, and might achieve success with it, we should beware of exaggerating the exceptions, particularly when we are arguing from fragments. One such exception seems to have been Timocles. There is a high incidence of personal and political references in what survives of him, and he is remarkable as a late exponent of this mode of comedy: a pro-Macedonian, who attacked, among others, Demosthenes and Hyperides, he was still writing after their deaths and during the dramatic career of Menander. The parallel with music and poetry perhaps has more to it than coincidence. The decline in quotable abuse might, one supposes, have an effect similar to that of the decline in music and poetry in making the general run of fragments of fourth-century comedy less exciting to read. But these two parallel

[1] Isocrates, *De pace* (8).14.
[2] Note for this point Aristophanes, fr. 700 K and Strattis, *Atalante* 3 K: Webster (1970) 28.
[3] *Samia* 603 with other references given by Gomme–Sandbach (1973) ad loc.

phenomena have one more common feature. It is that, since Aristophanes' younger years, both music and politics had been growing increasingly more complicated, and therefore less readily exploitable in terms of popular entertainment. The musical developments which contributed to the decline of the tragic as well as of the comic chorus are those which are reflected in the *Frogs* in the contrast between traditional choral lyric in the Aeschylean manner and the modernisms of Euripides, seen at their most characteristic in virtuoso arias for actors, something quite alien to choral writing.[1] In politics it was less easy by the fourth century, and had perhaps become progressively less easy since the plays of Aristophanes' younger years, for the evils of the day to be summed up in terms of the wickednesses of a Cleon or a Hyperbolus. Both *Ecclesiazusae* and *Plutus* are political comedies in the sense that they offer a solution, albeit a typically comic one, to the problems of life in Athens; but in both the solution, and the ills it seeks to remedy, are conceived rather in social and economic terms than specifically in terms of politics: this applies almost equally to the quasi-communistic state set up by the women who take over the Assembly in *Ecclesiazusae* and to the redistribution which follows the miraculous cure of Wealth in *Plutus*.

Some impression of the political atmosphere of the 390s can be gathered from the speech which Praxagora, the heroine of the *Ecclesiazusae*, rehearses for delivery in the Assembly. She knows how to make a political speech, as she explains, because she and her husband set up house on the Pnyx Hill 'when we were refugees' (243), and so she heard the speakers there. The precise reference of some of her allusions escapes modern scholars, and it may be that even for Aristophanes' audience the overall picture was of more importance than the detail.[2]

The speech, including interruptions, runs from 171 to 240. It portrays a mood of disillusionment which seems to go beyond the comic poet's habitual attack on things as they are. There has been a succession of increasingly bad leaders ('even if a man is good one day, he's bad for ten', 177f.); but the Assembly in its turn has shown itself more moved by a man's attitude to the rate for attendance money than his true worth or worthlessness. The Athenians' judgement of politics (the argument continues) is as inconstant as their judgement of politicians: 'now take the alliance – when we were considering it, they said we'd be ruined without it; once we got it, they were furious, and the proposer instantly took flight' (193–6). Then again: 'We need ships: the poor are for, the rich and the farmers against' (197f.). The charge of fickleness comes again at 823ff., where the proposer of a new tax is said to have won a

---

[1] See above, pp. 134f.

[2] See Ussher (1973) xx–xxv for discussion and for the dating of the play to 393 B.C. and not 392 from these references.

golden reputation from his idea until (inevitably) there were second thoughts and he was vilified; the tension between rich and poor is reflected again and again in this play and the *Plutus*, not least in the scenes with the personified figure of Poverty herself (415–618).

The New Order set up by the women in *Ecclesiazusae* has some striking features in common with that of Plato in *The republic*, though the nature of their relationship (if the two are related) remains an open question. For example, both political systems envisage community of land, money and possessions, with maintenance provided by the state. Meals, women and children are all nationalized, and we may note with Murray that the objection 'How will a man know his own son?' is a problem posed and answered by both systems, and an advantage of both is the absence of lawsuits.[1]

Ecclesiazusae is traditional comedy in that its mainspring is the enactment and illustration of a fantastic solution to a contemporary problem. Such a solution can take the form of escape into a Utopian future just as well as into a place far away or an idealized past, as we remarked in discussing *Birds* (p. 128 with n. 3). Nephelokokkygia, the ideal city of the birds, is in a sense a forerunner of *Ecclesiazusae*; but this time the scene is in Athens and not in the sky, and the innovators, as in *Lysistrata*, are nothing more bizarre than housewives taking over where they think their menfolk have failed them.[2] On the other hand, as we saw above, *Ecclesiazusae* is modern like *Plutus* in its emphasis on social and economic problems rather than on specific political or personal attack. We can perhaps call it equally modern, as opposed to *Clouds*, in that its satire has moved away from verbal wit and from the cartoon-like portraiture of a comic Socrates and taken a step towards criticizing ideas in the more general terms of their content and consequences. Aristophanes, who was not backward in stressing the novelty of his ideas, does so with emphasis for *Ecclesiazusae* (577–87), but this need mean no more than that they had not had full-dress treatment in a comedy before. The difficulty of postulating a circulated version of Plato's ideas in *The republic* early enough for *Ecclesiazusae* to draw on it is matched by the lack of any clear reference to the play in Plato, who must at all events have known it. If we suppose that *The republic* and *Ecclesiazusae* are essentially independent elaborations of a common stock of ideas (perhaps we need not postulate a lost treatise by some person unknown) the central interest from our point of view is still that an early fourth-century comedy takes the theme it does and pursues it for amusement in comic terms.

[1] Murray (1933) 188. See particularly *Eccl.* 597ff. with *Rep.* 416d–e; 657, 673ff. with 464d; 610ff. with 423e, 457c–d; 635ff. with 461c–d: Ussher (1973) xv–xx.

[2] The theme of women's rule is known from other plays, and some see a forerunner of *Lys.* and *Eccl.* in Pherecrates, *Tyrannis*: Ussher (1973) xv.

The tradition of *Clouds* continues in fourth-century comedy after *Ecclesia-zusae*, and can be recognized in references to Plato, the Academy and other philosophers and their pupils.[1] A scene which recalls the famous one of Socrates' Reflectory is narrated in a fragment of Epicrates:[2] in this, Plato conducts a seminar on the classification of living things – animals, trees and plants – in which the students have problems with a pumpkin and are patiently taken back to first principles when all have failed. The plain man's image of the intellectual is readily illustrated from some of the other references to Plato: the great man frowns in concentration, raising his eyebrows like a snail's horns; he walks up and down in thought, of course to no purpose; discussion with him is all idle talk, and he has a notion of the Good which can stand as proverbial for obscurity.[3] Pupils may be thin and wasted, like the half-dead associates of Socrates;[4] but the young or old Academician can also be thought of as an elegant, like the flatterers who waited on the great thinkers in Eupolis' philosophical comedy *Kolakes*, and he can be a smart young rhetorician, like the modern young of Aristophanes' day.[5]

The passage just cited on Plato's notion of the Good (Amphis 6 K) can be of further use to us in a more general aspect. It reads in full: 'But what good it can be that you are going to come by through her, master, is something that I understand less than I understand the Good of Plato.' 'Pay attention then', says the master. The context is the familiar one in which a man tells his slave or companion (and hence the audience) about his relationship with a woman, and meets with the incredulity, the worldly wisdom and the attempt to pass the whole thing off with a joke which are common human reactions (and hence good material for dramatists) in such situations.[6] As we have seen before, and can hardly recall too often, the status of allusions in comedy is vitally affected by their context, which in fragments is often much less easily inferred than in the present example. The element of satire against Plato in the reference to the Good is slight and good-humoured when it comes as part of a chat between slave and master, and when the emphasis of the scene is elsewhere. Two questions suggest themselves. Firstly: in considering allusions to tragedy in all their variety, we can see something of the process by which what began as satirical references stayed on and developed into part of the dramatic fabric

[1] For a survey, see Webster (1970) 50–6.
[2] Epicrates 11 K, cf. Ar. *Clouds* 133ff.
[3] Amphis, *Dexidemides*, 13 K; Alexis, *Meropis* 147 K; Alexis, *Parasitos* 180 K; Amphis, *Amphikrates* 6 K – all quoted among other passages by Diogenes Laertius, *Vit. Platonis* (3).26–8; for 'idle talk', cf. Ar. *Clouds* 1485 with *Tagenistai* 490 K and Eupolis 352 K (quoted above, p. 136).
[4] Aristophon, *Plato* 8 K, with Ar. *Clouds* 103, 504, 1112; *Birds* 1553ff.
[5] Antiphanes, *Antaios* 33 K, with Eupolis, *Kolakes* 159 K (above, p. 145f.); Ephippus, *Nauagos* 14K, with Ar. *Knights* 1375ff. (above, p. 143 with n. 2).
[6] Examples are the opening scenes of Menander, *Dyskolos* and *Misoumenos* and of Plautus, *Curculio* and *Pseudolus*.

of comedy; to what extent (we ask) can something similar be said of satire against Plato, the Pythagoreans and other intellectuals? And secondly: how far does comedy itself respond during the fourth century to developments in thought about politics, ethics, the craft of literature and other humane subjects? To answer the first question, as our example suggests, we need to know what characters in what situations are given allusions to philosophers or express ideas with a recognizable philosophical background;[1] on one aspect of the second question something will be said later on.

But to return once more to Aristophanes; it is interesting, and perhaps genuinely indicative of a trend in the development of comedy, that *Ecclesiazusae*, in illustrating the concept of the community of all property also produces what has been pointed out as the earliest scene in comedy in which two old men are clearly contrasted. The contrast is between the man who loyally brings out his household goods and forms them for the state occasion into the order of a festive procession; and on the other hand the sceptic, who finds all reasons for hanging back, but is keen enough to go when there is to be a free state banquet: they are the forerunners of such pairs in Menandrean comedy as Demeas and Nikeratos in the *Samia*, or Demeas and Micio in the *Adelphoi* as adapted by Terence.[2]

Athenaeus, as we have remarked, read fourth-century comedies voraciously (p. 147 with n. 2). Even a rapid inspection of one of the editions of comic fragments will show what a dominant part in our knowledge of comedy between Aristophanes and Menander is played by the quotations which Athenaeus puts on the lips of the scholars whose dinner-party is the subject of his *Deipnosophistai*. The range of the diners' conversation, though wide, is by no means universal: so it comes about that we have relatively rich material for some topics which Athenaeus regarded as germane to academic party conversation, such as cooks, food in variety, wine, wine-cups and hetaerae; but (even adding in our other material) we do not have the random sample of characters, motifs and dialogue which would result if the same amount of text were recovered by papyrological discovery from small pieces of ancient copies of the plays owing their preservation to chance. The word 'fragment' can mean more than one thing. Two immediate considerations arise. On the one hand, the fact that Athenaeus has special interests in certain themes and puts together passages which display them is one more factor to take into account when questions of repetitiveness or monotony in fourth-century comedy are raised. On the other hand, we know well that Greek comic poets were aware, as popular entertainers in other ages have been, that familiarity (with just a dash of

[1] See Webster (1970) 54–5 and (1950) 195 ff.
[2] *Eccl.* 728ff.; Webster (1970) 13.

157

something new) can be a powerful ingredient of success. With the help of Athenaeus' material we can explore some themes and their variants quite fully and attempt to mark out patterns of development which may illuminate the less well-documented areas that interest us. The figure of the *mageiros*, the professional caterer or cook, has been fully studied and can be quoted as an example.[1]

The cook, who is hired to cater for weddings and other special celebrations, is one of a group of characters who come together in plays with a love-intrigue theme. The theme itself and at least some of the character-types have fifth-century forerunners; but it is no doubt to the two generations after Aristophanes that we are to look for the basic development of what was to become, through Menander and the other writers of New Comedy in Greek and Latin, one of the most fruitful forms of fiction.

Young and old lovers and young and old hetaerae are characters we have met in earlier discussions.[2] The game of sexual pursuit can be complicated by rivalries within or across the age-groups; as helpers and confidants, there are available the household slaves, or the old dramatic type of boon companion, the parasite;[3] as hindrances, there can be stern fathers or domineering wives; the cook, the procurer and the moneylender all wait in the wings for their turn.[4]

In the formation of such fictional characters, the blend of fresh observation with literary inheritance is a fascinating one. Sometimes we may feel that the satirical portrait of a particular individual has been specially influential in forming a literary type. Needing an opponent in *Acharnians* for his hero's peace treaty with Sparta, Aristophanes brings on stage a contemporary military commander, Lamachus, in full hoplite gear with extravagantly plumed helmet; Lamachus rants and rages, but to no purpose, and he ends up with a battle and a wound for his efforts while Dicaeopolis enjoys women and wine. Here is a pattern both of a person and of a story which can be built on and transmuted. But of course, Lamachus is far from being the first soldier in literature. The Braggart Captain we all think of (taking our cue from Plautus and his *Miles gloriosus*) is not a regular officer like Lamachus, but a free-lance, a mercenary, corresponding in real life to those Greeks like Xenophon and many after him in the fourth century who sought their fortune in foreign wars, and looking back in literature to such ancestors as the wandering Orestes with his companion Pylades in Aeschylus, and perhaps as far as Archilochus.[5] One

[1] There are full studies by Giannini (1960) and Dohm (1964); see Handley (1965a) on 393 and index s.v. *cook*, and Berthiaume (1982).

[2] Above, pp. 139ff. on Ar. *Wasps*, Pherecrates, *Korianno* and other plays; p. 150 on *Ecclesiazusae* 877ff.

[3] Cf. above p. 146 with n. 1.

[4] Webster (1970) 63–7 gives a brief survey with references.

[5] Cf. Webster (1970) 64, 132: Archilochus 1ff. West, Aesch. *Cho.* 675 with Antiphanes, *Athamas* 16 K and the terracotta types listed by Webster–Green (1978) nos. AT 6–7.

attraction of service of this kind was the glamour of far away places and foreign despots' courts, and it is reflected in the tall story told by the soldier in Antiphanes' *Stratiotes* (202 K): 'Tell me, did you spend long in Cyprus?' 'All the time the war lasted.' 'Where, mostly?' 'In Paphos; and there was a remarkable piece of refinement to be seen there – you wouldn't have believed it.' 'What?' 'The King had pigeons to fan him at dinner, pigeons ....' (He wore perfume which attracted them, and had slaves scare them off and make them flap). The progress from satirical portrait to type was not, of course, necessarily regular or uniform. There are odd satirical references to contemporary soldiers (as to Lamachus) in fourth-century comedy, but satire against individuals is commoner in the case of hetaerae – perhaps not surprisingly, since they are part of the urban scene in the way that soldiers are not.[1] But the young girl with her lover in Aristophanes' *Ecclesiazusae* has her descendants in the girls who are cast as the fictional heroines of love-intrigue plots; and we hear of one in Antiphanes, *Hydria* (212 K):

> 'The man I'm talking about had a girl living next door to him, a hetaera, and he fell in love with her on sight; she was freeborn, but had no relations, no one to look after her – she was a good girl, one with a golden character, a hetaera in the true sense of "friend", when all the others spoil a good name with their bad ways.'

The typology of characters which can be built up from the fragments is complemented by representations of masks, actors and scenes in works of art, which give us much fuller evidence for fourth-century than for fifth-century comedy.[2] Having said much to bring out the continuity of comic traditions, we must also recognize that alongside their development of mythological comedy, the fourth-century dramatists were powerful innovators in the drama of everyday life, in the creation of comic fiction. Our difficulty in evaluating what they achieved is the inevitable one, that, for the lack of continuous Greek texts, we tend to think in terms of survivals from the age of Aristophanes and anticipations of Menander. There is a passage of Antiphanes which can be used to throw some light on the literary principles which comic fiction was developing, and it may help us to a conclusion.

Antiphanes' long dramatic career runs from within a year or so of the death of Aristophanes in the mid-380s until the Olympiad 334/331 B.C., ten years or more before the dramatic début of Menander in 321. Fragment 191, which is unfortunately undated, is part of a speech on the relative difficulty of composing tragedy and comedy; and it is plausibly suggested that the title of the play,

[1] Webster (1970) 63f. See also above, p. 131, on Timon of Athens as the archetypal misanthrope.
[2] Webster–Green (1978) with supplements published at intervals in *B.I.C.S.*; cf. p. 146 n. 2 above.

Poiesis, indicates that the speech was a prologue-speech spoken by the personified figure of Poetry herself. As a sign of the times, we can note in passing that a discussion of playwriting of this kind is something that a fifth-century poet would probably have handled, as Aristophanes does, by having the chorus speak for him in the parabasis.[1] Poetry (if it is Poetry) speaks for Antiphanes as follows:

> 'Tragedy is a lucky kind of writing in every way. Its plots, in the first place, are well known to the audience before a line is spoken; all the poet need do is remind them. Suppose I just say "Oedipus", they know the rest: father – Laius; mother – Jocasta; who his daughters and his sons were; what it is that he did, and what he will suffer. Or take the case of Alcmaeon...[which we here omit, partly because the text is not properly elucidated]...then, when they have no more to say and their plays have completely run dry, they raise the crane (*mechane*) like a finger and the spectators are satisfied. We can't do this. Everything has to be invented: new names, what happened in the past, the present circumstances, the end and the beginning. If a Chremes or a Pheidon leaves any of this out, he gets hissed off the stage, but your Peleus and your Teucer can do that.'

In interpreting this passage, we shall beware of treating Antiphanes as if he were writing an article on theatre and audience in the fourth century. We need to take what he says about tragedy and comedy much more as advertising material for the kind of play he is presenting than as documentation. That said, it can be seen that he is writing for an audience which likes to feel at home with its drama. Theatrical realities are present, in the shape of tragedy resolved by the *deus ex machina* and unsuccessful comedy hissed off the stage. Oedipus, Alcmaeon and other tragic heroes are alluded to in familiar terms, as in our time Hamlet or Hedda Gabler might be; but we need not go on to believe, as Antiphanes chooses to suggest, that a call for the name of Oedipus' father (any more than for that of Hamlet's uncle) would necessarily have met with a hundred per cent response.[2] What interests us above all is the concept of comedy as artistically constructed fiction, with an invented story, which must in fact be more than a story: it must be a plot, with a beginning, a middle (or present state) and an end, coherent and coherently presented; for incoherence (such is Antiphanes' self-defensive compliment to the audience) will meet with vigorous critical disapproval; while the characters, however idiosyncratic their circumstances, are to be people with names 'invented' by the author – in practice, as the two examples show, the invention often involved no more than a choice from a familiar stock.

Antiphanes, as we have just recalled, was old enough to have begun writing

[1] E.g. *Knights* (p. 107 above); cf. Sifakis (1971) 38ff.
[2] Aristotle, *Poetics* 1451b25, has it that even the best-known subjects of tragedy are known only to a few, though they give pleasure to all.

plays at or near the end of the lifetime of Aristophanes; but his conception here of organically constructed comedy about fictional people is closely akin to some of Aristotle's principles of dramatic composition, and may have been influenced by them; it anticipates, at least in essentials, what we find in Menander. 'Poetry', says Aristotle, 'tends to express the universal, History the particular' (*Poetics* 1451b6ff.). The distinction which interests him is between the way in which a man of a certain type will act, according to probability or necessity, and the particular, 'what Alcibiades did or suffered'. 'In Comedy', he continues, 'this is already clear: for comic poets construct their plot from probable incidents and then add names as they chance to come to mind.' One wonders how far comic practice nourished Aristotelian theory before the formulated principles in their turn influenced comic dramatists.

The Anonymus *De comoedia*, who was quoted near the beginning of this whole discussion for the number of plays of Middle Comedy, has this to say of their quality: 'The poets of Middle Comedy did not pretend to poetic style; they proceeded through familiar speech, and their virtues are those of prose – there is in them little work of the poet. They are all careful with their plots.'[1] If this is so it is not surprising that they do not lend themselves well to the gathering of colourful literary flowers, and that they may seem to be dull writers, especially when one takes into account the consideration that the authors whose quotations and excerpts provide the bulk of our fragments are hardly ever concerned, except incidentally, to illustrate the strictly dramatic virtues of the plays they use. One basis for plot-construction, we have seen, is in mythological comedy, with its pre-existing stories and characters. But for the design of plays with typical fictional characters, we depend on reconstruction from Latin adaptations and from the more traditional side of Menander's comedy. Plautus' *Menaechmi*, with its constant comedy of mistaken identity, can be taken with *Amphitruo* and (say) Menander's *Aspis* to give an idea of the ways in which poets of our period learnt to work out comic situations; and the existence of titles like *Homoioi* ('Two alike', Antiphanes and others) and *Didymoi* or *Didymai* ('Twins' of either sex, Anaxandrides, Antiphanes, Alexis and others) suggests that we are not dealing with isolated cases.[2]

One of the most productive techniques of mythological comedy – already pioneered, it must be allowed, by Euripides – was to subject the mechanisms of plot and the motivations of characters to the harsh light of the world we live in, to the standards of ordinary people, or rather, as Aristotle has it, of 'people worse than ourselves'.[3] If the traditional story pattern and the inherited behaviour pattern, whether the product of external divine agency or inner

[1] Anon. *De com.* II.49–52 Kaibel, III.42–5 Koster.
[2] For discussion of *Menaechmi* in this aspect see Webster (1970*b*) 67ff.
[3] Aristotle, *Poetics* 1448a16ff.

conviction, were to suffer erosion or distortion, some reinforcement was needed, some new standard of probable or acceptable human behaviour. It came with the fourth century's growing interest in the human individual and his relationships – in a word, with the science that came to be known as ethics. Fine distinctions between motives and personal qualities are the common ground of later fourth-century philosophers and of the higher reaches of the Comedy of Manners, with the foundation of which we credit Menander.

11. MENANDER AND THE NEW COMEDY

Menander's *Perikeiromene* takes its title from the incident which begins the action. 'The girl who has her hair cut off' has it cut off by the man she is living with, a young Corinthian who is a professional soldier. He cuts it off in a fit of fury when he is told that she let another man kiss her. She then leaves him. Here is part of a conversation between the soldier, Polemon, and a friendly neighbour, Pataikos:[1]

> POLEMON I've always treated her as my wife.
> PATAIKOS Don't shout at me. Who gave you her?
> POLEMON Gave me her? She did.
> PATAIKOS Very good. Perhaps she fancied you then, and now she doesn't.
>   She's left you because you're not treating her properly.
> POLEMON Not treating her properly...?

Polemon is deeply hurt by this, and not at all reassured to be told that violence will get him nowhere. The girl is her own mistress, and if he wants her back all he can do is try to persuade her; the man, if he can be found, can be brought to face a legal action, but the use of force would put Polemon himself in the wrong. 'Glykera has left me, Pataikos; she's left me, Glykera' – that is still the overpowering fact for Polemon; and (he urges) Pataikos must go and plead with her. 'If I ever did her any wrong at all...if I don't love, honour and cherish her...if you could just see her things...' At that, Pataikos backs away, but he is persuaded. Among the girl's clothes and jewellery, which for Polemon are a proof of his generosity, Pataikos will find the trinkets which were given her as a baby, and so discover that she is his own daughter. He had abandoned her together with a twin brother when their mother died after childbirth and he lost his livelihood in a shipwreck. It is the twin brother who is the cause of all the trouble. He is the man who was seen kissing Glykera; they had been brought up separately, and though he did not know who she was, she had been told about him. From these complications, one can see, will eventually come reconciliation and marriage.

All this seems a long way from Aristophanes, with his Trygaeus in *Peace*

---

[1] *Pk.* 239–43 (489–93 Sandbach) and continuing in what follows.

flying to Heaven on a dung-beetle to put an end to the war, or Praxagora in *Ecclesiazusae* packing the Assembly with women dressed as men in order to create her social revolution. But time has moved on. If it is rightly reckoned that Menander's first play, the lost *Orge* 'Anger' was produced in 321 B.C., that is the hundredth anniversary of the production of *Peace*; his death at about 50 in 292/291 or a neighbouring year is – near enough – a century after *Ecclesiazusae*. It is typical of the genre of New Comedy, the comedy of Menander and his contemporaries, that the plot of a play should be set in the domestic world of family relationships, and that it should have, prominently, what the cliché calls a love interest – anything from the intrigue by which a young man secures a desirable woman to a quarrel and reconciliation, as in *Perikeiromene*, between partners who are already attached. It is typical of Menander to have seen in this domestic world, which occupies the thoughts and daydreams of so many people for so much of their time, the material for a form of entertainment which would prompt serious reflection in its audiences as well as amusement. The balance is delicate. The headstrong and self-centred Polemon may make us laugh as he meets his match in the calm and civilized Pataikos; but if so, we laugh quietly, for there is a sense in which we are laughing at ourselves, at feelings we could admit to having experienced or could recognize among family and friends. Glykera's position in law and by the standards of fourth-century society was different, as commentators explain, from what it would be in twentieth-century Britain or many another modern society; but we overload the comedy if we make it, in any terms, too much of a tract on women's rights: the serious point, as is typical of Menander, is not just verbally asserted but woven into the plot, and it is that there are standards of equitable behaviour in human relationships which may lie deeper than the surface reactions of one person to another.

The Cairo codex of Menander was published in 1907. It gave, for the first time, large parts of *Epitrepontes* 'The Arbitrants', *Perikeiromene* and *Samia* 'The Woman of Samos' – three plays which were (not untypically) known beforehand from a total of about 20 lines of text between them in the form of identified quotations – and for good measure the beginning of *Heros* 'The Hero' and some lesser items.[1] This body of text, amounting to some 1,600 lines, was the basis of work on Menander for the next half-century. Around it there clustered a number of interesting lesser discoveries, sometimes from plays which could not be securely identified and have in some cases been identified since. From this material it became possible for the first time in the modern world to form a first-hand impression of the dramatic art of the author in such matters as the handling of dialogue, the articulation of plot through

---

[1] Gomme–Sandbach (1973) 39ff. and 50ff. give descriptions and lists of papyri. There has since been a new photographic edition of the Cairo codex with a preface by Koenen (1979).

sequences of scenes, and the delineation of character.[1] At the same time, the recovery of substantial portions of continuous Greek text gave a new impetus to the comparative study of Menander and his contemporaries with Latin adaptations of their plays by Plautus, Terence and other authors less fortunate in their survival.[2] There were now fresh reasons for taking an interest in the rich visual material relating to New Comedy, in the shape of scenes from plays, actors and masks represented in a wide range of media – terracottas, bronzes, mosaics, paintings, sculptures, gems – and produced over a period of several centuries for admirers of Greek comedy in all parts of the Graeco-Roman world.[3] A second stage of this story is briefly told in terms of a single event – the publication in 1959 from the Bodmer codex in Geneva of a play that is virtually complete, the *Dyskolos* or 'Misanthrope'. The third stage, that of the following twenty years, has not so far yielded any more complete plays, but the first and last of the three in the Bodmer codex, damaged at beginning and end, proved to be *Samia* and *Aspis* 'The shield'. When these followed the *Dyskolos* into print in 1969, they went together with the previously known remains to yield the last three acts of *Samia*, with portions of the first two; and the first two acts of *Aspis* with the beginning of the third and some fragments from later in the play.[4] Among other discoveries of the sixties and seventies were large portions of *Misoumenos* 'The man she hated' (1965ff.),[5] *Sikyonios (-oi)* 'The man – or men – from Sikyon' (1965) and a hundred-odd lines of *Dis exapaton* 'The double deceiver' (1968), many of them in poor condition, but giving much the most extensive text to date which is available for direct comparison with its adaptation into Latin, namely a stretch of the *Bacchides* of Plautus, beginning at 494ff. While work on these texts was in progress, there became known a most remarkable series of mosaics of scenes from Menander which were found in a house of the latter half of the third century A.D. at Chorapha, Mytilene: they are a fascinating complement to what we have learnt from the papyri and have opened up possibilities for the recognition of more illustrations of famous scenes from particular plays among the growing stock of visual material which has come down to us.[6]

This outline of the progress of rediscovery will be in place here if it serves to show how much the basis of modern criticism of Menander has been chang-

[1] Of course, many good and interesting things were said about Menander and New Comedy before 1907; see (e.g.) Lefèvre (1979) quoting Goethe and A. W. von Schlegel, and Leo (1895) III.
[2] Fraenkel (1922) remains exemplary in this field.
[3] E.g. Robert (1911); Webster (1969) gives an extensive catalogue, of which a revised edition is currently (1983) in preparation.
[4] *Aspis* absorbed 87 lines first published in 1913, and previously quoted as *Comoedia Florentina*; line references to *Samia* in books published before 1969 are to the 341 lines from the Cairo codex.
[5] Gomme–Sandbach (cf. p. 163 n. 1) under the sigla I, O10, O11; and add O19–O22, which are, respectively, *P.Oxy.* XLVIII 3368–71; for discussion, see Turner (1973) 15–21, 48–50 and (1978).
[6] Charitonidis–Kahil–Ginouvès (1970).

ing.[1] The impact of sheer novelty is complemented by the challenge of revaluing what we previously knew or thought we knew. Three questions at once suggest themselves: one asks what proportion of Menander's work we now have; whether there are likely to be more discoveries; and whether there are implications for the study of other writers of New Comedy. A recent calculation by W. G. Arnott reckons that the amount of Greek text available to us is something less than eight per cent of Menander's total output.[2] That would give a figure of the same order as our sample of Sophocles; for Aristophanes we can probably reckon that we have as much as 25 % to 30 % of the total amount of text known to the librarians at Alexandria. But the reality of the matter is both better and worse than the raw figures suggest. It is worse, in that we still only have one complete play of Menander in Greek; better in that there are eight (perhaps more) Latin plays by Plautus and Terence which are adapted from him. The list, with Greek titles in brackets, is as follows:

Plautus: *Aulularia* (*Apistos* or another); *Bacchides* (*Dis exapaton*); *Cistellaria* (*Synaristosai*); *Stichus* (*First Adelphoi*)

Terence: *Andria* (*Andria*, with additions from *Perinthia*); *Heauton Timoroumenos* (same title); *Eunuchus* (*Eunouchos*, with additions from *Kolax*); *Adelphoe* (*Second Adelphoi*, with a scene from Diphilus, *Synapothneskontes*).[3]

By a prudent estimate (leaving out of count many texts of unproved identity) there are now known more than fifty ancient copies of plays by Menander. These range in extent from the Bodmer and Cairo codices to scraps of a few letters only; and they range in date from the third century B.C. to the sixth or perhaps the seventh A.D.: Menander is in fact one of the best-represented ancient authors among those that survive on papyri.[4] The chances are therefore good that if collections of papyri continue to be published Menander will continue to be represented; and new methods of taking apart mummy cases in order to recover written papyri offer promising prospects for the future.[5] It is noticeable that though there are among papyri of Later Greek Comedy a number which do not appear, on stylistic or other grounds, to represent plays by Menander, there is very little which is certainly identifiable as a copy of a play by another writer in the genre.[6] It could well be, if enough papyri of the Hellenistic and early Roman period are recovered, that we shall be lucky enough to find and identify

---

[1] For more detail, see Arnott (1975) and (1979) xxvi–xxx, xlvii–lii; Handley (1979); Luppe (1980).

[2] Arnott (1979) xxx.

[3] Some doubt *Aulularia* (but the likeness to *Dyskolos* seems decisive); several other plays, including *Miles gloriosus* and *Pseudolus*, have been claimed as Menandrean.

[4] See for instance on an unidentified papyrus Handley (1975b) and (1977).

[5] See Maehler (1980).

[6] Examples are *P.Heid.* 183, third/second century B.C., Posidippus, *Apokleiomene*; and *P.Oxy.* 427, third century A.D., Antiphanes, *Anthropogonia*: respectively *CGFP* nos. 218 and *3.

a specimen of the work of Philemon, Diphilus or another of Menander's rivals and successors; but on present evidence the chances must be rated much lower than for Menander himself. Latin adaptations by Plautus from Philemon and Diphilus and by Terence from Apollodorus of Carystus do something to fill out the picture that can be formed from the Greek fragments, but the texts on which we depend for our knowledge of Menander's work are so much greater in extent as to make a just comparison problematical. If, on the other hand, it were possible to set aside a large part of our Menandrean material and reduce him to the size of a Philemon or a Diphilus, how much that is now taken for granted should we have to unlearn? We noted in our approach to fifth-century comedy that the new discoveries of Menander can be useful as a reminder of the differences between whole, partial and fragmentary knowledge (above, p. 104), and the point is equally to be taken now that we have come to Menander's own time. It will therefore be well to resume our attempt to form an impression of his literary qualities before we try to see how far the writing of others can contribute to an overall picture of New Comedy.

There is in Plutarch a story about Menander and playwriting which, true or not, has become virtually canonical in modern writing about him, ever since it was used by Wilamowitz to open his much-admired discussion of 'The Art of Menander'.[1] A friend is said to have pointed out that the time of the Dionysia was approaching 'and you haven't composed your comedy for it, have you?' 'Composed my comedy?' said Menander, 'I most certainly have composed it: I have my treatment of the theme worked out – I just have to set the lines to it.' It is perhaps a pity that we do not have Aristophanes on record in a similar situation, for there is a sense in which the two stand at opposite poles of comic writing. With Aristophanes, brilliance of language is primary, and sometimes we can see how stage spectacle and action are actually generated by a verbal concept transformed into visual terms.[2] With Menander, it is not that the dialogue is dashed off anyhow (one need only read some to test that); simply that the overall design of the play comes first. That Menander should have been conscious of this principle, even (as it might seem) to the point of being able to turn it, half-jokingly, against himself, is something which accords well with what we have seen earlier of the development of organized dramatic composition in comedy.[3] A similar insight can be derived, perhaps, from the very well-known portrait-relief of Menander sitting looking at the mask of a young man, which he is holding up in front of him, with two more masks on a table nearby.[4] This is one of a long series of representations in art of poets with masks,

---

[1] Plutarch, *Moralia* 347e; Wilamowitz-Moellendorff (1925) 119; cf. Handley (1965a) 10.
[2] See above, p. 136 with n. 4 and p. 137 with n. 1.
[3] See above, p. 148 with n. 1 and p. 161.
[4] Two versions are known: Webster (1969) nos. AS6 and IS10; Bieber (1961) figs. 316–17; on the series see Webster (1965) and Handley (1973).

and in showing Menander looking at one of a group such as this, the artist may well have been thinking of him precisely in the act of 'setting the lines' to the scene he has now reached in his plan.

It should follow, unless our impressions so far are seriously at fault, that plot and character-drawing in a comedy of this kind will be integrally related. A central feature of the design of the *Dyskolos* can be used to show how this is so.[1] The play is fashioned around a single character, Knemon the misanthrope, the 'Angry Old Man' who gives it its title. He is in fact on stage for about a quarter of the time the play would take to act – hardly more – and half of that quarter is allotted to Acts IV and V. For the rest, he is in the background, dominating the play largely through what we learn from others of him and his extraordinary way of life, and being built up for his one great moment, the major speech in Act IV at 708ff., made as if from his deathbed. The main line of the action is given from the first by the attempts of young Sostratos to gain Knemon's consent to marry his daughter. It is through the lover's story, with its ups-and-downs of unreliable helpers and unexpected allies, that the portrait of Knemon is built up; and as it proceeds the audience see him through the eyes of other characters. Thus, the god Pan gives a prologue speech, and with it the outline of the man, a sketch which will accumulate details as the play goes on and in some ways look different as it does so.[2] We next see Knemon through the eyes of a frightened slave whom he has chased off his land, and can observe the reactions of Sostratos and his friend Chaireas to this (81–146); then at last Knemon himself makes a brief appearance, and Sostratos is seen in his first direct confrontation (147–88); a little more is added by what we see of and hear from Knemon's daughter, and the first act ends with a portrait of Knemon as he appears to the slave from next door who inclines, as slaves do, to see the worst of things (22off.). This description could be continued further into the play, but perhaps enough has been said to suggest how the technique works. While the action itself flows in a plausibly motivated sequence (that is, we accept that the people we are seeing would probably or necessarily behave as they do if the given circumstances were real), the various characters are presented in such a way that we have a clue to the value of what they say about Knemon from what they themselves are shown to be; but in turn, by defining him, they also define themselves. Chaireas, for instance, is soon recognized by the audience as a specimen of a familiar dramatic type, the parasite, a man who makes friendship a profession. Of course he can help in a love-affair; of course he knows just what sort of man Knemon is; and of course, when the moment comes, he will deal with the matter 'first thing in the morning'.[3] In watching

---

[1] Cf. Handley (1965a) 11f.

[2] For references, see Handley (1965a) 23f. and index s.v. *prologue-speech*.

[3] See particularly 57ff., 125–34; and above p. 146 with n. 1.

the play, we see with a smile how hollow Chaireas is, but we also see how much more idiosyncratic a character Knemon is than Chaireas thinks. It happens that we have, in the hero of Plautus' *Aulularia*, a close dramatic relation of Knemon's, the self-centred old miser Euclio; and it also happens that in the broad structural terms with which we are dealing the plays are the mirror-image of each other, with Euclio very much in evidence at the beginning, and on stage in all for more than half, and possibly near three quarters of the play's acting time (to judge from Plautus' version as we have it); the lover's story, which corresponds to that of Sostratos, is correspondingly in the background until late on. The contrast in the presentation of the hero is very striking.[1]

It is sometimes said that there is no development of character in New Comedy, and it is perhaps useful to say so if the standard of comparison is the novel, or the kind of drama with an action extending over a considerable period of time. What does develop, and what gives a forward movement to plays with a serious interest in character, is the portrait which the audience is given, and the system of contrasts by which that portrait is built up and reinforced.[2] A character like Knemon differs from a real person in that he exists only in the linear dimension of the play's performance. For the purposes of the play, his character is what it is seen to be at a chosen moment; and a summation, such as we make for a programme note or an academic essay, is a creation which misses something of his essence. Just so, a retelling or summary of a plot made for the same purposes will easily trivialize and flatten action which was conceived in terms of a different medium than narrative.

If we now move a step away from the strategy of dramatic composition towards the tactics, narrative speeches can in fact be taken to illustrate some of the ways in which Menander varies his presentation of an incident. Our examples come from *Sikyonios*, *Misoumenos*, *Aspis* and *Dyskolos*. The action of the *Sikyonios* involves a slave and a young girl taking refuge at the sanctuary of Demeter at Eleusis. She will eventually prove to be freeborn and marry the hero, but at this point she and the slave are runaways, and in the narrative their status is being debated in front of a crowd which has gathered round. A debate of this sort can be presented by means of antithetical speeches from two actors, as is commonly done in drama: such a scene is the Arbitration from which *Epitrepontes* takes its title.[3] But by presenting a debate in narrative and not on the stage, as in *Sikyonios* 176–271, the dramatist exchanges the immediate impact of the speakers' presence for the ability to set a more elaborate scene in the audience's imagination; he can use more speakers, he can characterize them through the narrator's eyes, and – not least – he can abbreviate and select in a

---

[1] See p. 167 n. 1 above and *Entretiens Hardt* (1970) 100–1.

[2] See above, p. 157 with n. 2 and Webster (1950) 190ff.

[3] *Epitr.* 43–200 (219–376 S): the underlying pattern is that of the tragic agon, not the form we associate with Aristophanes.

way which would not work with direct presentation. On this occasion, a further dimension is given by echoing, in words and pattern, what was (and is) a classic example of its kind, Euripides' narrative in *Orestes* 866–956 of the debate in Argos which decided the fate of Orestes and Electra. The echo offers a kind of justification (if one were felt to be needed) for the unusual length and prominence – by Menandrean standards – of the narrative; but it also points the analogy between the slave and the girl in one perilous situation, and the tragic hero and heroine in another.[1]

The narrative which concerns us in *Misoumenos* is that of a quarrel. After a long search, Demeas has rediscovered his daughter, Krateia, a war-captive. He wants to ransom her from Stratophanes; Stratophanes wants to make her his wife; she utterly refuses, for he is at this time (in the words of the title) 'the man she hated': she had a special reason for doing so and – as it will prove – a mistaken one. All three parties are thus in a storm of conflicting emotions. Menander does not tackle the problems of managing this scene in direct presentation: it would have been a difficult peak to climb and to descend from. Instead, he brings on a slave, Getas, who has been there in the background, and is now reliving, quoting to himself and commenting on some of the high moments of the scene. He has an audience, in the shape of young Kleinias, who knows still less of what has been going on than the audience in the theatre; Kleinias paces up and down with the slave, listening, working things out for himself and eventually breaking in. The presentation thus exploits several different viewpoints at once, and blends almost the whole range of comic effects from high drama to farce. Something of this can perhaps be seen in a short excerpt:

> GETAS Lord help us, he couldn't just be reasonable about it, could he? It was pig versus mule, as they say. But that's not so bad as her – looks away, she does, while he's speaking. 'Oh, Krateia', he says, 'don't leave me, I beg you, don't. You'd never had a man when I took you, and I *was* your man, the first to love you and cherish you; and I do love you, Krateia, my dearest. What is there about me that pains you? I'll be dead, you'll see, if you leave me.' No answer, none.
> KLEINIAS What *is* all this?
> GETAS A barbarian, the woman is, a lioness.
> KLEINIAS Damn you, you *still* can't see me. How strange.
> GETAS Completely out of his mind. By Apollo here, I'd never have set her free...[2]

The interruptions to the narrative, which seem at first sight to reflect the randomness of real life, are in fact an integral part of its structure; and a similar technique

---

[1] See *Entretiens Hardt* (1970) 22f., and for more detail Handley (1965*b*) 47 with n. 10; on Menander and tragedy, Webster (1974) 56ff.; and cf. above p. 121 with n. 3 and p. 152 with n. 2.
[2] *Mis.* 302–15, taking for granted restorations etc. which do not affect the point being argued.

is used very effectively, if less elaborately, in the long narrative at the beginning of *Aspis*.[1]

The shield which gives *Aspis* its title is part of the spectacle that opens the play. It is broken; it is carried by the late owner's batman, and there follows a procession of captives with bundles and boxes, the spoils of a campaign. With the party, but somehow not of it, is an old man who for some time looks on in silence. The occasion is a sad one, strikingly so for the start of a comedy; the batman laments the loss of his young master, who had gone to war to provide a dowry for his sister and been killed. 'What an unexpected calamity, Daos.' 'Terrible.' 'Tell me, how did he die, what was the way of it?' The story proceeds, punctuated by comments from the old man. It was not a glorious campaign, but a tale of a force grown over-confident after easy success and good plunder; there was a surprise attack by night, and they were routed. The verse-rhythms are sombre, to match the mood of the story, and the manner is akin to that of tragedy, though without specific allusion or parody. The old man's interventions articulate the narrative, but they also gradually add a new colour to the scene. It becomes plain that his concern is no more than a mask for greed. He means to get his hands on the spoils, even if he has to marry his ward, the surviving child of the family, to do so. The plot proceeds through the intrigues by which he is frustrated, and comes to a peak with the return of the young soldier who had been supposed killed in battle: it was a case of mistaken identity, as Fortune, the prologue speaker, tells the audience immediately after the opening scene we have described. This is a remarkable piece of dramatic writing, and an interesting contrast with it is given by the narrative of a battle in Plautus' *Amphitruo*. Plautus makes a lyric of this, and there is a strong Roman colour to its language, but in Plautus we have war with 'the thunder of the captains and the shouting', not the death of a young mercenary after an ordinary military blunder.[2]

A further contrast is given by our last narrative, at the end of the *Dyskolos*, which looks back to the comic rather than to the tragic side of New Comedy's ancestry and is remarkable in being a musical scene – not, it is true, in any way resembling the full-blooded Plautine lyric of the *Amphitruo* narrative just mentioned, but at least with the accompaniment of a piper.[3] The slave Getas and the cook Sikon take revenge on Knemon, the old misanthrope, for the way in which he drove them from his door when they wanted to borrow a cooking-pot; and in a scene which is in effect a farcical reprise of the borrowing scenes of Act III they carry Knemon out from his house and go through a ballet-like routine of knocking at the door and shouting fantastic demands for party

---

[1] See Turner (1980) 9f. and 11, quoting Bozanic.
[2] *Amphitruo* 186–262, esp. 219–47, cf. Handley (1975a) 129f.
[3] *Dysk.* 880 (piper), 935–53 (narrative).

equipment. Finally Sikon forces the old man to listen to a recital of the proceedings at the betrothal feast which he has insisted on missing, and they then carry him in to the party under threat of being made to dance with them instead. Comedy has an interesting tradition of euphoric elevated style for descriptions of feasts and the like, for which it borrows freely from the language of higher poetry, especially perhaps dithyramb, and in calling old wine 'the Bacchic grizzlehead' (to take one phrase), Menander is alluding to this tradition, just as he is conscious in constructing the whole scene that comedy can by tradition end with a revel (and if the revel avoids the problem of shaping any more serious end, so much the better). As before, the narrative is punctuated by interruptions, and its festive note is diversified by Knemon's misery and Getas' triumphant sarcasm.[1]

The four narratives which have just been described and contrasted can be offered as a token of Menander's dramatic range; but they can also perhaps be taken together to make a fundamental point about his playwriting. Here, as so often, he takes a basically familiar situation, and diversifies it by giving it a novel context, a new variant, an unexpected additional dimension, an artifice of structure. One could show these same broad principles at work in his treatment of characters, when he takes typical figures, often recognizable from the outset by their costumes, masks and even by standard names; and then, in the way we have seen, he builds up through the action of the play a portrait which shows that the typical is not, in this or that way, what it seems to be on the surface. Examples ready to hand are Polemon, Stratophanes and Thrasonides, the three soldiers of *Perikeiromene*, *Sikyonios* and *Misoumenos*, each of whom is fixed by type in the tradition of the 'miles gloriosus', but is shown by the play as an individual with characteristics that evoke a response of sympathy and interest rather than superiority and ridicule.[2]

An important consequence of this concept of playwriting for the critic is that it matters very much to have a full context for whatever it is in a play by Menander that one wants to interpret. That, in the fragmentary state of much of the author, is something we very often do not have, or have to achieve by conjecture. To take a single example, fr. 111 'Whom the gods love, dies young' is several times quoted as a moral maxim in antiquity (and known in English from Byron); but in the context given by Plautus' adaptation (*Bacchides* 816f.) it is said by a slave at the expense of his elderly master.[3] It is appropriate here to remember that Menander is a poet of the Hellenistic Age. Though approaching by a different route, from concepts in social anthropology, T. B. L. Webster's treatment of the plays in his last book in terms of armatures and codes rather

[1] Cf. Handley (1965a) on 946–58; and see above, p. 113 with n. 5, p. 114 with n. 1, p. 116 with n. 4, p. 117 with n. 2 and p. 139 with nn. 1–2.
[2] See above, p. 158 with n. 5, and for New Comedy Hofmann and Wartenberg (1973).
[3] Handley (1968) 6, quoting Webster.

than tradition and innovation is extremely revealing if viewed in this light; and in regard to more detailed matters of language and dramaturgy both Sandbach and Arnott (in a discussion entitled 'The Cleverness of the Hellenistic Poet') have mapped out some interesting new territory.[1]

A difficulty which criticism of this kind of writing always faces is that of seeming to be too clever in turn (or indeed of being too clever).[2] Whether Menander's rivals and successors were often equally subtle is, as will have been plain from the state of the evidence, something very much harder to judge. Greek fragments apart, we know Philemon from Plautus' *Mercator*, *Mostellaria* and *Trinummus*, and Diphilus from *Casina*, *Rudens*, the fragmentary *Vidularia* (probably) and a scene in Terence's *Adelphoe*.[3] It is eminently credible from the scale on which some motifs are treated in the fragments that both poets had a more relaxed, more traditional, and in a sense more comic attitude to comic writing;[4] and a story which may be well found if not true has Menander saying to his rival 'Tell me, Philemon, don't you blush when you beat me?'[5] Philemon, on the evidence of the Latin plays, excelled in comedy of situation; in the Greek that we have the pompous heavy-footedness of some of his writing, as opposed to Menander, reminds one of Plautus as opposed to Terence, and suggests a man with broader rather than subtler theatrical effects in mind.[6] Diphilus, judging from *Rudens*, had a colourful way with a romantic comedy in a remote setting. Though the extent of Plautus' modifications is (as ever) a problem, it is likely that the original was both more expansive and more comic than *Dyskolos*.[7] A certain sharpness has been seen in his writing, both in some of his verbal felicities and in the way in which (both in *Casina* and in *Rudens*) there are groups of black-and-white (as opposed to Menandrean pastel) characters in confrontation.[8] But it remains hard to be confident from what we have of these authors that one is not imagining more than one sees.

It happens that, with the loss of Menander at the end of antiquity, the world of New Comedy reached modern times through Plautus and Terence. The idea of amusing, civilized fiction based on ordinary people's everyday affairs has proved to be an immensely fruitful one, with its myriad descendants and influences from ancient times onwards, and now including not only drama on radio and cinema or television screen, but above all, the novel. Popular fiction

[1] Webster (1974); Sandbach in *Entretiens Hardt* (1970) 111ff.; Arnott (1979) xxxviii–xlv.
[2] Cf. *Entretiens Hardt* (1970) 7f.
[3] Webster (1970) has well-documented chapters on Philemon, Diphilus and (from the next generation) Apollodorus of Carystus, from whom Terence took *Hecyra* and *Phormio*.
[4] E.g. long speeches by cooks, Philemon 79 K, Diphilus 43 K; and parasite, Diphilus 60–1 K; and compare Philemon 28 K with *Samia* 206ff., 98 K with *Georgos* 35ff., Diphilus 17 K. 11ff. with *Samia* 99f., 55 K with *Dyskolos* 402ff.
[5] Aulus Gellius, *N.A.* 17.4.　　[6] E.g. frs. 23, 69, 91, 106 K.
[7] Compare for instance *Rud.* 414–84 (asking for water) with *Dysk.* 189–214.
[8] Sharpness: e.g. 24 K with Menander, *Kolax* 85ff., and frs. 60, 72, 83, 91, 107 K.

of this kind has two very obvious characteristics: its characters and stories offer many people an escape into a world of wish-fulfilment, a world with which they can easily identify, but neater and more entertaining than the real one often is; and secondly, there is, to a greater or less degree, an enlightening or educating influence.[1] There is, of course, a very great part of human life, even everyday life, that does not enter into Menander's portrayal of it[2] (the same is often felt about others: for instance Jane Austen). There are times when our assent is strained by the role he accords to Fortune, or Ignorance, or whatever other divine or abstract force has contributed to the fashioning of a situation.[3] There are other ways also in which he is noticeably an ancient and not a modern writer, not least in regard to his characters' behaviour, which he often accounts for very precisely (this is part of the art of dramatic structure) but in ethical, not psychological (certainly not post-Freudian) terms.[4] The test of his rating through modern eyes could easily be the passage and the play from which we began: can Polemon and Glykera still survive in modern company?

[1] Cf. Thierfelder (1956) on Roman comedy in this regard.

[2] Handley (1965a) 12f. with some further references.

[3] See Webster (1950) 198ff.; Ludwig in *Entretiens Hardt* (1970) 45–110; Bozanic (1977) 145–58; Lefèvre (1979) 320–8.

[4] Handley (1965a) 13 and n. 3; Webster (1974) 43–55.

APPENDIX OF
AUTHORS AND WORKS

TRAGEDY

GENERAL WORKS

(1) Bibliography
Lesky, *TDH*
(2) Tragedy in general
Baldry, H. C., *The Greek tragic theatre* (London 1971)
Buxton, R. G. A., *Persuasion in Greek tragedy* (Cambridge 1982)
von Fritz, K., *Antike und moderne Tragödie* (Berlin 1962)
Garton, C., 'Characterization in Greek tragedy', *J.H.S.* 77 (1957) 247–54
Goldhill, S., *Reading Greek tragedy* (Cambridge 1986)
Gould, J., 'Dramatic character and "human intelligibility" in Greek tragedy', *P.C.Ph.S.* n.s.24 (1978) 43–63
Jones, J., *On Aristotle and Greek tragedy* (London 1962)
Kitto, H. D. F., *Greek tragedy*, 3rd ed. (London 1961)
idem, *Form and meaning in drama* (London 1956)
Knox, B. W. M., *Word and action: essays on the ancient theater* (Baltimore 1979)
Lattimore, R., *The poetry of Greek tragedy* (Baltimore 1958)
idem, *Story patterns in Greek tragedy* (London 1964)
Lesky, A., *Greek tragedy*, 2nd ed. (London 1967)
idem, *TDH*
Lloyd-Jones, H., *The justice of Zeus* (Berkeley & Los Angeles 1971)
Lucas, D. W., *The Greek tragic poets*, 2nd ed. (London 1959)
Pohlenz, M., *Die griechische Tragödie*, 2nd ed. (Göttingen 1954)
de Romilly, J., *L'évolution du pathétique d'Éschyle à Euripide* (Paris 1961)
eadem, *Time in Greek tragedy* (Ithaca, N.Y. 1968)
eadem, *La tragédie grecque* (Paris 1970)
Saïd, S., *La faute tragique* (Paris 1978)
Seeck, G. A. (ed.), *Das griechische Drama* (Darmstadt 1979)
Snell, B., *Scenes from Greek drama* (Berkeley & Los Angeles 1964)
Steidle, W., *Studien zum antiken Drama* (Munich 1968)
Taplin, O. P., *Greek tragedy in action* (London 1978)
Vernant, J.-P. and Vidal-Naquet, P., *Mythe et tragédie en Grèce ancienne* (Paris 1973), English tr. by J. Lloyd (Brighton 1981); Vol. II (Paris 1986)
Vickers, B., *Towards Greek tragedy* (London 1973)

Yale Classical Studies 25 (1977) ed. T. F. Gould and C. J. Herington
(3) Text, form, metre
Dale, A. M., *The lyric metres of Greek drama*, 2nd ed. (Cambridge 1968)
eadem, *Metrical analyses of tragic choruses*, fasc. I, *B.I.C.S.* suppl. XXI.1 (1971); fasc.
    II, *B.I.C.S.* suppl. XXI.2 (1981)
Duchemin, J., L'ἀγών *dans la tragédie grecque* (Paris 1945)
Jackson, J., *Marginalia scaenica* (Oxford 1955)
Jens, W. (ed.), *Die Bauformen der griechischen Tragödie* (Munich 1971)
Kranz, W., *Stasimon* (Berlin 1933)
Kraus, W., *Strophengestaltung in der griechischen Tragödie, S.A.W.W.* 231.4 (1957)
Nestle, W., *Die Struktur des Eingangs in der attischen Tragödie* (Stuttgart 1930: repr.
    Hildesheim 1967)
Page, D. L., *Actors' interpolations in Greek tragedy* (Oxford 1934)
Schadewaldt, W., *Monolog und Selbstgespräch* (Berlin 1926)

ORIGINS OF TRAGEDY

BIBLIOGRAPHY

(1) GENERAL: *DTC* (1st *and* 2nd edd.); H. Patzer, *Die Anfänge der griechischen Tragödie* (Wiesbaden 1962); G. F. Else, *The origin and early form of Greek tragedy* (Cambridge, Mass. 1965); A. Lesky, *Greek tragedy*, 2nd ed. (London 1967) chs. II–III; W. Burkert, 'Greek tragedy and sacrificial ritual', *G.R.B.S.* 7 (1966) 87–121; H. Lloyd-Jones, 'Problems of early Greek tragedy: Pratinas, Phrynichus, the Gyges fragment', *Estudios sobre la tragedia griega*, Cuaderno de la Fundación Pastor XIII (Madrid 1966); Lesky, *TDH* chs. I–III; F. R. Adrados, *Festival, comedy and tragedy: the Greek origins of theatre* (Leiden 1975). (2) THESPIS: *DTC* 69–89; Lesky, *TDH* 49–56. (3) PRATINAS, PHRYNICHUS: *DTC* 63–8; M. Pohlenz, 'Das Satyrspiel und Pratinas von Phleius', *Kleine Schriften* II (Hildesheim 1965) 473; Lesky, *TDH* 57–64. (4) GYGES FRAGMENT: E. Lobel, 'A Greek historical drama', *P.B.A.* 35 (1950) 3 12; D. L. Page, *A new chapter in the history of Greek tragedy* (Cambridge 1951): for bibliography see Lesky, *TDH* 536 n.30; R. A. Pack, *Greek and Latin literary texts from Graeco-Roman Egypt*, 2nd ed. (Ann Arbor 1965) 97 (on no. 1707).

TRAGEDY IN PERFORMANCE

BIBLIOGRAPHY

(1) GENERAL: *DFA*; R. C. Flickinger, *The Greek theater and its drama*, 4th ed. (Chicago 1936); A. W. Pickard-Cambridge, *The theatre of Dionysus in Athens* (Oxford 1946); A. Spitzbarth, *Untersuchungen zur Spieltechnik der griechischen*

Tragödie (Zurich 1946); M. Bieber, *The history of the Greek and Roman theater*, 2nd ed. (Princeton 1961); N. C. Hourmouziades, *Production and imagination in Euripides* (Athens 1965); T. B. L. Webster, *Monuments illustrating tragedy and satyr play*, 2nd ed., *B.I.C.S.* suppl. XX (1967); idem, *Greek theatre production*, 2nd ed. (London 1970); H. C. Baldry, *The Greek tragic theatre* (London 1971); E. Simon, *Das antike Theater* (Heidelberg 1972), tr. C. E. Vafopoulou-Richardson (London 1982); N. G. L. Hammond, 'The conditions of dramatic production to the death of Aeschylus', *G.R.B.S.* 13 (1972) 387–450; S. Melchinger, *Das Theater der Tragödie* (Munich 1974); P. Walcot, *Greek drama in its theatrical and social context* (Cardiff 1976); H.-D. Blume, *Einführung in das antike Theaterwesen* (Darmstadt 1978). (2) FESTIVALS: *DFA* 25–125; H.-J. Mette, *Urkunden dramatischer Aufführungen in Griechenland* (Berlin 1977); H. W. Parke, *Festivals of the Athenians* (London 1977) 104–6, 125–35. (3) THEATRE BUILDING: W. Dörpfeld and E. Reisch, *Das griechische Theater* (Athens 1896); Pickard-Cambridge, *Theatre* 1–74, 134–68; W. B. Dinsmoor, 'The Athenian theater of the fifth century', in *Studies presented to D. M. Robinson* I (St Louis 1951) 309–30; A. M. Dale, 'An interpretation of Aristophanes, *Vesp.* 136–210 and its consequences for the stage of Aristophanes', *J.H.S.* 77 (1957) 205–11 = *Coll. Papers* (Cambridge 1969) 103–18; A. von Gerkan and W. Müller-Wiener, *Das Theater von Epidauros* (Stuttgart 1961); P. Arnott, *Greek scenic conventions in the fifth century B.C.* (Oxford 1962) 1–43; K. J. Dover, 'The skene in Aristophanes', *P.C.Ph.S.* 192 (1966) 2–17; J. Travlos, *Pictorial dictionary of ancient Athens* (London 1971) 537–52; Melchinger, *Theater* 3–49, 82–111, 126–37. (4) STAGE MACHINERY: Pickard-Cambridge, *Theatre* 100–22; Arnott, *Conventions* 72–88; Hourmouziades, *Production* 93–198, 146–69; Melchinger, *Theater* 191–200. (5) PROPERTIES: J. Dingel, *Das Requisit in der griechischen Tragödie* (diss. Tübingen 1967). (6) SCENERY: H. Bulle, *Eine Skenographie*, 94th Winckelmannsprogramm (Berlin 1934); Pickard-Cambridge, *Theatre* 30–74, 122–7; Arnott, *Conventions* 91–106; Hourmouziades, *Production* 35–57; Simon, *Theater* 31–40; Melchinger, *Theater* 162–4. (7) ACTORS: J. B. O'Connor, *Chapters in the history of actors and acting in ancient Greece* (Chicago 1908); B. Hunningher, *Acoustics and acting in the theatre of Dionysus Eleuthereus* (Amsterdam 1956); *DFA* 126–76; P. Ghiron-Bistagne, *Recherches sur les acteurs dans la Grèce antique* (Paris 1976). (8) COSTUMES, MASKS, FOOTWEAR: *DFA* 177–209; Simon, *Theater* 17–31; Melchinger, *Theater* 201–16. (9) PRONOMOS VASE: P. E. Arias, M. Hirmer, B. B. Shefton, *A history of Greek vase painting* (London 1962) 377–80; F. Brommer, 'Zur Deutung der Pronomosvase', *A.A.* 1964, 110–14; E. Simon, 'Die "Omphale" des Demetrios', *A.A.* 1971, 199–206; H. Froning, *Dithyrambos und Vasenmalerei in Athen* (Würzburg 1971) 5–15. (10) ACTING AND PRODUCTION: K. Reinhardt, *Aischylos als Regisseur und Theologe* (Berne 1949); W. Steidle, *Studien zum antiken Drama* (Munich 1968); A. M. Dale, 'Seen and unseen on the Greek stage', *W.S.* 69 (1956) 96–106 = *Coll. Papers* 119–29; eadem, 'Interior scenes and illusion in Greek drama', *Coll. Papers* 259–71; O. P. Taplin, 'Significant actions in Sophocles' *Philoctetes*', *G.R.B.S.* 12 (1971) 25–44; D. Bain, *Actors and audience: a study of asides and related conventions in Greek drama* (Oxford 1977); O. Taplin, *The stagecraft of Aeschylus: observations on the dramatic use of exits and entrances in Greek tragedy* (Oxford 1977); D. J. Mastronarde, *Contact and discontinuity: some conventions of speech and action on the Greek tragic stage* (Berkeley & Los Angeles 1979); D. Bain, *Orders, masters and servants in Greek tragedy* (Manchester 1981).

AESCHYLUS

LIFE

b. 525/4 B.C. (?) at Eleusis, of eupatrid family. Fought at Marathon 490 and probably at Salamis; perhaps too at Plataea. Began competing at tragic festivals early in 5th c. and was first victorious in 484. Visited Sicily some time between 472 and 468 (revived *Persae*, produced *Aetnaeae*) and again in 458 or later. d. at Gela 456/5. May have been initiated into Eleusinian mysteries. Total no. of victories given as twenty-eight (Suda) or thirteen (*Life*). Sources: *Marm. Par.* 59 (birth); ibid. 50, *Life* (OCT 331–3), Suda s.v. 'Pratinas' (literary career); *Marm. Par.* 48, schol. on Aesch. *Pers.* 429, Paus. 1.14.5, *Life* 331.10–13 (military career). On his initiation see Lesky, *TDH* 65f., B. M. W. Knox, *The heroic temper* (Berkeley & Los Angeles 1964) 174 n.82; on Sicilian visits C. J. Herington, *J.H.S.* 87 (1967) 74–85; on political sympathies K. J. Dover, *J.H.S.* 77 (1957) 230–7 (*Eum.*); E. R. Dodds, *P.C.Ph.S.* n.s.6 (1960) 19–31 (*Oresteia*); A. J. Podlecki, *The political background of Aeschylean tragedy* (Ann Arbor 1966), reviewed by R. P. Winnington-Ingram, *Gnomon* 39 (1967) 641–6.

WORKS

Suda gives total no. of plays as ninety. A list in the MSS of A. (OCT 335) contains seventy-three titles but is demonstrably incomplete. Eighty-one (perhaps eighty-three) titles survive, but some may be duplicates. Numerals in the *Life* are probably corrupt. (1) EXTANT: Seven tragedies: *Persae* (produced 472), *Septem contra Thebas* (467), *Supplices* (460s: see H. Lloyd-Jones, *A.C.* 33 (1964) 356–74; Garvie, under *Studies* (2) below), *Oresteia* (*Agamemnon, Choephori, Eumenides*: 458), *Prometheus vinctus* (see Griffith, under *Studies* (2) below, 9–13). (2) LOST OR FRAGMENTARY (alphabetical by Greek titles, as in *TGF*: for the satyr plays see D. F. Sutton, *H.S.C.Ph.* 78 (1974) 123–30). *Athamas, Aegyptii, Aetnaeae, Alexander* (sat.? see Sutton 128–9), *Alcmene, Amymone* (sat.), *Argei, Argo, Atalanta, Bacchae, Bassarai* 'Bacchants', *Glaucus* (*pontios* 'of the sea' (sat.?) and *Potnieus* 'the Potnian'), *Danaides,* '*Dike* play' (sat.), *Diktyulci* 'Net drawers' (sat.), *Dionysou trophoi* 'Nurses of Diony-sus' (sat.?), *Hektoros lytra* 'Ransom of Hector' or *Phryges, Eleusinii, Epigoni, Edoni, Heliades, Heraclidae, Thalamopoioi* 'Bride-chamber builders' (sat.?), *Theoroi* 'Spec-tators' or *Isthmiastae* 'Those who went to the Isthmia' (sat.), *Threissae, Hiereiai* 'Priestesses', *Ixion, Iphigenia, Cabiri, Callisto, Cares* or *Europa, Cercyon* (sat.), *Kerykes* 'Messengers' (sat.), *Circe* (sat.), *Cressae, Laius, Lemnii, Leon* (sat.). *Lycurgus* (sat.), *Memnon, Myrmidones, Mysi, Neaniskoi* 'Youths', *Nemea, Nereides, Niobe, Xantriai* 'Wool-carders', *Oedipus, Ostologoi* 'Gatherers of bones' (sat.), *Hoplon krisis* 'Judgement of the arms', *Palamedes, Pentheus, Perrhaebides, Penelope, Polydectes, Prometheus (lyomenos* 'unbound', *pyrphoros* 'the fire-bearer' and (sat.) *pyrkaeus* 'the fire-kindler'), *Propompoi* 'Escorts', *Proteus* (sat.), *Salaminiae, Semele* or *Hydrophoroi* 'Water-carriers', *Sisyphus (drapetes* 'the fugitive' (sat.?) and *petrokylistes* 'the stone-roller' (sat.), *Sphinx* (sat.), *Telephus, Toxotides* 'Archeresses', *Hypsipyle* (sat.?), *Philoctetes, Phineus, Phorcides, Psychagogoi* 'Necromancers', *Psychostasia* 'Weighing of lives', *Orithyia*. For an attempt to group these into trilogies and tetralogies see Mette under *Texts and commentaries* below.

BIBLIOGRAPHY

(See A. Wartelle, *Bibliographie historique et critique d'Éschyle et de la tragédie grecque 1518–1974* (Paris 1978).)

TEXTS AND COMMENTARIES: TEXTS: H. Weil (BT, 1903); U. von Wila-mowitz-Moellendorff (Berlin 1914: repr. 1958); H. W. Smyth (Loeb, 1922–6: II rev. H. Lloyd-Jones 1957 to incl. principal papyrus fragments); D. L. Page (OCT, 1972). COMMENTARIES: (1) Complete. P. Groeneboom (Groningen 1928–52: lacks *Supp.*); H. J. Rose, 2 vols. (Amsterdam 1957–8). (2) Individual plays. *Oresteia*: G. Thomson (Cambridge 1938: with tr. and incl. work of W. G. Headlam: rev. ed. Prague 1966, without tr. but with scholia). *Ag.*: E. Fraenkel, 3 vols. (Oxford 1950: with tr.); J. D. Denniston and D. L. Page (Oxford 1957); J. Bollack and P. Judet de la Combe, 4 vols. (Lille 1981–). *Cho.*: U. von Wilamowitz-Moellendorff, *Aischylos Orestie* II (Berlin 1896); T. G. Tucker (Cambridge 1901); A. F. Garvie (Oxford 1986). *Pers.*: H. D. Broadhead (Cambridge 1960). *P.V.*: G. Thomson (Cambridge 1932: repr. New York 1979); M. Griffith (Cambridge 1983). *Sept.*: T. G. Tucker (Cambridge 1908); G. Italie (Leiden 1950); G. O. Hutchinson (Oxford 1985). *Supp.*: J. Vürtheim (Amsterdam 1928); H. Friis Johansen and E. W. Whittle, 3 vols. (Gyldendalske Boghandel 1980). *Dictyulci*: M. Werre deHaas (Leiden 1961). *Fragments. TGF* 3–128; Lloyd-Jones in Loeb II; H.-J. Mette, *Die Fragmente der Tragödien des Aischylos* (Berlin 1959); idem, *Der verlorene Aischylos* (Berlin 1963); idem, *Lustrum* 13 (1968) 513–34 and 18 (1975) 338–44; S. Radt, *Tragicorum Graecorum fragmenta* III (Berlin 1985). *Scholia.* O. L. Smith (BT: I, *Oresteia* and *Supp.*, 1976; II 2, *Sept.*, 1982); idem, *Studies in the scholia on Aeschylus. I: The recensions of Demetrius Triclinius, Mnemosyne* suppl. XXXVII (1975). *Pers.*: O. Dähndardt (BT, 1894); (Triclinian scholia) L. Massa Positano (Naples 1948). *P.V.*: C. J. Herington, *Mnemosyne* suppl. XIX (1972).

TRANSLATIONS: (1) PROSE: W. G. and C. E. Ş. Headlam (Bohn, London 1909). *Oresteia*: H. Lloyd-Jones, 3 vols. (Englewood Cliffs, N.J. 1970: with notes: repr. London 1979). *Pers.*: A. Podlecki (Englewood Cliffs, N.J. 1970: with notes). *Sept.*: C. M. Dawson (Englewood Cliffs, N.J. 1970: with notes). (2) VERSE: P. Vella-cott (Harmondsworth 1956–61); (ed.) W. Arrowsmith, *The Greek tragedy in new translations* (Oxford: *Pers.*, J. Lembke and C. J. Herington 1981; *P.V.*, J. Scully 1975;

Sept., A. Hecht and H. H. Bacon 1974; *Supp.*, J. Lembke 1975). *Oresteia*: R. Lattimore (Chicago 1953); R. Fagles (Harmondsworth 1977). *Ag.*: L. MacNeice (London 1936).

STUDIES: (1) GENERAL: U. von Wilamowitz-Moellendorff, *Aischylos Interpreta-tionen* (Berlin 1914); G. Murray, *Aeschylus, the creator of tragedy* (Oxford 1940); G. Thomson, *Aeschylus and Athens* (London 1941); F. Solmsen, *Hesiod and Aeschylus* (Ithaca, N.Y. 1949); K. Reinhardt, *Aischylos als Regisseur und Theologe* (Berne 1949); E. T. Owen, *The harmony of Aeschylus* (Toronto 1952); J. de Romilly, *La crainte et l'angoisse dans le théâtre d'Éschyle* (Paris 1958); R. D. Dawe, 'Inconsistency of plot and character in Aeschylus', *P.C.Ph.S.* n.s.9 (1963) 21–62; C. J. Herington, 'Aeschy-lus: the last phase', *Arion* 4 (1965) 387–403; H. D. F. Kitto, *Poiesis* (Berkeley & Los Angeles 1966) 33–115; (ed.) M. H. McCall, *Aeschylus: a collection of critical essays* (Englewood Cliffs, N.J. 1972); P. E. Easterling, 'Presentation of character in Aeschy-lus', *G.&R.* 20 (1973) 3–19; (ed.) H. Hommel, *Aischylos*, 2 vols., Wege der For-schung LXXXVII and CDLXV (Darmstadt 1974); M. Gagarin, *Aeschylean drama* (Ber-keley & Los Angeles 1976); O. Taplin, *The stagecraft of Aeschylus: observations on the dramatic use of exits and entrances in Greek tragedy* (Oxford 1977); V. Di Benedetto, *L'ideologia del potere e la tragedia greca* (Turin 1978); (ed.) E. G. Schmidt, *Aischylos und Pindar: Studien zu Werk und Nachwirkung* (Berlin 1981); T. G. Rosenmeyer, *The art of Aeschylus* (Berkeley, Los Angeles & London 1982); R. P. Winnington-Ingram, *Studies in Aeschylus* (Cambridge 1983). (2) INDIVIDUAL PLAYS: *Oresteia*: H. D. F. Kitto, *Form and meaning in drama* (London 1956) chs. I–III; E. R. Dodds, 'Morals and politics in the *Oresteia*', *P.C.Ph.S.* n.s.6 (1960) 19–31; A. Lebeck, *The Oresteia: a study in language and structure* (Washington 1971); C. W. Macleod, 'Politics and the *Oresteia*', *J.H.S.* 102 (1982) 124–44; S. Goldhill, *Language, sexuality, narrative: the Oresteia* (Cambridge 1984); D. J. Conacher, *Aeschylus' Oresteia: a literary commentary* (Toronto 1987). *Pers.*: K. Deichgräber, *N.A.W.G.* 1941; idem, *Der listensinnende Trug des Gottes* (Göttingen 1952); R. Lattimore, 'Aeschylus on the defeat of Xerxes', *Classical studies in honor of W. A. Oldfather* (Urbana, Ill. 1943) 82–93; R. P. Winnington-Ingram, 'Zeus in the *Persae*', *J.H.S.* 93 (1973) 210–19; G. Paduano, *Gli Persiani di Eschilo* (Rome 1978). *P.V.*: C. J. Herington, *The author of the Prometheus Bound* (Austin, Texas 1970); E. R. Dodds, 'The *Prometheus vinctus* and the progress of scholarship', *The ancient concept of progress* (Oxford 1973) 26–44; M. Griffith, *The authenticity of the Prometheus Bound* (Cambridge 1977); idem, 'Aeschylus, Sicily and Prometheus', in (edd.) R. D. Dawe et al., *Dionysiaca* (Cambridge 1978) 105–39; M. L. West, 'The Prometheus trilogy', *J.H.S.* 99 (1979) 130–48; D. J. Conacher, *Aeschylus' Prometheus Bound. a literary commentary* (Toronto 1980). *Sept.* (see Lesky, *T.H.XX* n 13; R. P. Winnington-Ingram, *Y.Cl.S.* 25 (1977) 1–45): K. Wilkens, *Die Interdependenz zwischen Tragödienstruktur und Theologie bei Aischylos* (Munich 1974); W. G. Thalmann, *Dramatic art in Aeschylus' Seven against Thebes* (New Haven & London 1978). On authenticity of closing scene see H. Lloyd-Jones, *C.Q.* n.s.9 (1959) 80–115; E. Fraenkel, *M.H.* 21 (1964) 58–64; R. D. Dawe, *C.Q.* n.s.17 (1967) 16–28; idem, in (edd.) Dawe et al., *Dionysiaca* (Cambridge 1978) 87–103. *Supp.*: R. P. Winnington-Ingram, 'The Danaid trilogy of Aeschylus', *J.H.S.* 81 (1961) 141–52; A. F. Garvie, *Supplices: play and trilogy* (Cambridge 1969). (3) STYLE: C. F. Kumaniecki, *De elocutionis Aeschyleae natura* (Cracow 1935); J. Dumortier, *Les images dans la poésie d'Éschyle* (Paris 1935; repr. 1975); W. B. Stanford, *Aeschylus in his style* (Dublin 1942); F. R. Earp, *The style of Aeschylus* (Cambridge 1948); O. Hiltbrunner, *Wiederholungs- und Motivtechnik bei Aischylos* (Berne 1950); A. Sideras, *Aeschylus Homericus*, Hypomnemata XXXI (Göttingen 1971); E. Petrounias, *Funktion und Thematik der Bilder bei Aischylos* (Göttingen 1976). (4) TEXT AND TRANSMISSION: A. Turyn, *The manuscript tradition of the tragedies of Aeschylus* (New York 1943); R. D. Dawe, *The collation and investigation of manuscripts of Aeschylus* (Cambridge 1964); idem, *A repertory of conjectures on Aeschylus* (Leiden 1965); A. Wartelle, *Histoire du texte d'Éschyle dans l'antiquité* (Paris 1971). (5) METRE: O. Schroeder, *Aeschyli cantica* (Leipzig 1907).

LEXICA: G. Italie, 2nd ed. (Leiden 1964: addenda by S. Radt); H. Holmboe, 6 vols. (Akademisk Boghandel 1971–3: lacks *Eum.*); H. E. Edinger, *Index analyticus Graecitatis Aeschyleae* (Hildesheim 1981).

SOPHOCLES

LIFE

b. 497/6 or 496/5 B.C. (*Marm. Par.* 56, *FGrH* 239) at Colonus, son of Sophillus. As a boy led paean of celebrations after Salamis. First competed at tragic festival in 468: won 1st prize with *Triptolemus*, beating Aeschylus (Plut. *Cimon* 8.8). Served as *hellenotamias* 443/2 (*IG* I² 202.36), as *strategos* with Pericles 441/0 (Androtion *FGrH* 324 F 38, Ion of Chios *FGrH* 392 F 6), possibly also with Nicias later (Plut. *Nicias* 15.2); *proboulos* 412/11 (Arist. *Rhet.* 1419a26–31, unless Arist. refers to a different Sophocles). Won 1st prize in 409 with Philoctetes (2nd *Hypoth.*). d. after Dionysia of 406 (*Vit. Eur.* 135.42ff.) and before Lenaea of 405 (Ar. *Frogs* 787ff.). Won eighteen victories at Dionysia = seventy-two plays (*IG* II² 2325). Total no. of victories (i.e. including some at Lenaea) was either twenty (*Life* 8) or twenty-four (Suda). Never placed lower than second. Served on embassies and was prominent in Athenian religious life, esp. in cult of Asclepius (*IG* II² 1252–3). Given posthumous hero cult under name of Dexion (*Et. Magn.* 256.6). Family: wife Nicostrate, son Iophon (tragic poet), concubine Theoris, son Ariston, grandson Sophocles (tragic poet). Sources: S. Radt, *Tragicorum Graecorum fragmenta* IV (Berlin 1977) 29 95. For S.'s political career see V. Ehrenberg, *Sophocles and Pericles* (Oxford 1954); L. Woodbury, *Phoenix* 24 (1970) 209–24; H. C. Avery, *Historia* 22 (1973) 509–14; for the *Life* see J. A. Fairweather, 'Fiction in the biographies of ancient writers', *Anc. Soc.* 5 (1974) 231–75; M. Lefkowitz, *The lives of the Greek poets* (London 1981) 75–87.

SOPHOCLES

WORKS

Suda gives total no. of plays as 123; titles of some 118 are known. (1) EXTANT: '
Tragedies: *Ajax, Antigone* (produced *c.* 442?), *Trachiniae, Oedipus tyrannus* (after
429?), *Electra, Philoctetes* (409), *Oedipus Coloneus* (posthumously prod. by grandson
Sophocles 401). For problems of dating see Lesky, *TDH*, on individual plays; H.-J.
Newiger, *G.G.A.* 209 (1967) 175–94. Also K. Schefold, *A.K.* 19 (1976) 71–8 (on
Ajax); (ed.) P. E. Easterling, *Trachiniae* (Cambridge 1982) 19–23. Satyr play:
Ichneutae 'Searchers' (substantial fragments). (2) LOST OR FRAGMENTARY (alphabetical
by Greek titles, as in *TGF* and Pearson: for the satyr plays see D. F. Sutton,
H.S.C.Ph. 78 (1974) 130–40). *Admetus* (sat.), *Athamas* A & B, *Ajax Locrus, Aegeus,
Aegisthus, Aethiopes, Aichmalotides* 'Captives', *Acrisius, Aleadae, Alexander, Aletes,
Alcmeon, Amycus* (sat.), *Amphiaraus* (sat.), *Amphitryon, Andromache* (?), *Andromeda,
Antenoridae, Atreus* or *Mycenaeae, Achaion syllogos* 'Gathering of the Achaeans',
Achilleos erastai 'Lovers of Achilles' (sat.), *Daedalus* (sat.), *Danae, Dionysiscus* (sat.),
Dolopes, Helenes apaitesis 'Demand for Helen', *Helenes gamos* 'Marriage of Helen'
(sat.), *Epigoni* (= *Eriphyle?*), *Eris, Hermione, Eumelus, Euryalus, Eurypylus, Eury-
saces, Heracleiscus* (sat.), *Heracles* or *Heracles at Taenarum* (= *Cerberus?*) (sat.),
Erigone, Thamyras, Theseus, Thyestes A & B, *Iambe* (sat.), *Iberes, Inachus* (sat.),
Ixion, Iobates, Hipponous, Iphigenia, Camici, Cedalion (sat.), *Clytemnestra, Colchides,
Creusa* (= *Ion?*), *Krisis* (sat.), *Kophoi* 'Dullards' (sat.), *Lacaenae, Laocoon, Larisaei,
Lemniae, Manteis* 'Seers' or *Polyidus, Meleager, Momus* (sat.), *Musae* (?), *Nauplius*
(*katapleon* 'ashore' and *pyrkaeus* 'the fire-kindler'), *Nausicaa* or *Plyntriai* 'Washer-
women', *Niobe, Odysseus akanthoplex* 'wounded by the prickle' or *Niptra* 'Foot-
washing', *Oecles, Oeneus* or *Schoeneus* (sat.: on authorship see p. 188), *Oenomaus,
Palamedes, Pandora* or *Sphyrokopoi* 'Hammerers' (sat.), *Peleus, Poimenes* 'Shepherds',
Polyxena, Priamus, Procris, Rhizotomoi 'Herbalists' or 'Sorcerers', *Salmoneus* (sat.),
Sinon, Sisyphus, Scythae, Scyrii, Syndeipnon 'Banquet' (sat.), *Tantalus, Teucer,
Telephus* (see Sutton 138), *Tereus, Triptolemus, Troilus, Tympanistai* 'Drummers',
Tyndareus, Tyro A & B, *Hybris* (sat.), *Hydrophoroi* 'Water-carriers', *Phaeaces,
Phaedra, Phthiotides, Philoctetes at Troy, Phineus, Phoenix, Phrixus, Phryges, Chryses.*
Also paeans (Suda): a fragment is preserved (*PMG* 737). Elegy to Herodotus (Plut.
Mor. 786b). Prose work *On the chorus* (Athen. 13.603ff.).

BIBLIOGRAPHY

TEXTS AND COMMENTARIES: TEXTS: A. C. Pearson (OCT, 1924: corr.
1928); A. Dain and P. Mazon (Budé, 1955–60); R. D. Dawe (BT, 1975–9, 2nd ed. 1984,
1985). COMMENTARIES: (1) Complete. L. Campbell, 2 vols. (1, 2nd ed., Oxford 1879; 11,
Oxford 1881); R. C. Jebb (Cambridge 1883 onwards, with tr.: *Aj.* 1896; *Ant.*, 3rd ed., 1900;
El. 1894; *O.C.*, 3rd ed., 1900; *O.T.*, 3rd ed., 1893; *Phil.*, 2nd ed., 1898; *Tr.* 1892); F.
Schneidewin and A. Nauck, rev. E. Bruhn (Berlin: *O.T.* 1910; *El.* 1912; *Ant.* 1913) and

L. Radermacher (*O.C.* 1909; *Phil.* 1911; *Aj.* 1913; *Tr.* 1914); J. C. Kamerbeek (Leiden: *Tr.* 1959; *Aj.*, 2nd ed. 1963; *O.T.* 1967; *El.* 1974; *Ant.* 1978; *Phil.* 1980; *O.C.* 1984). (2) Individual plays. *Aj.*: W. B. Stanford (London 1963); J. de Romilly (Paris 1976). *Ant.*: G. Müller (Heidelberg 1967); A. L. Brown, with tr. (Warminster 1987). *El.*: G. Kaibel (Leipzig 1896); J. H. Kells (Cambridge 1973). *O.T.*: O. Longo (Florence 1972); R. D. Dawe (Cambridge 1982). *Phil.*: T. B. L. Webster (Cambridge 1970). *Tr.*: O. Longo (Padua 1968); P. E. Easterling (Cambridge 1982). *Ichneutae*: V. Steffen (Warsaw 1960). *Inachus*: D. F. Sutton (Meisenheim am Glan 1979). *Fragments. TGF* 131–360; A. C. Pearson, 3 vols. (Cambridge 1917); D. L. Page, *Select papyri* III (Loeb, 1941) 12–53; R. Carden, *The papyrus fragments of Sophocles* (Berlin & New York 1974); S. Radt, *Tragicorum Graecorum fragmenta* IV (Berlin 1977). W. Willige, *Sophokles. Tragödien und Fragmente* (Munich 1966) gives a German tr. of the fragments. *Scholia.* W. Dindorf (Oxford 1852); P. N. Papageorgius (BT, 1888). *Aj.*: G. A. Christodoulou (Athens 1977). *O.C.*: V. de Marco (Rome 1952). *O.T.* (Byzantine scholia): O. Longo (Padua 1971).

TRANSLATIONS: (1) PROSE: *El.*: W. Sale (Englewood Cliffs, N.J. 1973: with notes). *O.T.*: T. Gould (Englewood Cliffs, N.J. 1970: with notes). (2) VERSE: E. F. Watling (Harmondsworth 1947–53); (edd.) D. Grene and R. Lattimore, in *The complete Greek tragedies* (Chicago 1959); R. Fagles and B. M. W. Knox, *Sophocles: the three Theban plays* (New York & London 1982); (ed.) W. Arrowsmith, *The Greek tragedy in new translations* (Oxford: *Ant.*, R. E. Braun 1974; *O.T.*, S. Berg and D. Clay 1978; *Tr.*, C. K. Williams and G. W. Dickerson 1978). *Tr.*: Ezra Pound (London 1956: repr. 1969); R. Torrance (Boston 1966).

STUDIES: (1) SURVEYS: H. Friis Johansen, *Lustrum* 7 (1962) 94–288; (ed.) H. Diller, *Sophokles* (Darmstadt 1967) 537–46 (Literatur-Übersicht); Lesky, *TDH* 169–274; H. Strohm, *A.A.H.G.* 24 (1971) 129–62; 26 (1973) 1–5; 30 (1977) 129–44; R. G. A. Buxton, *G.&R.* New surveys in the classics XVI (1984). (2) GENERAL: T. von Wilamowitz-Moellendorff, *Die dramatische Technik des Sophokles* (Berlin 1917); G. Perrotta, *Sofocle* (Milan 1935: repr. Rome 1963); C. M. Bowra, *Sophoclean tragedy* (Oxford 1944); K. Reinhardt, *Sophokles*, 3rd ed. (Frankfurt am Main 1947), English tr. by H. M. and F. D. Harvey (Oxford 1979); A. J. A. Waldock, *Sophocles the dramatist* (Cambridge 1951); C. H. Whitman, *Sophocles: a study of heroic humanism* (Cambridge, Mass. 1951); G. M. Kirkwood, *A study of Sophoclean drama* (Ithaca, N.Y. 1958); H. Diller, W. Schadewaldt, A. Lesky, *Gottheit und Mensch in der Tragödie des Sophokles* (Darmstadt 1963); A. Maddalena, *Sofocle*, 2nd ed. (Turin 1963); B. M. W. Knox, *The heroic temper* (Berkeley & Los Angeles 1964); R. M. Torrance, 'Sophocles: some bearings', *H.S.C.Ph.* 69 (1965) 269–327; (ed.) T. Woodard, *Sophocles, a collection of critical essays* (Englewood Cliffs, N.J. 1966); (ed.) H. Diller, *Sophokles*, Wege der Forschung XCV (Darmstadt 1967); T. B. L. Webster, *An introduction to Sophocles*, 2nd ed. (London 1969); W. Schadewaldt, *Hellas und Hesperien* I (Zurich & Stuttgart 1970) 369–434; G. H. Gellie, *Sophocles: a reading* (Carlton, Victoria 1972); R. W. B.

Burton, *The chorus in Sophocles' tragedies* (Oxford 1980); R. P. Winnington-Ingram, *Sophocles: an interpretation* (Cambridge 1980); C. Segal, *Tragedy and civilization: an interpretation of Sophocles* (Cambridge, Mass. 1981); A. Machin, *Cohérence et continuité dans le théâtre de Sophocle* (Quebec 1981); D. Seale, *Vision and stagecraft in Sophocles* (London 1982); V. Di Benedetto, *Sofocle* (Florence 1983, 1988). (3) INDIVIDUAL PLAYS: *Aj.*: B. M. W. Knox, 'The *Ajax* of Sophocles', *H.S.C.Ph.* 65 (1961) 1–37; M. Simpson, 'Sophocles' Ajax: his madness and transformation', *Arethusa* 2 (1969) 88–103; P. Burian, 'Supplication and hero cult in Sophocles' *Ajax*', *G.R.B.S.* 13 (1972) 151–6; M. Sicherl, 'The tragic issue in Sophocles' *Ajax*', *Y.Cl.S.* 25 (1977) 67–98. *Ant.*: R. F. Goheen, *The imagery of Sophocles' Antigone* (Princeton 1951); D. A. Hester,'Sophocles the unphilosophical', *Mnemosyne* 24 (1971) 11–59; H. Rohdich, *Antigone: Beitrag zu einer Theorie des sophokleischen Helden* (Heidelberg 1980). *El.*: H. Friis Johansen, 'Die *Elektra* des Sophokles: Versuch einer neuen Deutung', *C.&M.* 25 (1964) 8–32; C. P. Segal, 'The *Electra* of Sophocles', *T.A.Ph.A.* 97 (1966) 473–545; H.-J. Newiger, 'Hofmannsthals *Elektra* und die griechische Tragödie', *Arcadia* 4 (1969) 138–63; *O.C.*: I. M. Linforth, 'Religion and drama in "Oedipus at Colonus"', *Univ. of Calif. Publ. in Class. Phil.* 14.4 (1951); P. E. Easterling, 'Oedipus and Polynices', *P.C.Ph.S.* 13 (1967) 1–13; P. Burian, 'Suppliant and saviour: *Oedipus at Colonus*', *Phoenix* 28 (1974) 408–29. *O.T.*: B. M. W. Knox, *Oedipus at Thebes* (New Haven & London 1957); E. R. Dodds, 'On misunderstanding the *Oedipus Rex*', *G.&R.* 13 (1966) 37–49; A. Cameron, *The identity of Oedipus the king* (New York 1968); (ed.) M. J. O'Brien, *Twentieth-century interpretations of Oedipus Rex* (Englewood Cliffs, N.J. 1968). *Phil.*: O. P. Taplin, 'Significant actions in Sophocles' *Philoctetes*', *G.R.B.S.* 12 (1971) 25–44; P. Vidal-Naquet, 'Le *Philoctète* de Sophocle', in J.-P. Vernant and P. Vidal-Naquet, *Mythe et tragédie en Grèce ancienne* (Paris 1973) (Eng. tr. by Janet Lloyd, *Myth and tragedy in ancient Greece* (Brighton 1980)); J. U. Schmidt, *Sophokles Philoktet: eine Strukturanalyse* (Heidelberg 1973); P. E. Easterling, '*Philoctetes* and modern criticism', *I.C.S.* 3 (1978) 27–39. *Tr.*: P. E. Easterling, 'Sophocles' *Trachiniae*', *B.I.C.S.* 15 (1968) 58–69; C. P. Segal, 'Sophocles' *Trachiniae*: myth, poetry, and heroic values', *Y.Cl.S.* 25 (1977) 99–158. (4) STYLE: L. Campbell, *Sophocles* I, 2nd ed. (Cambridge 1879) 1–107; E. Bruhn, *Sophokles* erkl. von Schneidewin/Nauck, *Anhang* (Berlin 1899: repr. 1963); F. R. Earp, *The style of Sophocles* (Cambridge 1944); A. A. Long, *Language and thought in Sophocles* (London 1968); A. C. Moorhouse, *The syntax of Sophocles* (Leiden 1982). (5) METRE: O. Schroeder, *Sophoclis cantica* (Leipzig 1908); H. Pohlsander, *Metrical studies in the lyrics of Sophocles* (Leiden 1964); A. M. Dale, *Metrical analyses of tragic choruses*, fascs. I and II, *B.I.C.S.* suppl. XXI.1 (1971) and XXI.2 (1981). (6) TEXT: A. Turyn, *Studies in the manuscript tradition of the tragedies of Sophocles* (Urbana, Illinois 1952); R. D. Dawe, *Studies on the text of Sophocles*, 3 vols. (Leiden 1973–8).

LEXICON: F. Ellendt, 2nd ed. rev. H. Genthe (Berlin 1872: repr. Hildesheim 1958).

EURIPIDES

LIFE

b. 485/4 or 480 B.C., son of Mnesarchus (or Mnesarchides), of the deme of Phyle. d. 406 in Macedonia; his last years, 408–406 (?), were spent at the court of Archelaus in Pella. Competed at Dionysia on twenty-two occasions (first in 455), but won first prize only four times, the last time posthumously for the group of plays which included *Bacch.* and *I.A.* Apparently took no active part in public life (unlike Sophocles). Sources: ancient *Life* (ed. E. Schwartz, *Scholia in Euripidem* I (Berlin 1887) 1–8) and fragments of a *Life* by Satyrus (ed. G. Arrighetti (Pisa 1964)); Arist. *Rhet.* 2.6.20 with schol., Plut. *Nic.* 17 (alleged visit to Syracuse, elegy on those who died there); see P. T. Stevens, 'Euripides and the Athenians', *J.H.S.* 76 (1956) 87–94; M. Lefkowitz, 'The Euripides *Vita*', *G.R.B.S.* 20 (1979) 188–210. What biographical material we possess is unreliable: most of it obviously stems from comic travesties; cf. M. Lefkowitz, *The lives of the Greek poets* (London 1981) 88–104. There may be some truth to the Aristophanic hint (*Frogs* 1048) that he was unfortunate in his marriage, and it is certain that one of his sons (or perhaps a nephew), Euripides by name, was also a tragic poet. The one item of the anecdotal tradition which may have a basis in fact is the picture of E. as an intellectual recluse, the possessor of a large library (cf. Ar. *Frogs* 943 and 1409).

WORKS

Life gives total no. of plays as ninety-two, Suda as seventy-eight; latter figure probably represents no. of plays still available to Alexandrian scholars. (1) EXTANT: Tragedies (when approximate dates are given, these are based on the metrical criteria proposed by T. Zieliński, *Tragodoumenon libri tres* II (Cracow 1925)): *Alcestis* (produced 438: prosatyric), *Medea* (431), *Heraclidae* (c. 430), *Hippolytus* (428), *Andromache* (c. 425), *Hecuba* (c. 424), *Supplices* (c. 424), *Ion* (c. 418/17), *Electra* (417: perhaps 413), *Hercules furens* (c. 417), *Troades* (415), *Iphigenia in Tauris* (c. 413), *Helen* (412), *Phoenissae* (after 412, before 408), *Orestes* (408), *Bacchae* and *Iphigenia in Aulide* (both prod. posthumously, probably 405). Also *Rhesus* (if the extant play is by E., his earliest surviving work). Satyr play: *Cyclops*: see D. F. Sutton, *The date of Euripides' Cyclops* (Ann Arbor 1974). (2) LOST OR FRAGMENTARY (alphabetical by Greek titles, as in *TGF*: for the satyr plays see D. F. Sutton, *H.S.C.Ph.* 78 (1974) 140–3). *Aegeus, Aeolus, Alexander, Alcmeon through Corinth, Alcmeon through Psophis, Alcmene, Alope* or *Cercyon, Andromeda, Antigone, Archelaus, Auge, Autolycus,* (sat., possibly A & B: see D. F. Sutton, *Eos* 62 (1974) 49–53), *Bellerophon, Busiris* (sat.), *Danae, Dictys, Epeus, Erechtheus, Eurystheus* (sat.), *Theristai* 'Reapers' (sat.), *Theseus, Thyestes, Ino, Ixion, Hippolytus, Cadmus, Cresphontes, Cressae, Cretes, Lamia, Licymnius, Melanippe* (*hē sophē* 'the wise' and *hē desmotis* 'the prisoner'), *Meleager,*

EURIPIDES

Mysi, *Oedipus*, *Oeneus*, *Oenomaus*, *Palamedes*, *Peliades*, *Peleus*, *Plisthenes*, *Polyidus* or *Glaucus*, *Protesilaus*, *Stheneboea*, *Sisyphus* (sat.), *Sciron* (sat.), *Scyrii*, *Syleus* (sat.), *Telephus*, *Temenidae*, *Temenus*, *Hypsipyle*, *Phaethon*, *Philoctetes*, *Phoenix*, *Phrixus*, *Chrysippus*. Attributed by Alexandrians to Critias: *Pirithous*, *Rhadamanthus*, *Tennes* (see p. 89).

BIBLIOGRAPHY

(See C. Collard, *G.&R.* New surveys in the classics XIV (1981).)

TEXTS AND COMMENTARIES: TEXTS: R. Prinz and N. Wecklein (Leipzig 1877–1902); G. Murray (OCT, 1902–9); L. Méridier, L. Parmentier, H. Grégoire, F. Chapoutier, F. Jouan (Budé, 1926–83); BT (1964–: *Alc.*, A. Garzya 1980; *And.*, idem 1978; *Cyc.*, W. Biehl 1983; *Hec.*, S. G. Daitz 1973; *Hel.*, K. Alt 1964; *Heraclid.*, A. Garzya 1972; *Ion*, W. Biehl 1979; *I.T.*, D. Sansone 1981; *Or.*, W. Biehl 1975; *Supp.*, C. Collard 1984; *Tro.*, W. Biehl 1970); J. Diggle (OCT, 1981–), COMMENTARIES: (1) Complete. F. A. Paley (London 1857–74). (2) Selection. H. Weil (Paris 1905: *Hipp.*, *Med.*, *Hec.*, *I.A.*, *I.T.*, *El.* and *Or.*). (3) Individual plays. *Alc.*: A. M. Dale (Oxford 1954). *And.*: P. T. Stevens (Oxford 1971). *Bacch.*: E. R. Dodds, 2nd ed. (Oxford 1960); J. Roux, 2 vols. (Paris 1970–2). *Cyc.*: N. Wecklein (Leipzig 1903); J. Duchemin (Paris 1945); V. de Falco (Naples 1966); R. G. Ussher (Rome 1978); R. Seaford (Oxford 1984); W. Biehl (Heidelberg 1986). *El.*: J. D. Denniston (Oxford 1939: repr. 1954). *Hel.*: A. M. Dale (Oxford 1967); R. Kannicht, 2 vols. (Heidelberg 1969). *H.F.*: U. von Wilamowitz-Moellendorff (Berlin 1895; repr. Darmstadt 1959); G. W. Bond (Oxford 1981). *Hipp.*: W. S. Barrett (Oxford 1964). *Ion*: U. von Wilamowitz-Moellendorff (Berlin 1926: repr. 1969); A. S. Owen (Oxford 1939). *I.A.*: E. B. England (London 1891: repr. New York 1979). *I.T.*: M. Platnauer (Oxford 1938: repr. 1952). *Med.*: D. L. Page (Oxford 1938). *Or.*: W. Biehl (Berlin 1965); V. Di Benedetto (Florence 1965); M. L. West, with tr. (Warminster 1986); C. W. Willink (Oxford 1986). *Phoen.*: A. C. Pearson (London 1909: repr. New York 1979). *Supp.*: C. Collard, 2 vols. (Groningen 1975). *Tro.*: K. H. Lee (London 1976); S. A. Barlow, with tr. (Warminster 1986). *Fragments. TGF* 363–716; H. von Arnim, *Supplementum Euripideum* (Bonn 1913); B. Snell, *Supplementum* (Hildesheim 1964); C. Austin, *Nova fragmenta Euripidea in papyris reperta* (Berlin 1968); (edd.) G. A. Seeck *et al.*, *Euripides, Sämtliche Tragödien und Fragmente* VI (Munich 1981: with German tr. of the fragments). Bibliography: H.-J. Mette, 'Die Bruchstücke', *Lustrum* 12 (1967); 13 (1968) 284–403 and 569–71; 17 (1973–4) 5–26; 23–4 (1981–2). Discussion: H. van Looy, *Zes verloren Tragedies van Euripides* (Brussels 1964); T. B. L. Webster, *The tragedies of Euripides* (London 1967). *Fragmentary plays* (editions and discussions). *Aeolus*: S. Jäkel, *G.B.* 8 (1979) 101 18. *Alexander*: B. Snell, *Hermes* Einzelschriften V (1937); R. A. Coles, 'A new Oxyrhynchus papyrus: the hypothesis of Euripides' *Alexandros*', *B.I.C.S.* suppl. XXXII (1974). *Antiope*: J. Kambitsis (Athens 1972); B. Snell, *Scenes from Greek drama* (Berkeley & Los Angeles 1964) 70–98. *Archelaus*: A. Harder (Leiden 1985). *Cresphontes*: O. Musso (Milan 1974); A. Harder (Leiden 1985). *Cretans*: R. Cantarella (Milan 1963). *Erechtheus*: P. Carrara (Florence 1977); A. M. Diez (Granada 1975). *Hypsipyle*: G. W. Bond (Oxford 1963).

EURIPIDES

Phaethon: J. Diggle (Cambridge 1970). *Telephus*: E. W. Handley and J. Rea, *B.I.C.S.* suppl. v (1957). *Scholia*: E. Schwartz (Berlin 1887–91); O. L. Smith, *Scholia metrica anonyma in Euripidis Hecubam Orestem Phoenissas* (Copenhagen 1977); S. G. Daitz, *The scholia in the Jerusalem palimpsest of Euripides* (Heidelberg 1979).

TRANSLATIONS: (1) PROSE: *Alc.*: C. R. Beye (Englewood Cliffs, N.J. 1974: with notes). *Bacch.*: G. S. Kirk (Englewood Cliffs, N.J. 1970: with notes: repr. Cambridge 1979). *Ion*: A. P. Burnett (Englewood Cliffs, N.J. 1970: with notes). *I.A.*: K. Cavander (Englewood Cliffs, N.J. 1973: with notes). (2) VERSE: P. Vellacott (Harmondsworth, 1953–72: lacks *I.A.* and *Cyc.*); D. Grene and R. Lattimore, *The complete Greek tragedies* (Chicago 1953–72); (ed.) W. Arrowsmith, *The Greek tragedy in new translations* (Oxford: *Hipp.*, R. Bagg 1973; *I.T.*, R. Lattimore 1974; *Alc.*, W. Arrowsmith 1974; *Rhes.*, R. E. Braun 1978; *I.A.*, W. S. Merwin 1978; *Hel.*, J. Michie and C. Leach 1981; *Heraclid.*, H. Taylor and R. A. Brooks 1981; *Phoen.*: P. Burian and B. Swann 1981).

STUDIES: (1) GENERAL: G. Murray, *Euripides and his age* (London 1913); E. R. Dodds, 'Euripides the irrationalist', *C.R.* 43 (1929) 97–104; G. M. A. Grube, *The drama of Euripides* (London 1941); E. M. Blaiklock, *The male characters of Euripides* (Wellington, N.Z. 1952); W. H. Friedrich, *Euripides und Diphilos* (Munich 1953); L. H. G. Greenwood, *Aspects of Euripidean tragedy* (Cambridge 1953); G. Zuntz, *The political plays of Euripides* (Manchester 1955); H. Strohm, *Euripides: Interpretationen zur dramatischen Form* (Munich 1957); J. Jones, *On Aristotle and Greek tragedy* (London 1962) sect. IV; N. C. Hourmouziades, *Production and imagination in Euripides* (Athens 1965); F. Jouan, *Euripide et les légendes des chants cypriens* (Paris 1966); D. J. Conacher, *Euripidean drama* (Toronto 1967); H. Rohdich, *Die euripideische Tragödie* (Heidelberg 1968); W. Steidle, *Studien zum antiken Drama* (Munich 1968); R. P. Winnington-Ingram, 'Euripides poietes sophos', *Arethusa* 2 (1969) 127–42; A. P. Burnett, *Catastrophe survived* (Oxford 1971); G. Zuntz, 'Contemporary politics in Euripides', *Opuscula selecta* (Manchester 1972) 54–61; C. H. Whitman, *Euripides and the full circle of myth* (Cambridge, Mass. 1974); C. Collard, 'Formal debates in Euripides' drama', *G.&R.* 22 (1975) 58–71; A. Rivier, *Essai sur le tragique d'Euripide*, 2nd ed. (Paris 1975). (2) COLLECTIONS: *Entretiens VI: Euripide* (Fondation Hardt, Geneva 1960); (ed.) E. Segal, *Euripides: a collection of critical essays* (Englewood Cliffs, N.J. 1968); (ed.) E. R. Schwinge, *Euripides*, Wege der Forschung LXXXIX (Darmstadt 1968). (3) INDIVIDUAL PLAYS: *Alc.*: K. von Fritz, 'Euripides' Alkestis und ihre modernen Nachahmer und Kritiker', *A.&A.* 5 (1956) 27–70; (ed.) J. Wilson, *Twentieth-century interpretations of Euripides' Alcestis* (Englewood Cliffs, N.J. 1968); H. Erbse, 'Euripides' Alkestis', *Philologus* 116 (1972) 32–52. *And.*: A. Lesky, 'Der Ablauf der Handlung in der Andromache des Euripides', *A.A.W.W.* 84 (1947) 99–115 = *Ges. Schrift.* 144; H. Erbse, 'Euripides' Andromache', *Hermes* 94 (1966) 276–97; P. D. Kovacs, *The Andromache of Euripides: an interpretation* (Chico, Calif. 1980). *Bacch.* R. P. Winnington-Ingram, *Euripides and Dionysus* (Cambridge 1948: repr. Amsterdam 1969); J. de Romilly, 'Le thème du bonheur dans les *Bacchantes*', *R.E.G.* 76 (1963) 361–80; C.

186

EURIPIDES

Segal, *Dionysiac poetics and Euripides' Bacchae* (Princeton 1982). *El.*: K. Matthiessen, *Elektra, Taurische Iphigenie und Helena* (Göttingen 1964); M. J. O'Brien, 'Orestes and the gorgon: Euripides' *Electra*', *A.J.Ph.* 86 (1964) 13–39. *Hec.*: G. Kirkwood, 'Hecuba and Nomos', *T.A.Ph.A.* 78 (1947) 61–8; A. W. H. Adkins, 'Values in Euripides' *Hecuba* and *Hercules Furens*', *C.Q.* n.s.16 (1966) 193–219. *Hel.*: F. Solmsen, 'Onoma and Pragma in Euripides' *Helen*', *C.R.* 48 (1934) 119–21; A. P. Burnett, 'Euripides' *Helen*: a comedy of ideas', *C.Ph.* 55 (1960) 151–63; C. Segal, 'The two worlds of Euripides' *Helen*', *T.A.Ph.A.* 102 (1971) 553–614. *H.F.*: H. H. O. Chalk, 'Arete and Bia in Euripides' *Herakles*', *J.H.S.* 82 (1962) 7–18; J. C. Kamerbeek, 'Unity and meaning of Euripides' *Heracles*', *Mnemosyne* n.s.4.19 (1966) 1–16. *Heraclid.*: J. W. Fitton, 'The *Suppliant Women* and *Herakleidae* of Euripides', *Hermes* 89 (1961) 430–61; A. Lesky, 'On the *Heraclidae* of Euripides', *Y.Cl.S.* 25 (1977) 227–338; P. Burian, 'Euripides' *Heraclidae*: an interpretation', *C.Ph.* 72 (1977) 1–21. *Hipp.*: B. M. W. Knox, 'The *Hippolytus* of Euripides', *Y.Cl.S.* 13 (1952) 3–31 = *Word and action* (Baltimore 1979) 205–30; R. P. Winnington-Ingram, '*Hippolytus*: a study in causation', in *Entretiens VI: Euripide* (Fondation Hardt, Geneva 1960) 171–97. *Ion*: C. Wolff, 'The design and myth in Euripides' *Ion*', *H.S.C.Ph.* 69 (1965) 169–94; B. M. W. Knox, 'Euripidean comedy', *Word and action* (Baltimore 1979) 250–74. *I.A.*: D. L. Page, *Actors' interpolations in Greek tragedy...with special reference to Euripides' Iphigeneia in Aulis* (Oxford 1934). *I.T.*: G. Zuntz, 'Die *Taurische Iphigenie* des Euripides', *Die Antike* 9 (1933) 245–54. *Med.*: P. E. Easterling, 'The infanticide in Euripides' *Medea*', *Y.Cl.S.* 25 (1977) 177–91; B. M. W. Knox, 'The *Medea* of Euripides', *Y.Cl.S.* 25 (1977) 193–225 = *Word and action* (Baltimore 1979) 295–322. *Or.*: N. A. Greenberg, 'Euripides' *Orestes*: an interpretation', *H.S.C.Ph.* 66 (1962) 157–92; E. Rawson, 'Aspects of Euripides' *Orestes*', *Arethusa* 5 (1972) 155–67; W. Burkert, 'Die Absurdität der Gewalt und das Ende der Tragödie: Euripides' *Orestes*', *A.&A.* 20 (1974) 97–109. *Phoen.*: H. D. F. Kitto, 'The final scenes of the *Phoenissae*', *C.R.* 53 (1939) 104–11; E. Fraenkel, 'Zu den *Phoenissen* des Euripides', *S.B.A.W.* 1963, 1; J. de Romilly, 'Les Phéniciennes d'Euripide', *R.Ph.* 39 (1965) 28–47; E. Rawson, 'Family and fatherland in Euripides' *Phoenissae*', *G.R.B.S.* 11 (1970) 109–27. *Rhes.*: W. Ritchie, *The authenticity of the Rhesus of Euripides* (Cambridge 1964); H. D. F. Kitto, 'The *Rhesus* and related matters', *Y.Cl.S.* 25 (1977) 317–50. *Tro.*: T. C. W. Stinton, *Euripides and the judgment of Paris* (London 1965); G. L. Koniaris, '*Alexander, Palamedes, Troades, Sisyphus* – A connected tetralogy? A connected trilogy?', *H.S.C.Ph.* 77 (1973) 87–124; R. Scodel, *The Trojan trilogy of Euripides* (Göttingen 1980). (4) TEXT AND TRANSMISSION: A. Turyn, *The Byzantine manuscript tradition of the tragedies of Euripides* (Urbana 1957); G. Zuntz, *An inquiry into the transmission of the plays of Euripides* (Cambridge 1965); V. D. di Benedetto, *La tradizione manoscritta euripidea* (Padua 1965); S. G. Daitz, *The Jerusalem palimpsest of Euripides* (Berlin 1970); K. Matthiessen, *Studien zur Textüberlieferung der Hekabe des Euripides* (Heidelberg 1974); J. Diggle, *Studies on the text of Euripides* (Oxford 1981). (5) STYLE: W. Breitenbach, *Untersuchungen zur Sprache des euripideischen Lyrik* (Stuttgart 1934: repr. Hildesheim 1967); W. Ludwig, *Sapheneia: ein*

Beitrag zur Formkunst im Spätwerk des Euripides (Tübingen 1954); E. R. Schwinge, *Die Verwendung der Stichomythie in den Dramen des Euripides* (Heidelberg 1968); S. A. Barlow, *The imagery of Euripides* (London 1971); K. H. Lee, *Index of passages cited in Breitenbach, etc.* (Amsterdam 1979).

CONCORDANCE: J. H. Allen and G. Italie (Berkeley & Los Angeles 1954), supplemented by C. Collard (Groningen 1971).

MINOR TRAGIC POETS

LIVES, FRAGMENTS, INDEXES

The ancient testimonia are assembled in B. Snell, *Tragicorum Graecorum fragmenta* I (Göttingen 1971). This volume also contains the fragments themselves, thus replacing Nauck's *TGF* 719–833. Snell's volume has no *index verborum*: for Nauck's edition there is an index to the whole, *Tragicae dictionis index spectans ad Tragicorum Graecorum Fragmenta* (Petersburg 1892: repr. Hildesheim 1962). Discussion and bibliography in Lesky, *TDH* 523ff.; B. Snell, *Szenen aus griechischen Dramen* (Berlin 1971); G. Xanthakis-Karamanos, *Studies in fourth-century tragedy* (Athens 1980).

INDIVIDUAL AUTHORS

Achaeus: C. Drago, 'Achaeo: un satirografo minore del V secolo', *Dioniso* 5 (1936) 231–42. Agathon: P. Leveque, *Agathon* (Paris 1955). Chaeremon: C. Collard, 'On the tragedian Chaeremon', *J.H.S.* 90 (1970) 22–34. Critias: D. F. Sutton, 'Critias and atheism', *C.Q.* 31 (1981) 33–8. Ezechiel: H. Jacobson, *The Exagoge of Ezekiel* (Cambridge 1983). Ion of Chios: A. von Blumenthal, *Ion von Chios. Die Reste seiner Werke* (Stuttgart & Berlin 1935).

SATYR PLAYS

WORKS

Euripides' *Cyclops*: see D. F. Sutton, *The date of Euripides' Cyclops* (Ann Arbor 1974). Considerable papyrus fragments of Aeschylus' *Dictyulci*, 'Dikē play' and *Theoroi* or *Isthmiastae*, Sophocles' *Ichneutae* and *Inachus*, and anonymous *Oeneus* or *Schoeneus* (Sophoclean authorship made more likely by *P. Oxy.* 2453; cf. introd. to Page, under *Commentaries* below). Hypotheses of Euripidean satyr plays in *P. Oxy.* 27.2455. For lost plays see *Appendix* entries for Aesch., Soph. and Eur.; also D. F. Sutton, 'A handlist of satyr plays', *H.S.C.Ph.* 78 (1974) 107–43. Bibliographical refs. in R. A. Pack, *The Greek and Latin literary texts from Graeco-Roman Egypt*, 2nd ed. (Ann Arbor 1965) s.v. 'satyr play' and individual authors.

GREEK COMEDY

BIBLIOGRAPHY

(See Schmid–Stählin I 2 79–86 and individual authors; Guggisberg (1947), under *Studies* (1) below.)

TEXTS AND COMMENTARIES: TEXTS: W. Steffen *Satyrographorum Graecorum fragmenta* (Poznań 1952). COMMENTARIES: As for tragedians. Papyrus texts (often abbrev.) with tr. and comm. in H. Lloyd-Jones, *Aeschylus* II (Loeb, 1957) and D. L. Page, *Select papyrii* III (Loeb, 1941).

MONUMENTAL EVIDENCE: F. Brommer, *Satyrspiele*, 2nd ed. (Berlin 1959); T. B. L. Webster, *Monuments illustrating tragedy and satyr play*, 2nd ed., *B.I.C.S.* suppl. XX (1967) 148; A. D. Trendall and T. B. L. Webster, *Illustrations of Greek drama* (London 1971) ch. II.

STUDIES: (1) GENERAL: W. Aly, 'Satyrspiel', *RE* IIA.2 (1925) 235–47; W. Süss, *De Graecorum fabulis satyricis* (Dorpat 1929); L. Campo, *I drammi satireschi della Grecia antica* (Milan 1947); P. Guggisberg, *Das Satyrspiel* (Zurich 1947); L. E. Rossi, 'Il drama satiresco attico', *D. Arch.* 6 (1972) 248–302; N. C. Hourmouziades, *Satyrika* (Athens 1974); B. Seidensticker, 'Das Satyrspiel', in (ed.) G. A. Seeck, *Das griechische Drama* (Darmstadt 1979) 204–57; W. Steffen, *De Graecorum fabulis satyricis* (Wrocław 1979); D. F. Sutton, *The Greek satyr play* (Meisenheim am Glan 1980); idem, 'Satyr plays and children in the audience', *Prudentia* 13 (1981) 71–4. (2) AESCHYLUS: A. Setti, 'Eschilo satirico', *A.S.N.P.* 17 (1948) 1–36; R. G. Ussher, 'The other Aeschylus', *Phoenix* 31 (1977) 287–99. (3) SOPHOCLES: W. N. Bates, 'The satyr-dramas of Sophocles', in *Classical studies presented to Edward Capps* (Princeton 1936) 14–23; W. Steffen, 'De Sophoclis indagatoribus quaestiones aliquot', *Poznańskie Towarzystwo Przyjaciół Nauk* 11 (1949) 83–112. (4) EURIPIDES: W. Wetzel, *De Euripidis fabula satyrica quae Cyclops inscribitur cum Homerico comparata exemplo* (Wiesbaden 1965); A. P. Burnett, *Catastrophe survived* (Oxford 1971), index s.v. 'satyric motifs'; L. E. Rossi, 'Il *Ciclope* di Euripide come *Komos* mancato', *Maia* 23 (1971) 10–38; W. Steffen, 'The satyr-dramas of Euripides', *Eos* 69 (1971) 203–26.

GREEK COMEDY

GENERAL WORKS

(1) List of poets (259 in all)
Austin, C., *Z.P.E.* 14 (1974) 201–25
(2) Fragments
Austin, *CGFPap*
Austin, C. and Kassel, R., *Poetae comici Graeci* IV, *Aristophon–Crobylus* (Berlin & New York 1983); III, 2 *Aristophanes* (1984); V, *Damoxenus–Magnes* (1986)

189

Edmonds, J. M., *Fragments of Attic comedy*, 3 vols. (Leiden 1957–61: with tr.: much speculative restoration)

Kaibel, *CGF* (Epicharmus and other Doric writers)

Kock, *CAF*, with J. Demiańczuk, *Supplementum comicum* (Cracow 1912)

Meineke, A., *Fragmenta comicorum Graecorum*, 5 vols. (Berlin 1839–57: history of comedy vol. I, word index by H. Iacobi vol. v)

Olivieri, A., *Frammenti della commedia greca e del mimo...*, 2 vols., 2nd ed. (Naples 1946: Epicharmus etc., with comm.)

(3) Inscriptional records

Geissler, P., *Chronologie der altattischen Komödie* (Berlin 1925: repr. with addenda 1969)

Mette, H.-J., *Urkunden dramatischer Aufführungen in Griechenland* (Berlin & New York 1977)

Pickard-Cambridge, *DFA* 101–25

(4) Other archaeological material (representations of scenes, actors, masks etc.)

Bieber, M., *The history of the Greek and Roman theater*, 2nd ed. (Princeton 1961: 870 illustrations)

Brea, L. Bernabò, *Menandro e il teatro greco nelle terracotte liparesi* (Genoa 1981)

Pickard-Cambridge, *DFA*

idem, *DTC* (origins)

Seeberg, A., *Corinthian komos vases*, *B.I.C.S.* suppl. XXVII (1971: origins)

Trendall, A. D., *Phylax vases*, 2nd ed., *B.I.C.S.* suppl. XIX (1967)

Webster, T. B. L., *Monuments illustrating Old and Middle Comedy*, 3rd ed. by J. R. Green, *B.I.C.S.* suppl. XXXIX (1978)

idem, *Monuments illustrating New Comedy*, 2nd ed., *B.I.C.S.* suppl. XXIV (1969)

(5) Ancient and medieval writings on comedy

Kaibel, *CGF*

Koster, W. J. W., *Scholia Graeca in Aristophanem* I I a (Groningen 1975)

(6) History

Herter, H., *Vom dionysischen Tanz zum komischen Spiel* (Iserlohn 1947: origins)

Lesky 233–40, 417–52, 633–7, 642–65

Meineke, A., under (2) above

Pickard-Cambridge, *DTC* (origins)

Schmid, W., in Schmid–Stählin IV 2 (1946) 1–470 (5th c.)

Webster, T. B. L., *Studies in later Greek comedy*, 2nd ed. (Manchester 1969: 4th c. to Menander)

(7) Special studies

Arnott, W. G., 'From Aristophanes to Menander', *G.&R.* 19 (1972) 65–80

Berk, L., *Epicharmus* (Groningen 1964: see also *DTC* 230–90)

Bonnanno, M. G., *Studi su Cratete comico* (Padua 1972)

Breitholz, L., *Die dorische Farce* (Stockholm 1960)

Descroix, J., *Le trimètre iambique des iambographes à la comédie nouvelle* (Mâcon 1931)

Dohm, H., *Mageiros* (Munich 1964)

Fraenkel, E., *De media et nova comoedia quaestiones selectae* (Göttingen 1912)

Gil, L., 'Comedia ática y sociedad ateniese', *Estudios clásicos* 18 (1974) 61–82, 151–86; 19 (1975) 59–88

Hofmann, W. and Wartenberg, G., *Der Bramarbas in der antiken Komödie, Abh. Ak. Wissenschaften DDR* 1973, 2

Hunter, R. L., *Eubulus: the fragments* (Cambridge 1983)

Oeri, H.-G., *Der Typ der komischen Alten* (Basel 1948)

Pieters, L., *Cratinus* (Leiden 1946)

Schwarze, J., *Die Beurteilung des Perikles durch die attische Komödie* (Zurich 1936)

Sifakis, G. M., *Parabasis and animal choruses* (London 1971)

Wehrli, F., *Motivstudien zur griechischen Komödie* (Zurich 1936)

White, J. W., *The verse of Greek comedy* (London 1912)

Wiemken, H., *Der griechische Mimus: Dokumente zur Geschichte des antiken Volkstheaters* (Bremen 1972)

(8) Surveys

Dover, K. J., in *FYAT* (on comedy generally, c. 1900–68)

Kraus, W., *A.A.H.G.* 24 (1971) 161–80 (Old Comedy and Epicharmus)

idem, *A.A.H.G.* 28 (1975) 1–18 (4th c. comedy excluding Menander)

Murphy, C. T., *C.W.* 49 (1956) 201–11, 65 (1972) 261–73 (Aristophanes and Old Comedy)

ARISTOPHANES

LIFE AND WORKS – EXCURSUS

Aristophanes, son of Philippus, of the deme Kydathenai in Athens (Kirchner, *Prosop. Att.* 2090), was probably in his late 'teens when his first play, the lost *Daitales* ('Banqueters'), was staged in 427 B.C.; his birth-date is accordingly put at about 445 (*Clouds* 528–31 and schol.; Anon. *De com.* II 43f. Kaibel, III 38 Koster). The play was well received, and took second prize; in the next year *Babylonians* (also lost) won a first, and more firsts came in the two following years with *Acharnians* and *Knights* (for sources see *General works* for 'Greek Comedy' under (3) 'Inscriptional records'). This was a brilliant start, and when the selection of the eleven plays that survive was made, five were chosen from the first seven years of A.'s career: they are *Acharnians*, 425; *Knights*, 424; *Clouds*, 423; *Wasps*, 422; *Peace*, 421.

Like some of his contemporaries, A. sometimes gave plays to other people to produce. He is defensive about this in *Knights*, which was his first independent production (512ff.); the practice is reflected in the joke that he was 'born on the fourth', like Heracles, to toil for others (Ameipsias, fr. 28 K *et al.*; cf. Plato com. frs. 99–100 K with *P. Oxy.* 2737 fr. 1 ii 10ff. = *CGFPap* 56, 44ff.). None the less, when Cleon, who was his fellow-demesman, took offence at the political content of *Babylonians*, it seems likely to have been A. himself and not his producer Callistratus who was brought before the Council by the offended politician and denounced for 'slandering the city in front of foreigners' (that is, in a play produced at the Dionysia; cf. *Ach.* 377–82, 502ff., 630ff. with schol. on 378, 503; *Wasps* 1284–91 and schol.).

By the time of his references to the affair in *Acharnians*, A. was already working on his all-out attack on Cleon in *Knights*, apparently with some collaboration with his rival and close contemporary Eupolis, over which the two exchanged hard words (*Ach.* 300ff.; *Clouds* 553f. with schol., quoting Eupolis, *Baptai* (78 K); *Knights* 1288ff. with schol.); for what it is worth, Cratinus, who had been written off by A. in the *Knights* as an old drunkard who was once supremely powerful and popular, appears in this matter to have sided with Eupolis (*Knights* 526ff. with schol. on 531).

These personal references perhaps have their nearest modern counterparts in the world of the revue theatre or of the satirical magazine. No doubt they reflect some of the pressures that were felt by a writer of topical comedy competing for production and success at one of the two annual festivals in Athens; but just how deep the feelings were is hard to say. Two of his rivals' jokes (that he was going bald and that he was of suspect Athenian status because of a connexion with Aegina) A. ingeniously tries to neutralize by adopting them (*Clouds* 540, *Knights* 550, *Peace* 767ff., *Ach.* 653f.). The other side of the early success-story is to be seen in his disappointment over *Clouds*, which came third to the play *Pytine* ('Wine-flask') by Cratinus and the *Konnos* of Ameipsias, which (gallingly) brought in Socrates, like the *Clouds* (*Wasps* 1043ff.; *Clouds* 530ff.; Cratinus, *Pytine* frs. 181–204 K; Ameipsias, *Konnos* frs. 7–12 K).

The passage of *Clouds* just cited comes from a part of the play composed for a revised edition, which is the one that survives, probably not long before 417. There A. looks back with pride to the *Knights*, and criticizes his rivals for the sameness of their repeated attacks on Hyperbolus, by contrast with his own ventures into new fields. The death of Cleon and the ending of the war in 421 had certainly changed the scene in which A. had his early thrills and spills by removing two of his main preoccupations. But, little as we know about his personal circumstances in earlier times, we now know less, since, whether speaking with the voice of a character or that of a chorus in a parabasis, he has less to say for himself. The plays which survive from his 'middle period', 420–400, from about age 25 to about 45, are *Birds* (414), *Lysistrata* (411), *Thesmophoriazusae* (411) and *Frogs* (405); and though Euripides is a character in the last two of these (as earlier in *Acharnians*) we have no outside information about their personal relationship, if any existed.

Beneath all the variety of theme in the plays there are trends which show the direction in which comedy was developing. There is less immediate political engagement, and a growing social interest; lyric still flourishes, but largely above and beyond its traditional function in epirrhematic syzygies and other patterned sequences of scenes; but if we argue from these trends to changes in A.'s personal attitude to politics and music, we are merely arguing in circles. There are still, as earlier, passages which show that he was eminently conscious of the comic tradition in which he worked and of his own competitive position (e.g. *Second Thesmophoriazusae* (prob. 407/6) frs. 333–4 K; *Frogs* 1–14). Whether he had, or expressed, strong theoretical views on playwriting we have no way to tell: when Plato in the *Symposium* has Socrates attempt to question Agathon and A. about the writing of tragedy and comedy, it is at the end of a very long party, and A., amusingly enough, is the first to fall asleep (*Symp.* 223d); perhaps the practical criticism of the second half of *Frogs* was nearer to his own temperament.

From the twenty years between *Frogs* and the presumed date of A.'s death in the mid-380s we have two plays, *Ecclesiazusae* (393 or 392?) and *Plutus* (388), which are conspicuous by their diminution of the role of the chorus and their turn away from the lively topicalities of the fifth-century plays to a less colourful style and a more generalized approach to the affairs of the time. A. had sons who were comic poets, Philippus (*Prosop. Att.* 14460), Araros (*Prosop. Att.* 1575)) and possibly another (?Philetaerus, *Prosop. Att.* 14253; ?Nicostratus, *Prosop. Att.* 11038). It is an interesting reflection of his continuing status as a comic writer that later critics could see in his last two plays, the lost *Kokalos* and *Aiolosikon*, what they recognized as anticipations of Middle and New Comedy (Platonius, I 31f. Kaibel, I 29f. Koster; *Vit. Ar.* XI 69f. D.–D., XXVIII 54f. Koster); it is also interesting that these plays by a man nearing 60 with a long career behind him could be handed over for production to someone of the next generation, his son Araros, with a view to increasing his standing with the public (*Plut.* arg. III Coulon = IV Dübner, *et al.*). The Alexandrian Library catalogued forty-four plays in all, of which four were thought doubtfully authentic or spurious (Anon. *De com.* II 47f. Kaibel, III 41 Koster, *et al.*).

Sources: Cantarella's edition of A. sets out most of the relevant texts in the Prolegomena, I 135ff.; for some friends of A. see Sterling Dow, *A.J.A.* 73 (1969) 234–5, discussing *IG* II² 2343; for portraits G. M. A. Richter, *Portraits of the Greeks* I (London 1965) 140, with T. B. L. Webster, *Monuments illustrating Old and Middle Comedy*, 3rd ed. by J. R. Green, *B.I.C.S.* suppl. XXXIX (1978), under AS1.

BIBLIOGRAPHY

TEXTS AND COMMENTARIES: TEXTS: F. W. Hall and W. M. Geldart (OCT, 1906–7: with fragments); V. Coulon and H. van Daele (Budé, 1923–30 and later corrected reprints); B. B. Rogers (Loeb, 1924: with verse tr.); R. Cantarella (Milan 1949–64: with prolegomena and Italian prose tr.); A. Sommerstein (Warminster 1980–7: *Ach., Knights, Clouds, Wasps, Peace, Birds,* with tr. and notes). COMMENTARIES: (1) The eleven plays. B. B. Rogers (London 1902–16: with verse tr. as Loeb); J. van Leeuwen, 12 vols. incl. prolegomena (Leiden 1893–1906). (2) Individual plays. *Ach.*: W. W. Rennie (London 1909); W. J. M. Starkie (London 1909: with parallel tr.). *Knights*: R. A. Neil (Cambridge 1901). *Clouds*: W. J. M. Starkie (London 1911: with parallel tr.); K. J. Dover (Oxford 1968). *Wasps*: W. J. M. Starkie (London 1897); D. M. MacDowell (Oxford 1971). *Peace*: H. Sharpley (London 1905); M. Platnauer (Oxford 1964). *Birds*: T. Kock and O. Schroeder (Leipzig 1927); P. I. Kakrides (Athens 1974: in Greek). *Lys.*: U. von Wilamowitz-Moellendorff (Berlin 1927); J. Henderson (Oxford 1987). *Frogs*: T. G. Tucker (London 1906); L. Radermacher, *S.A.W.W.* 1921, 2nd ed. by W. Kraus (Vienna 1954); W. B. Stanford, 2nd ed. (London

1963). *Eccl.*: R. G. Ussher (Oxford 1973). *Plut.*: K. Holzinger, *S.A.W.W.* 218.3 (1940). *Fragments.* See *General works* under 'Greek Comedy'. For *Daitales* ('Banqueters') see A. C. Cassio, *Banchettanti: i frammenti* (Pisa 1977). *Scholia.* W. Dindorf and F. Dübner (Paris 1842 and reprints: obsolete, but not yet replaced for all plays); W. J. W. Koster *et al.* (in progress: Groningen 1960–). *Birds*: J. W. White (Boston & London 1914). *Lys.*: G. Stein (Göttingen 1891). Also G. Zuntz, *Die Aristophanes-Scholien der Papyri*, 2nd ed. (Berlin 1975); W. G. Rutherford, *A chapter in the history of annotation = Scholia Aristophanica* III (London 1905). See further T. Gelzer, *Gnomon* 33 (1961) 26–34, and for work on the scholia and the textual transmission generally idem under *Studies* (1) below, *Aristophanes der Komiker* 1548–63.

TRANSLATIONS: W. Arrowsmith, D. Parker *et al.*, *The complete Greek comedy* (Ann Arbor 1961–: *Ach.* 1961; *Clouds* 1962; *Wasps* 1962; *Birds* 1961; *Lys.* 1964; *Frogs* 1962; *Eccl.* 1967); D. Fitts (New York 1962: *Birds, Lys., Thes., Frogs*); D. Barrett (*Wasps, Birds, Thes., Frogs, Eccl.*) and A. Sommerstein (*Ach., Knights, Clouds, Peace, Lys., Plut.*) (Harmondsworth, 1964–78); P. Dickinson, 2 vols. (Oxford 1970).

STUDIES: (1) SURVEYS: K. J. Dover, *Lustrum* 2 (1957) 52–112; T. Gelzer, *Aristophanes der Komiker* (Stuttgart 1971) = *RE* suppl. XII 1391–1570; R. G. Ussher, *G.&R.* New surveys in the classics XIII (1979); see *General works* (8) under 'Greek Comedy'. (2) GENERAL: C. Pascal, *Dioniso: saggio sulla religione e la parodia religiosa in Aristofane* (Catania 1911); W. Süss, *Aristophanes und die Nachwelt* (Leipzig 1911); G. Murray, *Aristophanes, a study* (Oxford 1933); Q. Cataudella, *La poesia di Aristofane* (Bari 1934); V. L. Ehrenberg, *The people of Aristophanes*, 2nd ed. (London 1951: 3rd ed. New York 1972: reprints); W. Süss, 'Scheinbare und wirkliche Inkongruenzen in den Dramen des Aristophanes', *Rh.M.* 97 (1954) 115–59, 229–54, 289–316; H.-J. Newiger, *Metapher und Allegorie* (Munich 1957); T. Gelzer, *Der epirrhematische Agon bei Aristophanes* (Munich 1960); E. Fraenkel, *Beobachtungen zu Aristophanes* (Rome 1962); C. F. Russo, *Aristofane, autore di teatro* (Florence 1962); P. Händel, *Formen und Darstellungen in der aristophanischen Komödie* (Heidelberg 1963); C. H. Whitman, *Aristophanes and the comic hero* (Cambridge, Mass. 1964); J. Taillardat, *Les images d'Aristophane*, 2nd ed. (Paris 1965); P. Rau, *Paratragodia* (Munich 1967); K. J. Dover, *Aristophanic comedy* (London 1972); G. E. M. de Ste Croix, *The origins of the Peloponnesian war* (London 1972) App. xxix 'The political outlook of Aristophanes'; J. Sánchez Lasso de la Vega, 'Realidad, idealidad y politica en la comedia de Aristofane', *C.F.C.* 4 (1972) 9–89; A. Sommerstein, 'On translating Aristophanes', *G.&R.* 20 (1973) 140–54; E. B. Spyropoulos, *L'accumulation verbale chez Aristophane* (Thessaloniki 1974); J. Henderson, *The maculate muse: obscene language in Attic comedy* (New Haven & London 1975); B. A. Sparkes, 'Illustrating Aristophanes', *J.H.S.* 95 (1975) 122–35; C. W. Dearden, *The stage of Aristophanes* (London 1976); W. Kraus, 'Aristophanes und Sokrates', *Sprachwissenschaftliche Beiträge zur Literaturwissenschaft* (Öst. Akad. der Wissenschaften) 7 (1976) 161–79; H. Schareika, *Der Realismus der attischen Komödie* (Frankfurt am Main, Berne & Las Vegas 1978); F. Heberlein,

Pluthygieia: zur Gegenwelt bei Aristophanes (Frankfurt am Main 1980). (3) INDIVIDUAL
PLAYS: *Knights*: M. Pohlenz, *N.A.W.G.* 1952 = *Kl. Schr.* II 511ff.; O. Navarre, *Les
cavaliers d'Aristophane: étude et analyse* (Paris 1956); M. Landfester, *Die Ritter des
Aristophanes* (Amsterdam 1967). *Wasps*: U. von Wilamowitz-Moellendorff, *S.D.A.W.*
1911 = *Kl. Schr.* I 284ff.; G. Paduano, *Il giudice giudicato: le funzioni del comico nelle
Vespe di Aristofane* (Bologna 1974). *Birds*: E. Fraenkel, *Kleine Beiträge* (Rome 1964)
427–67 with *Beobachtungen zu Aristophanes* (Rome 1962) 58–99; H. Hofmann,
Mythos und Komödie (Hildesheim 1976) 70–229. *Thes.*: H. Hansen, 'Aristophanes'
Thesmophoriazusae: theme, structure, production', *Philologus* 120 (1976) 165–85. (4)
METRICAL STUDIES: Descroix and White in *General works* (7) under 'Greek Comedy'.
P. Pucci, 'Aristofane ed Euripide', *M.A.L.* ser. 8 x.5 (1961) 273–423; C. Prato, *I
canti di Aristofane* (Rome 1962); A. M. Dale, *Lyric metres of Greek drama*, 2nd ed.
(Cambridge 1968) and (1969) under (5) below; T. McEvilley, 'Development in the
lyrics of Aristophanes', *A.J.Ph.* 91 (1970) 257–76; E. Domingo, *La responsión
estrofica en Aristofane* (Salamanca 1975). (5) COLLECTED STUDIES (items in these
collections are *not* listed separately above; the obelus indicates that all or much of the
material is reprinted from elsewhere). Κωμῳδοτραγήματα: *studia Aristophanica in
honorem... W. J. W. Koster* (Amsterdam 1967: a miscellany); † (ed.) D. J. Littlefield,
Twentieth-century interpretations of the Frogs (Englewood Cliffs, N.J. 1968); A. M.
Dale, *Collected papers* (Cambridge 1969: see esp. nos. †3, †8, †9, †11, †14, †15, 21–5,
mainly on staging and on the nature of verse); † (ed.) H.-J. Newiger, *Aristophanes
und die alte Komödie* (Darmstadt 1975: with introd. and long bibliography, 487–510);
(ed.) J. Henderson, *Aristophanes: Essays in interpretation*, *Y.Cl.S.* 26 (1980).

LEXICA: O. J. Todd (Cambridge, Mass. 1932: based on OCT: corrections by
W. K. Pritchett, *C.Ph.* 51 (1956) 102); H. Dunbar, new ed. by B. Marzullo (Hildesheim
1973).

MENANDER

LIFE AND WORKS–EXCURSUS

Menander, son of Diopeithes, of the deme Kephisia (Kirchner, *Prosop. Att.* 9875),
was born in 342/1 B.C.; he died in 292/1 or a neighbouring year (*IG* XIV 1184 and
other sources; but there are conflicts of evidence). He was remembered as having been
a pupil of Theophrastus, Aristotle's successor as head of the Peripatetic School
(Diog. Laert. 5.36), and also as a contemporary of Epicurus, who, though born in
Samos, did his military service in Athens and was in the same ephebe class as M.
(Strabo 14.638). It may have been through Theophrastus and his circle that M. came
into contact with a somewhat older contemporary, Demetrius of Phalerum, and
formed a friendship which is said to have put him in peril at the time of Demetrius'
overthrow from his governorship of Athens in 307 (Diog. Laert. 5.79). M. thus seems
to have moved in the higher circles of Athenian intellectual and political life; but we

do not know of any political engagement or activity on his part, nor of intellectual interests outside his writing for the theatre. Like Aristophanes and other comic poets, he began early; and he had early successes. In spite of disagreements between sources, we can probably say that his first production came in 321 with the lost play *Orge* ('Anger') and that it won a first (Jerome, *Chron.* 1696; Anon. *De com.* II 69ff. Kaibel, III 57ff. Koster). It is not certain what lies behind the tradition that associates M. with Alexis (who was producing comedies in Athens at least as early as the 350s). They are thought of as nephew and paternal uncle (Suda, s.v. Ἄλεξις, at the same time describing Alexis as from Thurii in south Italy); or as pupil and master (Anon. *De com., loc. cit.*): some critics presumably saw a special affinity in their work.

M. is variously credited with 105, 108 and 109 plays (Aulus Gellius 17.4.4 knows of all three figures); nearly all of these are now known at least by title, though the existence of alternative titles complicates the reckoning now as (no doubt) in antiquity. Dating is difficult because we have few firm records, and there are problems both in translating what may seem to be logical sequences of literary development into a chronological sequence and in trying to use as evidence for precise dating events mentioned in the plays as part of the background of fictional characters' lives. Apart from the (probable) initial success of *Orge* in 321, *Dyskolos* (or *Misanthrope*) won first prize at the Lenaean festival in 316 (production notice in the Bodmer codex), and an unidentified play at the Dionysia in the next year (*Marm. Par. B* ep.14). M.'s total of eight victories in thirty years (Gell. *loc. cit.*) is an eminently respectable, though not spectacular score, and there must have been many disappointing occasions. One of these was in 312, when his *Heniochos* ('Charioteer') came fifth (*IG* II² 2323a, 36f.); by 301, when a production of the *Imbrians* had to be postponed, the number of his plays was reckoned in the seventies (*P. Oxy.* 1235, 103ff.). Soon after his death, if not within his lifetime, a portrait statue by the sons of Praxiteles, Cephisodotus and Timarchus, was set up in the theatre of Dionysus; only its inscribed base now survives (*IG* II² 3777), but the influence of this work on the numerous later portraits appears to have been considerable.

M.'s plays became classics of the theatre within a generation or so of his death; and from 240 B.C. onwards Latin comedies adapted from him and other fourth-century playwrights were being performed at festivals in Rome. He was a much-favoured author throughout the Hellenistic age and later antiquity, as can be seen from numerous references to him and from the frequency of fragmentary copies of the plays in collections of excavated papyri. M. was still being read and copied in the sixth, perhaps the early seventh century (*P. Berol.* 21199), but after the Byzantine Dark Ages is only known from quotations and from Latin versions (at least eight plays by Plautus and Terence are based on him) until his renaissance in modern times. Our knowledge of his work has been transformed by the progressive recovery of new texts in the 19th and 20th centuries, most notably from the Cairo codex (*P. Cair.* J 43227), published in 1907, and from the Bodmer codex (1959, 1969). Studies and commentaries written before or between the stages of rediscovery have useful material and valuable insights, but will inevitably mislead if used without forethought.

MENANDER

Sources: most of the relevant texts are set out in the Testimonia at the beginning of vol. II of Koerte–Thierfelder's BT ed.; for portraits see G. M. A. Richter, *Portraits of the Greeks* (London 1965) with S. Charitonidis, L. Kahil, R. Ginouvès, *Les mosaïques de la maison du Ménandre à Mytilène*, *A.K.*, Beiheft VI (1970) 27–31, E. Lissi Caronna, *B.A.* 52 (1967) 41–2 and B. Ashmole, *A.J.A.* 77 (1973) 61.

BIBLIOGRAPHY

TEXTS AND COMMENTARIES: TEXTS: Collected plays and fragments: A. Koerte (BT: I, *Reliquiae in papyris et membranis vetustissimis servatae*, 3rd ed. 1938, repr. with addenda 1955, 1957; II, *Reliquiae apud veteres scriptores servatae*, rev. and augmented by A. Thierfelder, 2nd ed. 1959); D. del Corno, vol. I (Milan 1967: contents similar to Koerte I, but without *Samia* and '*Com. Flor.*' = *Aspis*: with Italian prose tr.); J.-M. Jacques (Budé: I 1, *Samia*, 1971: I 2, *Dyskolos*, 2nd ed., 1976); F. H. Sandbach, *Reliquiae selectae* (OCT, 1972: omits shorter quoted fragments: corrected repr. 1976); W. G. Arnott, vol. I (Loeb, 1979: *Aspis–Epitrepontes*). See also *CGFPap*. *Sententiae*: W. Görler, Μενάνδρου Γνῶμαι (Berlin 1963); S. Jaekel (BT, 1964) with D. Hagedorn and M. Weber, *Archiv für Papyrusforschung* 3 (1968) 15–50 and R. Führer, *Zur slavischen Übersetzung der Menandersentenzen* (Königstein 1982). COMMENTARIES: A. W. Gomme and F. H. Sandbach (Oxford 1973: goes with OCT). One or more plays: *Aspis* and *Samia*: C. Austin, 2 vols. (Berlin 1969–70: I, text with app. crit. and indexes; II, *Subsidia interpretationis*); F. Sisti (Rome: *Aspis*, 1971; *Samia*, 1974). *Dyskolos*: E. W. Handley (London & Cambridge, Mass. 1965); J. Martin, *L'atrabilaire*, 2nd ed. (Paris 1972). *Epitrepontes*: U. von Wilamowitz-Moellendorff, *Das Schiedsgericht* (Berlin 1925); V. de Falco, 3rd ed. (Naples 1961). *Hydria*: K. Gaiser, *A.H.A.W.* 1977, 1 (conjectural reconstruction from *CGFPap* adesp. nov. 244 and other sources). *Misoumenos*: E. G. Turner, *The lost beginning of Menander, Misoumenos* (London 1978) = *P.B.A.* 73 (1977) 315–31, and *P. Oxy.* 48 (1981) and 3368–71 (new text of lines 1–100). *Phasma*: E. G. Turner, *G.R.B.S.* 10 (1969) 307–24. *Samia*: see above with *Aspis*; D. M. Bain (Warminster 1983). *Sikyonios*: R. Kassel (Berlin 1965: critical ed.).

TRANSLATIONS: L. Casson (New York 1971); P. Vellacott, 2nd ed. (Harmondsworth 1973: includes select shorter fragments: with Theophrastus, *Characters*). *Epitrepontes*, *Perikeiromene* (reconstructed versions in verse): G. Murray, *The arbitrants* (London 1945), *The rape of the locks* (London 1945). *Samia* (version for broadcasting: blank verse): E. G. Turner (London 1972).

STUDIES: (1) SURVEYS: A. Koerte, *RE* XV.1 (1931) 707–61, with H.-J. Mette, *RE* suppl. XII (1970) 854–62; H.-J. Mette, *Lustrum* 10 (1965) 5–211; 11 (1966) 139–49; 13 (1968) 535–68; W. G. Arnott, 'Menander: discoveries since the *Dyskolos*', *Arethusa* 3 (1970) 49–70; idem, 'Menander, Plautus, Terence', *G.&R.* New surveys in the classics IX (1975); W. Kraus, *A.A.H.G.* 26 (1973) 31–56; E. W. Handley, 'Recent

MENANDER

papyrus finds: Menander', *B.I.C.S.* 26 (1979) 81–7; W. Luppe, 'Literarische Texte: Drama', *Archiv für Papyrusforschung* 27 (1980) 233–50. (2) GENERAL: C. Préaux, 'Ménandre et la société athénienne', *C.E.* 32 (1957) no. 63, 84–100; eadem, 'Les fonctions du droit dans la comédie nouvelle', *C.E.* 35 (1960) no. 69, 222–39; T. B. L. Webster, *Studies in Menander*, 2nd ed. (Manchester 1960); A. Dain, 'La survie de Ménandre', *Maia* 15 (1963) 278–309; A. Barigazzi, *La formazione spirituale di Menandro* (Turin 1965); K. Gaiser, 'Menander und der Peripatos', *A.&A.* 13 (1967) 8–40; P. Flury, *Liebe und Liebessprache bei Menander, Plautus und Terenz* (Heidelberg 1968); A. Blanchard, 'Recherches sur la composition des comédies de Ménandre', *R.E.G.* 73 (1970) 38–51; T. B. L. Webster, *Studies in later Greek comedy*, 2nd ed. (Manchester 1970); W. T. MacCary, 'Menander's soldiers: their names, roles and masks', *A.J.Ph.* 93 (1972) 279–98; J. S. Feneron, 'Some elements of Menander's style', *B.I.C.S.* 21 (1974) 81–95; N. Holzberg, *Menander: Untersuchungen zur dramatischen Technik* (Nürnberg 1974); T. B. L. Webster, *An introduction to Menander* (Manchester 1974); D. del Corno, 'Alcuni aspetti del linguaggio di Menandro', *Studi classici e orientali* 24 (1975) 13–48; A. G. Katsouris, *Linguistic and stylistic characterization: tragedy and Menander* (Ioannina 1975); M. G. Ferrero, 'L'asindeto in Menandro', *Dioniso* 47 (1976) 82–106; K. Treu, 'Die Menschen Menanders', in (ed.) R. Mueller, *Mensch als Mass aller Dinge* (Berlin 1976) 399–421; M. Marcovich, 'Euclio, Knemon and the Peripatos', *I.C.S.* 2 (1977) 192–218; S. M. Goldberg, *The making of Menander's comedy* (London, Berkeley & Los Angeles 1980); E. G. Turner, 'The rhetoric of question and answer in Menander', *Themes in drama* 2 (1980) 1–23. (3) INDIVIDUAL PLAYS: *Adelphoi II*: O. Rieth, *Die Kunst Menanders in den Adelphen des Terenz* (Hildesheim 1964). *Aspis*: H. Lloyd-Jones, *G.R.B.S.* 12 (1971) 175–95. *Dis exapaton*: E. W. Handley, *Menander and Plautus* (London 1968 and – in German – as Wege der Forschung CXXXVI (1973): deals with the text corresponding to Plautus, *Bacchides* 494ff.); K. Gaiser, *Philologus* 114 (1970) 51–87; V. Pöschl, *S.H.A.W.* 1973, 4. *Dyskolos*: A. Schäfer, *Menanders Dyskolos: Untersuchungen zur dramatischen Technik* (Meisenheim am Glan 1965). *Hypobolimaios*: M. Kokolakis, *Athena* 66 (1962) 9–114. *Misoumenos*: T. B. L. Webster, 'Woman hates soldier: a structural approach to Greek comedy', *G.R.B.S.* 14 (1973) 287–99. *Samia*: H.-D. Blume, *Menanders Samia: eine Interpretation* (Darmstadt 1974); H. Lloyd-Jones, *Y.Cl.S.* 22 (1972) 119–44. *Sikyonios*: H. Lloyd-Jones, *G.R.B.S.* 7 (1966) 131–57 (quotes the Greek extensively). *Theophoroumene*: E. W. Handley, *B.I.C.S.* 16 (1969) 88–101 (quotes extensively). (4) SOME SHORTER GENERAL DISCUSSIONS: G. Murray, *Aristophanes* (Oxford 1933) 221–63; A. W. Gomme, *Essays in Greek history and literature* (Oxford 1937) 249–95; L. A. Post, *From Homer to Menander* (Berkeley, Cal. 1951); E. Lefèvre, 'Menander', in (ed.) G. A. Seeck, *Das griechische Drama* (Darmstadt 1979) 307–53. Webster (1974) 111–93, under (2) above, gives 'summary reconstructions of all the plays of which anything useful can be said'. (5) PRODUCTION AND COSTUME: See *General works* (4) under 'Greek Comedy' and add: T. B. L. Webster, 'The masks of Greek comedy', *Bull. John Rylands Library* 32 (1949) 97–136; idem, 'Menander: production and imagination', *Bull. John Rylands Library* 45 (1962) 235–72; Charitonidis *et al.* under

Life and works above *ad fin.* (6) COLLECTED STUDIES: C. Corbato, *Studi Menandrei* (Trieste 1965); F. Zucker, *Menanders Dyskolos als Zeugnis seiner Epoche* (Berlin 1965); (ed.) E. G. Turner, *Entretiens XVI: Ménandre* (Fondation Hardt, Geneva 1970).

INDEXES (partial coverage only): Koerte, BT ed. II, supplemented (mainly from *Dysk.*) by H.-J. Mette, *ed. Dysk.*, 2nd ed. (Göttingen 1961). *Aspis* and *Samia*: Austin I, under *Commentaries* above. *Dysk.*: H. Lloyd-Jones, *ed. Dysk.* (OCT, 1960). *Mis.* (most of), *Sik.* and some other pieces: *CGFPap*. *Sententiae*: Jaekel, BT ed.

METRICAL APPENDIX[1]

(1) BASIC PRINCIPLES

(A) STRESSED AND QUANTITATIVE VERSE

In metres familiar to speakers of English, rhythm is measured by the predictable alternation of one or more stressed syllables with one or more unstressed syllables (distinguished by the notation – and ∪, or ′ and ×). Consequently, it is word-accent that determines whether or not a word or sequence of words may stand in a certain part of the verse. Thus the word *Hellenic* may occupy the metrical unit represented by the notation ∪–∪ by virtue of the stress imparted to its second syllable in everyday pronunciation. In contrast, the rhythms of classical Greek metres are measured by the predictable alternation of one or more 'heavy' syllables with one or more 'light' syllables (defined below, and distinguished by the notation – and ∪), so that in the construction of Greek verse the factor of primary importance is not word-accent but syllabic 'weight'. Thus the word Ἑλλήνων, although accented in normal speech on the second syllable, consists for metrical purposes of three heavy syllables, and for this reason can only occupy the metrical sequence –––. Verse constructed upon this principle is conventionally designated *quantitative*: it should be emphasized that this term refers to the quantity (or 'weight') of syllables, and that throughout this account such quantity is described by the term 'heavy' and 'light' to distinguish it from the intrinsic length of vowels; unfortunately, both syllabic weight and vowel-length are still generally denoted by the same symbols, – and ∪.

(B) SYLLABIFICATION

A syllable containing a long vowel or diphthong is heavy (e.g. the first syllables of δῶρον and δοῦλος).

A syllable containing a short vowel is light if it ends with that vowel (e.g. the first syllable of θέρος), but heavy if it ends with a consonant (e.g. the first syllable of θέρμος).

---

[1] References by name only are to bibliography under (4) below.

To decide whether or not a short-vowelled syllable ends with a consonant (and thus to establish its quantity), the following rules should be observed:[1] (i) word-division should be disregarded; (ii) a single consonant between two vowels or diphthongs belongs to the succeeding syllable (thus λέγω → *lĕ–go*; πάθεν ἄλγεα → *pă–thĕ–nal-ge–a*); (iii) of two or more successive consonants, at least one belongs to the preceding syllable (thus λέμμα → *lēm–ma*; φίλτατε ξένων → *phĭl–ta–tēk–se–non*).

Note: the rough breathing does not count as a consonant (except in the case of ῥ, which normally makes the preceding syllable heavy; see West 15–16); 3, ξ and ψ count as two (*ʒd, ks* and *ps*).

To (iii) there is an important exception. In the case of the combination of a plosive and a liquid or nasal consonant (πβφ, τδθ, κγχ followed by λ or ρ, or by μ or ν), the syllabic division may be made either between the consonants (e.g. πατρός → *pāt–ros*) or before them (e.g. *pă–tros*), resulting in *either* a heavy *or* a light preceding syllable. However, when two such consonants belong to different parts of a compound or to two different words, the division is always made between them, giving a heavy preceding syllable e.g. ἐκλέγω → *ēk–le–go* not *ĕ–kle–go*; ἐκ λόγων → *ēk–lo–gon*, not *ĕ–klo–gon*). Lastly, when, after a short final vowel, these consonants begin the next word, the division is nearly always (except in epic) made before them, giving a light preceding syllable (e.g. ὁ κλεινός → *hŏ–klei–nos*).

See further West 15–18.

(C) ACCENT

The accent of ancient Greek was basically one of pitch (i.e. 'tonal'). It had a negligible influence on the construction of recited verse (though it clearly affected the melody of the spoken line), and in lyric verse was completely subordinate to the requirements of the musical accompaniment. Whether there was also an element of stress in the accentuation of classical Greek (either related to the tonal accent or independent of it), and, if there was, whether it had any significant effect on the construction of recited verse, are matters of debate: see Allen (1973) 274–334, (1974) 120–5, 161–7 (with bibliography 161; see also M. L. West, *Gnomon* 48 (1976) 5–6).

A fundamental change in accentuation took place by gradual stages in later antiquity. By the latter part of the 4th c. A.D. the tonal accent had been replaced by a 'dynamic' one: i.e. the accented syllable was no longer differentiated by variation of pitch but by stress. This change was reflected in the structure of verse, which ceased to be quantitative and came to be based on the opposition of stressed and unstressed syllables; see Allen (1974) 119–20, West 162–4.

---

[1] The resulting division is practical only; for the difficulties involved in an absolute definition of the syllabic unit see Allen (1973), esp. 27–40.

(2) TECHNICAL TERMS

Anceps ('unfixed'): term used to describe a metrical element which may be represented by either a heavy or a light syllable. The final element of many Greek metres is regularly of this nature, but not in certain lyric metres in which there is metrical continuity (*synaphea*) between as well as within lines. In this account the convention is followed of marking final anceps as heavy.

Antistrophe: see *Strophe*.

Aphaeresis: see *Synecphonesis*.

Arsis: see *Thesis*.

Caesura ('cutting') and *diaeresis*: division between words within a verse is traditionally termed *caesura* when occurring inside a foot or metron, and *diaeresis* when occurring at the end of a foot or metron (but cf. M. L. West, *C.Q.* n.s.32 (1982) 292–7). The varied distribution of these plays an important part in avoiding monotony in the construction of verse; in particular, the caesura prevents a succession of words co-extensive with the feet or metra of a line.

Catalexis: the truncation of the final syllable of one colon or metron in relation to another (e.g. the pherecratean is the catalectic form of the glyconic; see under (3b) below).

Contraction: the substitution of one heavy syllable for two light ones.

Correption: see *Elision*.

Crasis: see *Synecphonesis*.

Diaeresis: see *Caesura*.

Elision and *hiatus* ('cleft'): a short final vowel is generally suppressed or *elided* when immediately preceding another vowel. When it is not elided in these circumstances it is said to be in *hiatus*; by the process of *correption* (commonest in early epic and elegy) a long vowel or diphthong in hiatus (either within a word or at word-juncture) may be scanned short to make a light syllable. See further West 10–15.

Epode: (1) A two-line period in which a short line follows a longer line (e.g. Archilochus uses iambic trimeter plus dactylic hemiepes, hexameter plus iambic dimeter etc.). (2) See *Strophe*.

Prodelision: see *Synecphonesis*.

Responsion: see *Strophe*.

Resolution: the substitution of two light syllables for a heavy one.

Strophe: metrical structure used by the dramatists and lyric poets, made up of one or more periods and recurring in the same form either once (when the second strophe is called the *antistrophe*) or more often. *Triadic structure* denotes the scheme in which two strophes (strophe and antistrophe) are followed by a third of different metrical form (*epode*); the scheme may be repeated *ad lib*.

Synaphea: see *Anceps*.

Synecphonesis: the merging into one syllable either of two vowels within a word (e.g. θεός as a monosyllable) or of a final diphthong or long vowel (or ό, ά, τό, τά) and an initial vowel; when the second word begins with ε (generally ἐστι) this is known as *prodelision* or *aphaeresis* (e.g. ποῦ 'στιν). According to whether or not the synecphonesis is indicated in writing, it is sometimes termed *crasis* (e.g. καὶ ἐγώ → κἀγώ) or *synizesis* (e.g. ἦ οὐ as a monosyllable).

Synezesis: see *Synecphonesis*.

Thesis and *arsis*: terms used originally to designate those parts of Greek verse accompanied by the setting down and raising of the foot (i.e. the down beat and up beat). Since the terms are now generally used in the opposite of their original meanings, West recommends abandoning them and using substitutes such as *ictus* for the down beat.

Triadic structure: see *Strophe*.

Units of analysis:

Period: metrical structure, sometimes extending over many written lines (e.g. the Sapphic strophe), (i) whose boundaries do not cut into a word, (ii) within which there is metrical continuity (synaphea), and (iii) whose final element is anceps.

Colon: single metrical phrase of not more than about twelve syllables (e.g. the glyconic); generally cola are subdivisions of periods, though some may be used as short periods in themselves.

Metron: the rhythm of some verse is regular enough to be divided into a series of identical or equivalent units known as metra, and the period may be described according to the number of metra it contains (dimeter, trimeter, tetrameter, pentameter, hexameter = metron × 2, 3 etc.).

Foot: metrical unit which is identical with the metron in some types of verse (e.g. dactylic), a division of it in others (e.g. in iambic, trochaic and anapaestic verse there are two feet in each metron).

(3) COMMON METRES

For the sake of simplicity only the most basic characteristics of each metre are given here. For the numerous divergencies regarding anceps, resolution, position of caesura etc., see Dale, Raven and West. The notation used below is basically that of West: − = heavy, or final anceps; ∨ = light; × = anceps; ≤ = usually heavy; ⌒ = usually light; ∪∪ = resolvable heavy; ⌣⌣ = contractible pair of lights).

(a) Stichic verse (constructed by repetition of same metrical line; chiefly intended for recitation or recitative, though some stichic metres were sung)

Iambic tetrameter catalectic:

$$\times -\cup-|\ \times -\cup-|\times -\cup-|\cup--$$

(very common metre of comedy, used mainly for entries and exits of chorus and in contest scenes)

Iambic trimeter:

$$ \times -\cup-|\times -\cup-|\times -\cup- $$

(principal metre of dramatic dialogue; used by iambographers as an 'informal' metre for satirical and abusive poetry; used by Archilochus in alternation with a shorter line (hemiepes, iambic dimeter etc.) to form an epode)

Choliambus or scazon:

$$ \times -\cup-|\times -\cup-|\times --- $$

(= iambic trimeter with heavy in place of final light; used for satirical and scurrilous poetry (Hipponax, Callimachus, Herodas), for philosophical invective (Timon) and for fable (Babrius))

Trochaic tetrameter catalectic:

$$ -\cup-\times\,|-\cup-\times\,|-\cup-\times\,|-\cup- $$

(apparently (Arist. *Poet.* 1449a21) the original metre of tragic dialogue, but in extant tragedy (where it is associated with scenes of heightened tension) far less common than the iambic trimeter; very common in comedy, particularly in the epirrhemes of the parabasis (see pp. 358ff.))

Dactylic hexameter:

$$ -\cup\cup|-\cup\cup|-\cup\cup|-\cup\cup|-\cup\cup|-- $$

(regular metre for epic, pastoral and didactic poetry; also used for oracles, riddles, hymns and laments; occasionally found in drama; used by Archilochus in alternation with a shorter line (hemiepes, iambic dimeter etc.) to form an epode)

Dactylic 'pentameter' (properly = hemiepes × 2):

$$ -\cup\cup-\cup\cup-|-\cup\cup-\cup\cup- $$

(almost invariably following the hexameter to form the elegiac couplet, which is regarded as an entity and hence as stichic (or 'distichic'); used for a wide variety of themes (sympotic, military, historical, descriptive, erotic) and the standard metre for epigram)

Anapaestic tetrameter catalectic:

$$ \overline{\cup\cup}-\overline{\cup\cup}\,|\cup\cup-\overline{\cup\cup}-|\overline{\cup\cup}-\overline{\cup\cup}-|\cup\cup-- $$

(dignified metre, very common in comic dialogue)

(b) Non-stichic verse (constructed by combination and expansion of different metrical cola and metra; chiefly intended for singing, either solo (monody) or choral, to the accompaniment of music and/or dance)

The principal units may be classified as follows (though n.b. units from different categories are frequently found in combination):

Iambic: based on metron ×–∪–; commonest sequences are of dimeters and trimeters; often combined with other cola.

Trochaic: based on metron –∪–×; commonest sequences are of dimeters and trimeters; often combined with other cola.

lekythion:	–∪–⏞|–∪–	(= catalectic dimeter)
ithyphallic: .	–∪–∪|––	
scazon:	–∪–× |–∪–× |–∪–× |–––	

Dactylic: based on metron –∪∪; commonest sequences are of from two to six metra; often combined with iambics and trochaics.

hemiepes: –∪∪–∪∪–

Dactylo-epitrite: based on the hemiepes (–∪∪–∪∪–) and cretic (–∪–), which may be preceded, separated or followed by an anceps which is normally heavy (epitrite = –∪––; for the terminology see West 70); particularly common in Pindar and Bacchylides.

Anapaestic: based on metron ∪∪–∪∪–; traditionally a marching metre, and particularly associated with parts of drama where movement takes place on stage; commonest sequence is of dimeters, often ending in a paroemiac (∪∪–∪∪–\|∪∪–– = catalectic dimeter).

Dochmiac: based on metron ∪––∪–; associated with scenes of great excitement; very common in tragedy, rare in comedy except in parodies; commonest sequences are of metra and dimeters; often combined with iambics, cretics and bacchii (= ∪––).

Cretic: based on metron –∪– or –∪∪∪ ('first paeon') or ∪∪∪– ('fourth paeon'); common in comedy, rare in tragedy; commonest sequences are of dimeters, trimeters and tetrameters.

Ionic: based on metron ∪∪–– (minor ionic) or ––∪∪ (major ionic); associated with cult, and with the exotic and barbaric; commonest sequences are of dimeters and trimeters; often found in combination with the anacreontic = ∪∪–∪–∪––.

Aeolic: term sometimes used to include other cola of asymmetrical length, but here restricted to those containing as a nucleus the choriamb (–∪∪):

glyconic:	× × |–∪∪–|∪–
pherecratean:	× × |–∪∪–|–
telesillean:	× |–∪∪–|∪–
reizianum:	× |–∪∪–|–
hipponactean:	× × |–∪∪–|∪––
hagesichorean (or enoplian):	× |–∪∪–|∪––
aristophanean:	–∪∪–|∪––
dodrans:	–∪∪–|∪–
adonean:	–∪∪–|–

Some Aeolic cola are used as periods in themselves; more often they are used to form longer periods, (i) by combination with other cola (Aeolic or otherwise), (ii) by the addition of prefix or suffix (e.g. addition of bacchius to glyconic gives the phalaecian = ×× |‒◡◡‒|◡‒◡‒‒), or (iii) by dactylic or choriambic expansion from within (e.g. choriambic expansion of glyconic gives the lesser asclepiad = × × |‒◡◡‒‒◡◡‒|◡‒). Two common Aeolic strophes based on Aeolic cola are the Sapphic (= ‒◡‒× |‒◡◡‒| ◡‒‒ (three times) plus ‒◡◡‒|‒ = adonean) and the Alcaic (= × ‒◡‒× |‒◡◡‒|◡‒ (twice) plus × ‒◡‒× ‒◡‒‒ plus ‒◡◡‒◡◡‒|◡‒‒); for different analyses of these strophes see West 32–3, Raven 77–9, *OCD* 683.

(4) BIBLIOGRAPHY

Allen, W. S., *Accent and rhythm* (Cambridge 1973)

idem, *Vox Graeca*, 2nd ed. (Cambridge 1974)

Dale, A. M., *The lyric metres of Greek drama*, 2nd ed. (Cambridge 1968)

eadem, *Metrical analyses of tragic choruses*, fasc. I, *B.I.C.S.* suppl. XXI.1 (1971); fasc. II, *B.I.C.S.* suppl. XXI.2 (1981)

Maas, P., *Greek metre*, tr. H. Lloyd-Jones (Oxford 1962)

Raven, D. S., *Greek metre*, 2nd ed. (London 1968)

Sommerstein, A. H., *The sound pattern of ancient Greek* (Oxford 1973)

West, M. L., *Greek metre* (Oxford 1982)

White, J. W., *The verse of Greek comedy* (London 1912)

Wilamowitz-Moellendorff, U. von, *Griechische Verskunst* (Berlin 1921)

WORKS CITED IN THE TEXT

Arnim, H. von (1913). *Supplementum Euripideum*. Bonn.
Arnott, W. G. (1975). *Menander, Plautus, Terence. G. & R.*, New surveys in the classics IX.
(1979). *Menander* I. Loeb. London & Cambridge, Mass.
Baldry, H. C. (1953). 'The idler's paradise in Greek comedy', *G. & R.* 22: 49–60.
Barlow, S. A. (1971). *The imagery of Euripides: a study in the dramatic use of pictorial language*. London.
Berthiaume, G. (1982). 'Les rôles du *mágeiros*: étude sur la boucherie, la cuisine et le sacrifice dans la Grèce ancienne', *Mnemosyne* suppl. LXX.
Bieber, M. (1961). *The history of the Greek and Roman theater*. 2nd ed. Princeton, N.J.
Björck, G. (1950). *Das alpha impurum und die tragische Kunstsprache*. Uppsala.
Blanchard, A. (1970). 'Recherches sur la composition des comédies de Ménandre', *R.E.G.* 83: 38–51.
Bonanno, M. G. (1972). *Studi su Cratete comico*. Padua.
Bozanic, N. (1977). 'Structure, language and action in the comedies of Menander'. Diss. London.
Bruns, I. (1896). *Das literarische Porträt der Griechen im fünften und vierten Jahrhundert vor Christi Geburt*. Berlin.
Burnyeat, M. F. (1977). 'Socratic midwifery, Platonic inspiration', *B.I.C.S.* 24: 7–16.
Butcher, S. H. (1891). *Some aspects of the Greek genius*. London.
Cassio, A. C. (1977). *Aristofane, Banchettanti: i frammenti*. Pisa.
Charitonidis, S., Kahil, L. and Ginouvès, R. (1970). *Les mosaïques de la maison du Ménandre à Mytilène. Antike Kunst*, Beiheft 6. Bern.
Coffey, M. (1976). *Roman satire*. London.
Coleman, R. G. G. (1972). 'The role of the Chorus in Sophocles' *Antigone*', *P.C.Ph.S.* n.s. 18: 4–27.
Conacher, D. J. (1967). *Euripidean drama*. Toronto.
Connor, W. R. (1971). *The new politicians of fifth-century Athens*. Princeton, N.J.
Constantinides, E. (1969) 'Timocles *Ikarioi satyroi*: a reconsideration', *T.A.Ph.A.* 100: 49–61.
Dale, A. M. (1954). *Euripides, Alcestis*. Oxford.
(1959). 'The Hoopoe's song', *C.R.* 9: 199–200 = *Collected papers* (1969) 135–6.
Davies, M. I. (1969). 'Thoughts on the Oresteia before Aischylos', *B.C.H.* 93: 214–60.
Denniston, J. D. and Page, D. L. (1957). *Agamemnon*. Oxford.
Dodds, E. R. (1929). 'Euripides the irrationalist', *C.R.* 43: 97–104.
(1951). *The Greeks and the irrational*. Berkeley & Los Angeles.
(1960). *Euripides, Bacchae*. 2nd ed. Oxford.

Dohm, H. (1964). *Mageiros*. Zetemata XXXII. Munich.

Dover, K. J. (1954). 'Greek comedy', in *FYAT*.

(1968). *Aristophanes' Clouds*. Oxford.

Easterling, P. E. (1973). 'Presentation of character in Aeschylus', *G. & R.* 20: 3–19.

(1978). 'The second stasimon of *Antigone*', in R. D. Dawe, J. Diggle, P. E. Easterling, ed. *Dionysiaca*. Cambridge.

Ehrenberg, V. L. (1951). *The people of Aristophanes*. 2nd ed. Oxford. (3rd ed. New York 1962.)

Eliot, T. S. (1926). Introduction to *Savonarola: a dramatic poem*, by Charlotte Eliot. London.

Entretiens Hardt (1970). *Ménandre: Entretiens* 16. Geneva.

Fraenkel, E. (1922). *Plauteinisches im Plautus*. Berlin. (Revised as *Elementi plautini in Plauto*, Florence 1960.)

(1950). 'Some notes on the Hoopoe's song', *Eranos* 48: 75–84 = *Kleine Beiträge* I (1964) 453–61.

Garvie, A. F. (1969). *Aeschylus' Supplices: play and trilogy*. Cambridge.

Gelzer, T. (1956). 'Aristophanes und sein Sokrates', *M.H.* 13: 65–93.

(1960). *Der epirrhematische Agon bei Aristophanes*. Zetemata XXIII. Munich.

(1976). 'Some aspects of Aristophanes' dramatic art in the *Birds*', *B.I.C.S.* 23: 1–14.

Ghiron-Bistagne, P. (1976). *Recherches sur les acteurs dans la Grèce antique*. Paris.

Giannini, A. (1960). 'La figura del cuoco nella commedia greca', *Acme* 13: 135–216.

Gomme, A. W. (1938). 'Aristophanes and politics', *C.R.* 52: 97–119. (Repr. in D. A. Campbell, ed., *More essays in Greek history and literature* (Oxford 1962).)

(1956). *A historical commentary on Thucydides* II. Oxford. (See also Gomme *et al.* (1945–70).)

Gomme, A. W. and Sandbach, F. H. (1973). *Menander: a commentary*. Oxford.

Griffith, M. (1977). *The authenticity of Prometheus Bound*. Cambridge.

Händel, P. (1963). *Formen und Darstellungen in der aristophanischen Komödie*. Heidelberg.

Handley, E. W. (1953). 'XOPOY in the *Plutus*', *C.Q.* n.s. 3: 55–61.

(1959). Review of H. J. Newiger, *Metapher und Allegorie*, in *J.H.S.* 79: 166–7.

(1965a). *The Dyskolos of Menander*. London & Cambridge, Mass.

(1965b). 'Notes on the *Sikyonios* of Menander', *B.I.C.S.* 12: 38–62.

(1968). *Menander and Plautus: a study in comparison*. (Inaugural lecture) London.

(1969). 'Notes on the *Theophoroumene* of Menander', *B.I.C.S.* 16: 88–101.

(1973). 'The poet inspired?', *J.H.S.* 93: 104–8.

(1975a). 'Plautus and his public: some thoughts on New Comedy in Latin', *Dioniso* 46: 117–32.

(1975b). 'Some new fragments of Greek comedy', *Proc. xiv int. congr. papyrologists, 1974*, 133–48.

(1977). 'P. Oxy. 678: a fragment of New Comedy', *B.I.C.S.* 24: 132–4.

(1979). 'Recent papyrus finds: Menander', *B.I.C.S.* 26: 81–7.

(1982a). 'P. Oxy. 2806: a fragment of Cratinus?', *B.I.C.S.* 29: 109–17.

(1982b). 'Aristophanes' rivals', *Proc. Class. Ass.* 79: 23–5.

Handley, E. W. and Rea, J. R. (1957). *The Telephus of Euripides*. B.I.C.S. suppl. v.

Harrison, E. B. (1976). 'The Portland Vase: thinking it over', in L. Bonfante and H. von Heintze, edd., *Essays in memoriam Otto J. Brendel*. Mainz.

Henderson, J. (1975). *The maculate muse: obscene language in Attic comedy*. New Haven.

Herington, C. J. (1970). *The author of the Prometheus Bound*. Austin, Texas.

Hofmann, H. (1976). *Mythos und Komödie*. Spudasmata xxx. Hildesheim.

Hofmann, W. and Wartenberg, G. (1973). 'Der Bramarbas in der antiken Komödie', *Abh. der Akad. der Wiss. der DDR*, 1973.2.

Hunter, R. L. (1979). 'The comic chorus in the fourth century', *Z.P.E.* 36: 23–38.

Jones, J. (1962). *On Aristotle and Greek tragedy*. London.

Knox, B. M. W. (1964). *The heroic temper*. Berkeley & Los Angeles.

(1976). 'Euripides' Medea', *Y.Cl.S.* 25: 193–206.

Koenen, L. (1979). *The Cairo codex of Menander (P. Cair. J 43277)*. A photographic edition prepared under the supervision of Henry Riad and Abd el-Kadr Selim, with a preface by L. Koenen. London, Institute of Classical Studies.

Körte, A. (1893). 'Archäologische Studien zur alten Komödie', *J.D.A.I.* 8: 61–93.

Lattimore, R. (1958). *The poetry of Greek tragedy*. Baltimore.

Lefèvre, E. (1979). 'Menander', in G. A. Seeck, ed., *Das griechische Drama*, 307–53. Darmstadt.

Leo, F. (1895). *Plautinische Forschungen*. 2nd ed. 1912. Berlin.

Lloyd-Jones, H. (1956). 'Zeus in Aeschylus', *J.H.S.* 76: 55–67.

(1957). *Aeschylus* II. 2nd ed. Loeb.

(1966). 'Problems of early Greek tragedy: Pratinas, Phrynichus, the Gyges fragment', *Estudios sobre la tragedia griega*, Cuaderno de la Fundación Pastor XIII. Madrid.

(1971). *The justice of Zeus*. Berkeley & Los Angeles.

Long, A. A. (1968). *Language and thought in Sophocles*. London.

Ludwig, W. (1970). 'Die plautinische Cistellaria und das Verhältnis von Gott und Handlung bei Menander', in *Entretiens Hardt* 16: 43–110.

Luppe, W. (1980). *Literarische Texte: Drama. Archiv für Papyrusforschung* 27: 233–50.

MacDowell, D. (1971). *Aristophanes, Wasps*. Oxford.

Maehler, H. (1980). 'A new method of dismounting papyrus cartonnage', *B.I.C.S.* 27: 120–2.

Mazon, P. (1904). *Essai sur la composition des comédies d'Aristophane*. Paris.

Mette, H. J. (1959). *Die Fragmente der Tragödien des Aischylos*. Berlin.

Murray, G. (1933). *Aristophanes: a study*. Oxford.

Muscarella, O. W. (1974). *Ancient art: The Norbert Schimmel Collection*. Mainz.

Mussche, H. F. and others (1965). *Thorikos* III. Brussels.

Nestle, W. (1901). *Euripides. Der Dichter der griechischen Aufklärung*. Stuttgart.

Newiger, H.-J. (1957). *Metapher und Allegorie: Studien zu Aristophanes*. Zetemata XVI. Munich.

Norwood, G. (1931). *Greek comedy*. London.

Oeri, H. G. (1948). *Der Typ des komischen Alten: seine Nachwirkungen und seine Herkunft*. Basel.

Owen, A. S. (1936). 'The date of the Electra of Sophocles', in *Greek poetry and life, Essays presented to Gilbert Murray*, ed. C. Bailey and others. Oxford.

Page, D. L. (1942). *Greek literary papyri*. London.

Payne, H. (1931). *Necrocorinthia*. Oxford.

Philippson, R. (1932). 'Sokrates' Dialektik in der Wolken', *Rh.M.* 81: 30–8.

Pickard-Cambridge, A. W. (1946). *The theatre of Dionysus at Athens*. Oxford.

Pollitt, J. J. (1974). *The ancient Greek view of art: criticism, history and terminology*. New Haven & London.

Radermacher, L. (1951). 'Artium scriptores. Reste der voraristotelischen Rhetorik', *S.A.W.W.* 227: 3.

Rau, P. (1967). *Paratragodia: Untersuchung einer dramatischen Form des Aristophanes.* Zetemata XLV. Munich.

Reinhardt, K. (1947). *Sophokles.* 3rd ed. Frankfurt am Main.

Robert, C. (1911). *Die Masken der neueren attischen Komödie.* Hallisches Winckelmannsprogr. XXV. Halle a. S.

Russell, D. A. and Winterbottom, M. (1972). *Ancient literary criticism.* Oxford.

de Ste Croix, G. E. M. (1972). *The origins of the Peloponnesian War.* London.

Schmid, W. (1948). 'Das Sokratesbild der Wolken', *Philologus* 97: 209–28.

Schwarze, J. (1971). *Die Beurteilung des Perikles durch die attische Komödie und ihre historische und historiographische Bedeutung.* Zetemata LI. Munich.

Seeberg, A. (1971). *Corinthian Komos vases. B.I.C.S.* suppl. XXVII.

Sifakis, G. M. (1971). *Parabasis and animal choruses.* London.

Simon, E. (1971). 'Die "Omphale" des Demetrios', *A.A.*: 199–206.

(1972). *Das antike Theater.* Heidelberg. (Tr. C. E. Vafopoulou-Richardson (1982) London.)

Snell, B. (1953). *The discovery of the mind: the Greek origins of European thought,* tr. T. G. Rosenmeyer. Oxford.

Sutton, D. F. (1974*a*). *The date of Euripides' Cyclops.* Ann Arbor.

(1974*b*). 'A handlist of satyr plays', *H.S.C.Ph.* 78: 107–43.

Taplin, O. (1975). 'The title of Prometheus Desmotes', *J.H.S.* 95: 184–6.

Thierfelder, A. (1956). 'Römische Komödie', *Gymnasium* 63: 326–45.

Torrance, R. M. (1965). 'Sophocles: some bearings', *H.S.C.Ph.* 69: 269–327.

Trendall, A. D. (1967). *Phlyax vases.* 2nd ed. *B.I.C.S.* suppl. XIX.

Trendall, A. D. and Webster, T. B. L. (1971). *Illustrations of Greek drama.* London.

Turner, E. G. (1952). *Athenian books in the fifth and fourth centuries.* Inaugural lecture. 2nd ed. 1978. London.

(1973). *The papyrologist at work. G.R.B.S.* monograph VI.

(1976). 'A fragment of Epicharmus? (or Pseudoepicharmea?)', *W.S.* 89: 48–57.

(1978). 'The lost beginning of Menander, *Misoumenos*', *Proc. Brit. Acad.* 73: 315–31.

(1980). 'The rhetoric of question and answer in Menander', *Themes in Drama* 2: 1–23.

Ussher, R. G. (1973). *Aristophanes, Ecclesiazusae.* Oxford.

Vermeule, E. (1966). 'The Boston Oresteia Krater', *A.J.A.* 70: 1–22.

Vickers, B. (1973). *Towards Greek tragedy.* London.

Webster, T. B. L. (1950). *Studies in Menander.* 2nd ed. 1960. Manchester.

(1952). 'Chronological notes on Middle Comedy', *C.Q.* n.s. 2: 13–26.

(1959). *Greek art and literature, 700–530 B.C.* London.

(1965). 'The poet and the mask', in M. J. Anderson, ed., *Classical drama and its influence: essays presented to H. D. F. Kitto,* 3–13. London.

(1967). *The tragedies of Euripides.* London.

(1969). *Monuments illustrating New Comedy.* 2nd ed. *B.I.C.S.* suppl. XXIV.

(1970). *Studies in later Greek comedy.* 2nd ed. Manchester.

(1974). *Menander: an introduction.* Manchester.

Webster, T. B. L. and Green, J. R. (1978). T. B. L. Webster, *Monuments illustrating Old and Middle comedy,* 3rd ed. rev. and enlarged by J. R. Green. *B.I.C.S.* suppl. XXXIX.

Wehrli, F. R. (1948). *Motivstudien zur griechischen Komödie*. Zurich & Leipzig.

West, M. L. (1974). *Studies in early Greek elegy and iambus*. Berlin & New York.

Wilamowitz-Moellendorff, U. von (1925). *Menander: Das Schiedsgericht*. Berlin.

(1962). *Kleine Schriften* IV. Berlin.

Wilson, A. M. (1974). 'A Eupolidean parallel for the rowing scene in Aristophanes' *Frogs*', *C.Q.* n.s. 24: 250–2.

Winnington-Ingram, R. P. (1948). 'Clytemnestra and the vote of Athena', *J.H.S.* 68: 130–47.

(1965). 'Tragedy and Greek archaic thought', in M. J. Anderson, ed., *Classical drama and its influence*. London.

Zieliński, T. (1885). *Die Gliederung der altattischen Komödie*. Leipzig.

Zuntz, G. (1955). *The political plays of Euripides*. Manchester.

INDEX

Main references are distinguished by figures in bold type. Main references to the Appendix (which should normally be consulted for basic details of authors' lives and works, and for bibliographies) are given in italic figures.